MiFID 2
CASTING NEW LIGHT ON EUROPE'S CAPITAL MARKETS

REPORT OF THE ECMI-CEPS TASK FORCE ON THE MiFID REVIEW

CHAIR   PIERRE FRANCOTTE
Former Chief Executive Officer, Euroclear
General Manager, PLF International

RAPPORTEURS   DIEGO VALIANTE
Research Fellow, ECMI & CEPS

KAREL LANNOO
Chief Executive Officer and Senior Research Fellow
CEPS & ECMI

CENTRE FOR EUROPEAN POLICY STUDIES
BRUSSELS

Acknowledgements

The rapporteurs gratefully acknowledge the contributions provided by all participants in the Task Force, and in particular by the Chair, Pierre Francotte, who went to extraordinary lengths to ensure that all members were fully heard. A list of participants is provided at the end of this report. Mirzha J. de Manuel Aramendía provided valuable research assistance and extensive operational support. Editing and other tasks related to the administration of the Task Force were provided by Anne Harrington, Margarita Minkova, Isabelle Tenaerts and Jackie West. All errors should only be attributed to the rapporteurs.

Disclaimer

The views expressed in this report do not necessarily reflect the views and positions of all members involved in the Task Force. The members do not necessarily agree with all positions put forward and do not necessarily endorse any reference to academic and independent studies. A sound and clear set of principles has guided the drafting process, in order to preserve a neutral approach to divergent views. All members were given ample opportunity to express their views and – if well-grounded – they are reflected in the final text. Wherever fundamental disagreement arose, the rapporteurs have made sure that all views have been explained in a clear and fair manner. The content of the report, however, can be only attributed to the rapporteurs. Data included in the text have been generally considered as 'material and relevant'.

ISBN 978-94-6138-081-4
© Copyright 2011, ECMI and CEPS.

All rights reserved. No part of this publication may be reproduced, stored in a retrieval system or transmitted in any form or by any means – electronic, mechanical, photocopying, recording or otherwise – without the prior permission of the Centre for European Policy Studies and the European Capital Markets Institute.

European Capital Markets Institute
And Centre for European Policy Studies
Place du Congrès 1, B-1000 Brussels
Tel: (32.2) 229.39.11 Fax: (32.2) 219.41.51
Website: www.ceps.eu

TABLE OF CONTENTS

Preface i
Executive Summary 1
1. Introduction 16
   1.1 The MiFID review 16
2. The Markets in Financial Instruments Directive 21
   2.1 The legislative process 21
   2.2 The legal structure 23
3. The Impact of the MiFID on European Markets: Some evidence from cash equity markets 28
   3.1 Introduction 28
   3.2 A more competitive environment 30
   3.3 The introduction of new technologies 36
   3.4 Evolution in market microstructure and brokerage services 39
   3.5 A more comprehensive transparency regime 41
   3.6 Greater investor protection 42
4. A 'Renewed' Transparency Regime 44
   4.1 The role of transparency in financial markets 44
   4.2 Pre-trade transparency for cash equities: Benefits and costs 49
        4.2.1 Dark liquidity 55
        4.2.2 Pre-trade transparency waivers: where do we stand? 59
        4.2.3 A consolidated quote system 65
   4.3 What pre-trade transparency for non-equity instruments? 66
   4.4 Post-trade transparency regime: Fixing 'bugs' and extending scope 70
        4.4.1 The trade reporting regime for shares 75
        4.4.2 Challenges with data consolidation 76
        4.4.3 Bond markets 85
        4.4.4 Structured financial products 93
        4.4.5 Over-the-counter derivatives 95

5. Reshaping Market Structure 100
- 5.1 Introduction 100
- 5.2 Securities markets as network industry 100
  - 5.2.1 Markets Multi-sidedness and Securities Markets 102
- 5.3 Competition and fragmentation 107
- 5.4 Classification and obligations of trading venues: A 'new' role for internalisation? 117
  - 5.4.1 Shedding light on over-the-counter equity trading ... 121
- 5.5 Some aspects of market microstructure for organised trading 134
  - 5.5.1 Market setting: The role of trading mechanisms 135
  - 5.5.2 The evolution of trading: Market efficiency and financial stability 143
- 5.6 Access to market infrastructures for equities: What's next? 158

6. Provision of Investment Services 164
- 6.1 The nature of investment services and investors 165
- 6.2 Fiduciary duties 169
- 6.3 Organisational rules 174
  - 6.3.1 Investment advice: Striking the right balance 181
- 6.4 Conduct of business rules 185
  - 6.4.1 Conflicts of interests under MiFID 186
  - 6.4.2 Client categorisation 189
  - 6.4.3 Suitability and appropriateness tests 192
  - 6.4.4 Grasping the definition and economics of 'best execution' obligations 198

7. A New Regime for Commodity Derivatives 205
8. Conclusions 214
References 220
Annex I. List of Acronyms 238
Annex II. The objectives of the Task Force 240
Annex III. Market Infrastructure overview 242
Annex IV. Figures and Tables Illustrating Equity Markets 249
Annex V. List of Task Force Participants 259

List of Figures

Figure 1. Interaction with main EU regulatory actions 19
Figure 2. MiFID timeline 20
Figure 3. MiFID original principles 24
Figure 4. Impact of the crisis on EEA equity turnover and volumes
(lit & dark) 29
Figure 5. Registered trading venues in the European Economic Area (EEA)
and breakdown for equities 31
Figure 6. Bid/ask average spread and implicit volatility on
EuroSTOXX, FTSE100 and CAC40 33
Figure 7. EEA equity markets – 2010 pan-European market shares 34
Figure 8. Most liquid EU shares by execution venue 35
Figure 9. Pre-trade transparency and market quality 51
Figure 10. Market depth and OTC activity 52
Figure 11. Current use of waivers 62
Figure 12. Data vendors' market shares (all asset classes) 79
Figure 13. Average quotes per minute 84
Figure 14. Average daily number of IRS trades by currency 95
Figure 15. Average daily number of new IRS trades by maturity 96
Figure 16. Primary securities markets 104
Figure 17. Secondary securities markets 105
Figure 18. Cost structures with (A) and without (B) size externalities 109
Figure 19. Market fragmentation versus liquidity fragmentation 112
Figure 20. 2009 Exchanges revenues by activity
(main European markets) 116
Figure 21. Trading platforms and MiFID 118
Figure 22. Transparency obligations for venues under MiFID 124
Figure 23. Broker-dealer crossing system 125
Figure 24. Proposal for broker dealer crossing system (BCSs) 127
Figure 25. OTC 'printed' vs 'actual' equity trading 130
Figure 26. Dealer markets (trading models) 141
Figure 27. Average trade size on SETS 144
Figure 28. Average value of orders executed for most liquid
European shares 145

Figure 29. Aggregated S&P 500 market depth 148
Figure 30. Shifting the regulatory centre of gravity................................ 157
Figure 31. Equity landscape before and after MiFID and the
Code of Conduct 161
Figure 32. General clauses 174
Figure 33. Exemptions for commodity instruments and firms 206

List of Tables
Table 1. The MiFID review 17
Table 2. Share of HFT by trading venue (shares of order books) 37
Table 3. EEA trading venues' volumes (thousands of shares;
by order book) 41
Table 4. Dark liquidity in the EU (% of total EEA trading)* 56
Table 5. Dark liquidity in the EU (% of EEA RMs, MTFs and
BCNs trading)* 56
Table 6. MTFs run/owned by exchanges 116
Table 7. Auction versus dealer markets 140

List of Boxes
Box 1. Defining 'dark' in securities trading 31
Box 2. Defensive Strategies 54
Box 3. Transaction reporting: Current regime and CESR's proposals 72
Box 4. The US consolidated tape and quote 82
Box 5. Investing in bonds 87
Box 6. The TRACE experience 92
Box 7. A case study of national stock exchanges:
Next steps after the demutualisation 115
Box 8. The regime for systematic in|ternalisers 120
Box 9. Organised trading for OTC derivatives: EU and US discussions 127
Box 10. OTC equity transaction type standards 131
Box 11. The role of issuers 133
Box 12. Order types 137
Box 13. The US 'flash crash': what can be learned? 146
Box 14. Regulatory shift: the 'growing' role of macro regulators 156
Box 15. A new regime for investment advice: the FSA's proposal 183
Box 16. MiFID and asset management at a crossroads 197

PREFACE

The Task Force aimed to shed new light on the main aspects of the Markets in Financial Instruments Directive (MiFID), drawing on the vast practical experience of the Task Force members, the timely input given by regulators and the European Commission and the benefit of a substantial body of academic research and analysis.

It was acknowledged at the outset of the Task Force's work that the revision of MiFID was to be more than an ordinary assessment conducted a few years after the introduction of a new directive, and that it was important to take into account the lessons of the financial crisis in a context of growing uncertainty about the future of Europe's capital markets. It was believed that the review represented a significant opportunity to strengthen the role of the internal market and to regain investors' confidence, which had been badly damaged by the recent financial crisis. As noted in the G20 context, MiFID is part of the process of strengthening the effectiveness of regulation, especially in areas that had previously been unregulated. Greater transparency, investor protection and market stability are some of the main steps that will give financial markets sounder, safer and more resilient foundations.

MiFID is one piece in a broader legislative and regulatory framework regarding the financial markets and it is important to ensure that the revised MiFID maintains appropriate coherence with other current and forthcoming laws and regulations, whose interplay in the implementation process should preserve legal certainty and a properly harmonised regime for investment services.

The work of the Task Force and the final report, independently drafted by the rapporteurs, come at a crucial moment for the MiFID review. Through the Task Force, the industry has sought to make a contribution that can play a major role in supporting the work of public authorities to disentangle the effects of the crisis from the issues raised by separate market failures or regulatory and supervisory gaps. The report is therefore an attempt to make a thoughtful qualitative and quantitative analysis of the major problems at stake and where feasible, to put forward proposals that take into account market developments and reflect the latest findings in the academic literature.

The Task Force was composed of market participants from practically all relevant segments of the securities industry, whose interests and sensitivities clearly did not always coincide. Therefore a consensus could not realistically be reached on a number of important issues, but it did create a unique opportunity for the Task Force to lay out the issues in a fair and balanced way and to articulate the arguments of the different views of these industry segments, providing legislators, regulators and supervisors with a deeper insight into market views and the state-of-art literature. The issues at stake are often arcane and highly technical, but the way in which they are tackled by the public authorities in the coming months will have a major impact not only on the functioning of the financial markets and on the competitive position of the various players involved in the chain between investors and issuers, but also, most importantly, on the well-being of large and small investors and business units in Europe.

This is why the Task Force felt that it was more important to articulate the issues and the different views that prevail than to purport to submit elusive and vague consensus positions or high-level conclusions to which each and all members of the Task Force could agree. The latter approach would mask the real issues at stake and be an ineffective basis on which public authorities could make their own policy decisions.

This objective guided the discussions in the five intense meetings held in the second half of 2010. A key factor of success was going to be that all segments of the industry would be able to express their views in an open and constructive way, that the rationale for the various views would be fully articulated and understood, and that reliable supporting data would be provided to allow for a neutral and balanced assessment. It is to the credit of all Task Force members that, notwithstanding the complexity and sensitivity of the issues, they have successfully met this challenge. And it is to the credit of the rapporteurs that they have produced a report that sums up these issues in a lucid and balanced way. While this report will not make the task of the public authorities seeking to define the future path of MiFID altogether easy, it should at least allow it to be placed on a stronger factual and conceptual basis. If one considers the complexity of the task, this is a worthwhile outcome.

Pierre Francotte
Chairman of the Task Force

EXECUTIVE SUMMARY

The review of the Markets in Financial Instruments Directive (MiFID) is a worthwhile but delicate exercise, coming at a time of great uncertainty for the economic outlook and the impact of re-regulation in Europe. The review is an opportunity to boost investor confidence and strengthen the resilience, efficiency and transparency of financial markets and instruments. Investor protection and market efficiency should remain the guiding principles of the Directive, but it must also be compatible with the growing demand for market safety and financial stability. This report is therefore an opportunity to contribute to the debate led by the European Commission and the new European Securities and Markets Authority (ESMA) by providing an articulated and balanced position on MiFID.

While initially limited to strengthening conduct of business requirements and reviewing mandatory areas, several factors now call for a more extensive review of the Directive. New priorities have emerged as the debate on the causes of the financial crisis has advanced and new institutions have been established on both sides of the Atlantic to monitor markets and macro-prudential risks. Also, the advantages of technological innovation are seen differently today than they were before the crisis.

The functional approach of MiFID is set to become more prescriptive, in line with other forthcoming legislation and the G20 objective to leave no area of financial markets unregulated. By reducing the number of exemptions and extending the scope of the Directive, the breadth of implementing measures will expand, together with the role of ESMA and national supervisors. In this context, there will be almost no scope for self-regulation. Instead, the task will fall upon supervisors to keep rules up to date with fast-moving market innovation.

The objective of the review is to improve market integrity, stability and efficiency, as well as investor protection. Given the breadth of the

changes foreseen, this Task Force has chosen to focus on three core areas:
1) Transparency
2) Market structure
3) Provision of investment services

While the review has identified some regulatory gaps, it mainly seeks to improve the way in which the Directive is implemented and enforced by national authorities. The European Commission and ESMA should minimise the risk of adding layers of regulation where failures are the result of inadequate supervision or enforcement. Clarifying intended scopes of current regulation may help to create a more harmonised framework of supervisory practices. Most importantly, the review should clarify ambiguities in the legal text when the application of the law is inconsistent.

Investors should benefit from the new MiFID. The revision of the legal text should aim at solving legal and market divergences across Europe, and make sure that the benefits of the new competitive environment are spread along the value chain and passed on to final users, retail and wholesale investors, as appropriate.

When it comes to assessing the effects of MiFID, it is difficult to disentangle the impact of regulation from the effects of the recent financial crisis. Nevertheless, the creation of a harmonised regulatory framework for the provision of investment services in Europe is a paramount achievement of the Directive.

MiFID has changed European capital markets in many ways. It has brought greater competition between trading venues and between investment firms both on trading costs and execution services. It has also contributed to substantial investments in technology for trading and platforms. The growth of dark trading venues, such as MTF (multilateral trading facility) dark pools and broker-dealer crossing networks (BCNs), has been another interesting consequence of the new environment. Finally, the Directive has widened the scope of transparency requirements, harmonised the framework of business conduct rules and improved the protection for investors.

Still, there is scope to bring more clarity to some definitions and further harmonise rules and supervisory practices. In other areas, such as market quality (price formation) and integrity, the impact of the Directive is not yet apparent, since evidence remains fairly controversial and inconclusive.

Transparency

Transparency plays a crucial role in the smooth functioning of financial markets and the monitoring of systemic risk. It also ensures that the process of price formation works well, through efficient price discovery mechanisms. Regulatory action is needed in some respects, however, not only to take stock of the recent financial crisis but also to assess the experience gained since the transposition of the Directive.

Transparency is no panacea for market failures, however. Ill-defined transparency requirements would harm efficiency in less-liquid markets with no increase of investor protection or reduction of systemic risk. Conversely, markets could become less-liquid and thus more volatile. Hence, regulatory intervention should be proportional to the structure of each market and take into account the dynamics through which orders find their market-clearing price.

Retail and wholesale markets are intrinsically different due to their divergent market structures. Yet, the design of transparency requirements should not only look at the nature of investors, but also at the characteristics of the market itself. The Commission may need to launch a public consultation in order to request data that would constitute a technical basis on which to better distinguish retail and wholesale actors for each financial instrument.

Equity markets

Pre-trade transparency supports the smooth functioning of venues' trading mechanisms, as well as efficient price discovery and implementation of best execution policies.

Under certain conditions, pre-trade transparency may impair market liquidity. Hence, MiFID introduced waivers, which should be retained. A move towards a more rule-based approach should be balanced with flexible application and ongoing supervision in order to meet market needs. However, conflicting views between members emerge when discussing the breadth of these exemptions.

Turning to post-trade disclosure, the financial crisis called for a further layer of market transparency. A new regime should include the disclosure of aggregate data on capital markets to monitor systemic risk and increase market integrity and efficiency. The extension of trade reporting to both shares admitted to trading only on MTFs or organised trading facilities and to equity-like instruments would be helpful, since all these instruments serve similar purposes. However, for other financial instruments, the mere extension of the rules for equities would most likely generate inconsistencies, given their diverse nature.

In the post-MiFID environment, several aspects have contributed to reducing the *quality of data* and hindering its consolidation. The MiFID review should look at the standardisation of both data formats (code identifiers, etc.) and flags to solve issues in some specific areas (e.g. OTC trades). The relevance of trade flags stems from the support they offer to liquidity discovery mechanisms across trading venues. Market initiatives should reduce the number of trade flags, currently around 50, to fewer than 10 across Europe.

In this regard, ESMA should guide the currently industry-led initiatives to improve standardisation and reduce inconsistencies. However, either the Commission or ESMA should be able to impose consistency if commercial initiatives do not lead to a satisfactory solution within a reasonable timeframe.

The *disclosure of data in real-time* is fundamental for the efficiency of price formation processes. New technologies can help reduce delays. However, reducing the maximum allowed for trade reporting from three minutes to one minute misses the point; regulators' supervision should make sure that firms are not taking more than real time for other reasons than technical delays. In any case, the legal obligation is to report 'as close to real time as possible' and should be duly enforced. The industry is working to make all market data that is not subject to delays freely available after 15 minutes, in line with ESMA's recommendations. Moreover, delays should be permitted in specific circumstances, with appropriate calibration for trades done at the end of the day.

Despite the importance of a consolidated quotation system, priority should be given to removing obstacles to the use of *consolidated post-trade data solutions*. In particular, it is important to improve investor access to both pre- and post-trade data. The challenge is to promote beneficial competition for end investors and support best execution.

To achieve consolidation, formats would need to be standardised and granularity increased, which would curb costs for users and increase accessibility. Some market participants have already committed to reduce costs for final users by unbundling fees for pre- and post-trade data; a step in the right direction that data vendors and distributors would do well to follow. When lower data collection costs are realised, they should be passed-on to final users. Regulators and competition authorities should draw attention to potentially unfair market practices and anti-competitive market conditions that impede markets from offering data solutions at a 'reasonable' cost, rather than attempting to define when a cost is actually 'reasonable'.

The US experience with the unintended consequences of a consolidated tape run by a public entity should suggest alternative solutions. Consolidated tapes can be designed and offered by competing data operators (so-called 'Approved Public Arrangements' or APAs), once the rules of the game have been clearly defined and duly enforced. These tapes could cover not only shares but also other financial instruments admitted to trading on regulated markets (RMs), MTFs or organised trading facilities (OTFs), as long as a sound regime has been put in place.

Regulators should set the conditions to facilitate the consolidation and timely delivery of data to investors in real time, fully unbundled through APAs. Operators would have to meet strict requirements and be responsible for the detection of multiple publications (misreporting or double-counting). Only if the industry fails to meet these conditions, ESMA should adopt the necessary arrangements to set a single consolidated tape in the EU.

Confidential *transaction reporting* to regulators serves the integrity of financial markets. Extending the scope of the reporting may reduce the risk of manipulation on less-liquid markets and improve market integrity and surveillance. Disclosure would then cover all financial instruments admitted to trading on RMs, MTFs and OTFs, with no distinction as to where and how they are actually traded. This move would need to be coordinated with other EU initiatives, such as the review of the Market Abuse Directive (MAD), and the harmonisation of current supervisory practices across Europe. Information should be meaningful and not overburden regulators' supervisory activities.

Bond markets

A strong push towards pre-trade public disclosure for non-equity financial instruments would require a rethink of the current market structure for less-liquid asset classes, and consequently a shift in the intermediation towards auction markets and from a mainly institutional demand to a more retail and small professional one to ensure a constant and sufficient demand over time. Pre-trade transparency is, therefore, strictly needed in auction markets in order to stimulate investors' willingness to bid, since they are able to see other parties' binding commitments in advance.

Some market participants agree that available data are sufficient and that further pre-trade transparency is not really needed. Instead, at this stage, they believe regulators should focus on improving post-trade disclosure.

Other market participants, however, believe that an *ad hoc* pre-trade transparency for bonds would be appropriate. This regime would apply waivers, and would cover bonds listed on regulated markets or multilateral trading facilities or organised trading facilities, whether order-driven, quote-driven or inter-dealer platforms. Information should be more easily available, to help price discovery and open the market to retail and small professional investors.

A transparency regime for bond markets should provide meaningful information to stimulate price discovery. The speed, breadth and depth of information should be designed around 'dynamic' liquidity measures. Since there is not a single measure of liquidity readily available, transparency requirements should be developed on an instrument-by-instrument basis. This task should rather be left to secondary legislation, such as Level 2 implementing measures or binding technical standards.

Liquidity is a dynamic aspect, which may take different forms according to the characteristics of the financial instrument and the trading mechanism. This reality should be taken into account which allows exemptions or deferred publication in order to preserve an efficient and sound price formation process. Dynamic measures of liquidity can be designed around criteria such as frequency of trades, overall turnover or prospective liquidity, product standardisation or transaction size. Finally, since data are fragmented, data formats and flags may need to be further standardised for the purpose of pre-trade transparency.

Derivatives and structured financial products

Derivatives and structured products are mainly traded on a bilateral basis. These trades occur either purely 'over-the-counter' or through 'inter-dealer platforms' under a request-for-quote (RFQ) model. A *pre-trade transparency regime,* therefore, should be designed in a different way than for auction markets. Liquidity in dealer markets, such as markets for bonds, derivatives and structured products, is underpinned by quote-driven auctions, inter-dealer platforms or bilateral negotiations. To function well, bilateral markets (interdealer or purely bilateral) need less pre-trade transparency than order-driven ones, such as equity markets. Executable prices might thus not always be consistently available. The current market structure, however, does not impede future market developments in the years to come towards a different structure of intermediation and nature of the demand.

Current MiFID rules on transparency were devised for equities, so applying them bluntly to derivatives and structured products could generate unintended consequences for the incentives for dealers to provide liquidity by using their private information. They could potentially exit illiquid products and confine their activities to those that are inherently more liquid. Pre-trade transparency for complex non-equity products would only work by first changing the way these products are traded and the nature of the demand, which would need to be constant and sufficiently high over time (as for auction markets).

A *post-trade transparency* regime for derivatives and structured products should be more detailed and tailored to the nature of these products. Where listed on RMs and/or MTFs, the regime could be designed with the same methodology employed for bonds, but its implementation should follow a phased approach.

Exemptions and due calibrations should be allowed in order to preserve efficient price formation and guarantee the effective monitoring of systemic risk. Calibrations should take into account the nature of these markets and each financial instrument, rather than a division into broader categories (e.g. by asset classes). A mere application of post-trade transparency to a general list of instruments would definitely hamper market liquidity. As for bond markets, measurements of liquidity should be taken into account with due care to avoid adverse consequences in terms of liquidity for wholesale participants.

The extension of trade reporting to non-equity markets can be facilitated by current infrastructures, thereby reducing costs. It is critical, however, that transparency requirements remain independent from the eligibility criteria for trading and clearing. In effect, the requirements to access a central counterparty clearing (CCP) are not based only on liquidity itself but also on technical and legal aspects. Hence, the mere eligibility for the clearing of an instrument is not an appropriate test for transparency purposes, nor is it appropriate to assess the level of liquidity or the frequency of trades.

Structured financial products (SFPs) and OTC derivatives are good tools to free capital back to the real economy and better allocate risks and resources. They help spread credit risk and transfer it to those who are more able to bear it. However, the financial crisis has taught us that spreading risk among counterparties through complex instruments does not ultimately cancel it out.

Information about the underlying assets and net exposures should always be publicly available in aggregate level to monitor systemic risk. Regulators should have access to data via reporting, especially through trade repositories. During times of financial distress, aggregated information on net exposures would help contain herd behaviour set off by market opacity.

Trade repositories have sufficient skills and capabilities to collect and aggregate information about net exposures. Financial institutions would need to disclose information on net exposures in a way that does not compromise the confidentiality of sensitive information, but at the same time provides meaningful information (more detailed) to regulators and to the market. Trade repositories would then be able to aggregate this information and offer a global picture.

Narrowing exemptions for commodity derivatives under MiFID may have a substantial impact on the business of non-financial companies. Some market participants advocate these changes as an important step towards a more level playing field, with greater transparency and investor protection, while others ask for further research on the consequences of narrowing these exemptions, in terms of costs of hedging relevant exposures. The need for consistency across several regulations in the commodity business probably demands a more articulated answer.

'Curbing speculation' is a vague objective, given that the distinction between hedging and speculative trading remains highly controversial. Regulators, instead, should shed light on the risks of price manipulation that arise from the accumulation of dominant net positions in future and derivatives markets. Strengthening supervisory powers, especially through position limits, could help to control price manipulation, in particular for physical markets or markets for non-storable commodities (e.g. electricity), but would not necessarily mitigate systemic risk. A more effective alternative would be to use position management tools to impede net sizes reaching a dominant position.

Market structure

Competition among trading venues on execution services and among investment firms on the provision of other investment services have generated positive effects, such as lower trading costs. Competition needs, however, to be fair and based on a level playing field among MiFID official trading venues. Markets benefit today from the interaction of various groups of users and platforms.

Being a vital part of the network, competition appears where markets are contestable, not only from a technological standpoint but also in terms of fair market practices. This implies the need to lower barriers to entry and exit for users and platforms (contestability), including sunk costs, as well as to monitor market practices in a dynamic way.

This report also acknowledges the importance of ensuring a harmonised approach in the application of MiFID requirements for official trading venues. Regulated markets and multilateral trading facilities should be subject to *convergent legal obligations and supervisory oversight* across member states. This convergence already exists in some European countries such as the UK.

On the classification of *broker-dealer crossing networks (BCNs)*, the Task Force discussed two different views.

On the one side, it is argued that some OTC trading escapes MiFID rules on pre-trade transparency for trading platforms and systematic internalisers, and does not provide sufficient post-trade information. It also alleged that it escapes MTFs' rules on access, discretion and surveillance. In this view, some of the BCNs would perform the same function as RMs and MTFs, while others may be more akin to systematic internalisers. BCNs would operate as 'multilateral' trading mechanisms by matching trades as 'riskless' counterparty. BCNs that do not meet the definition of OTC trading would rather be classified either as multilateral trading platforms or systematic internalisers (SIs). Otherwise, pre-trade transparency obligations would be circumvented to the detriment of price discovery, investor protection and market integrity.

Conversely, other market participants believe that advanced brokerage, offered to wholesale counterparties through BCNs, meets the MiFID definition of OTC trading. They note that trades may fall below the standard market size only after splitting them to reduce market impact. These 'child' orders would then be internally matched, but mostly routed to external trading venues, such as RMs and MTFs. The Directive, in their view, would actually refer to 'parent' orders, since fiduciary duties and conduct of business rules apply to them as a whole. Finally, a Broker-dealer Crossing System (BCS) should not be considered 'multilateral' since the dealers assume risks when providing best execution and other conduct of business arrangements, which neutral platforms do not provide.

OTC equity trading plays an important role in financial markets, in particular when it comes to the best execution of complex institutional orders. Therefore, the review of MiFID should not ban these trading activities. The review should rather clarify the criteria that define 'OTC trades' with proper flexibility, in particular what kinds of trades are subject to OTC requirements under MiFID (e.g. 'child' or 'parent' orders). In addition, it should foster the availability of data in order to allow the full assessment and enforcement of best execution rules. Finally, it should ensure that price formation processes and market quality are preserved and, if possible, improved.

The data employed in the run-up to the MiFID review by the Committee of European Securities Regulators (CESR) to ascertain the size of OTC equity trading are not sufficiently accurate. Analysis based on this data cannot be considered conclusive and has probably led to an overestimation of the size of this market. More effort needs to be made to assess market quality in Europe with accuracy and to clarify the actual size of OTC equity trading, its origin and its impact on price formation processes. There is a compelling need to improve the quality of market data by reducing inconsistencies and increasing granularity through the use of harmonised flags.

The G20 called for derivatives to be further standardised and traded on electronic platforms, 'where appropriate'. A greater push towards standardisation and organised trading should balance the benefits of a more transparent and orderly setting with the costs incurred by a potentially lower availability of customised derivatives, which would mean a greater possibility to leave some risk in the system not properly hedged. These proposals raise challenges for regulators and market participants with regard to investor choice, market liquidity and efficiency, and potential overlaps with the MTF regime. The MiFID review needs to address them in a way that is proportional and consistent with the European Market Infrastructure Regulation (EMIR) and other relevant EU directives.

Financial market infrastructures are networks that can operate in a competitive environment. MiFID and competent authorities may need to strengthen actions to keep barriers to entry and exit low, giving due attention to economies of scale and scope, and other potential efficiencies. The Code of Conduct improved price transparency. More remains to be done, however, to solve existing commercial and technical challenges and increase accessibility through unbundling and interoperability of current infrastructures.

Ultimately, MiFID favours freedom of access by investment firms to competing market infrastructures. In effect, while the original Directive envisaged non-discriminatory access to competing infrastructures, the transposition of this provision and its enforcement have been inconsistent across EU member states, in particular in relation to the definition of the 'legitimate commercial ground' to deny access. The review of MiFID should try to bridge these inconsistencies, together with other legislative proposals such as the European Market Infrastructure Regulation (EMIR), Securities Law Directive (SLD) and Central Securities Depositories Regulation (CSDR).

Promoting structural changes in non-equity markets to give easier access to retail investors may raise conflicting views. For some market participants, the market for fixed income securities should remain wholesale and dealer-driven. In their view – even though a commendable objective – *direct retail access* to non-equity instruments may destabilise these markets, as it may generate higher volatility with no liquidity enhancements. These effects would ultimately heighten risks for retail investors, given the increasing complexity of fixed income securities. Instead, other stakeholders firmly support the opening of bond markets to retail investors. They believe greater transparency would be a liquidity driver for these markets. Under proper delays and exemptions, the potentially negative impact of retail trading activities would be fairly limited.

Issuers are important actors for innovation and a more efficient allocation of resources in our economies. Some market participants believe that issuers should be duly informed and agree where their shares are traded in secondary markets. This proposal, however, does not find wide support among both market participants and policy-makers, since in their view it raises relevant issues of market efficiency, legal entitlement of the right and conflicts of interest.

The systemic importance of modern capital markets highlights the inner tensions between financial stability, market efficiency and technological innovation. A well-functioning market must balance efficiency and safety to avoid disequilibria. The *role of technology* in the configuration of market infrastructure has become ever more important. Markets are redesigning their infrastructures thanks to innovative technology. In short, speed and volume will probably continue to grow, but trading venues may have to deal with more frequent crises and outages.

Technological innovations and techniques have brought revolutionary changes to trading. Among these changes, there are major benefits, such as better order management and control of market impact; or more efficient and faster feed of information into prices. Both these changes generate gains in terms of lower spreads and better price discovery that benefit participants throughout the value chain.

However, modern trading also presents a number of challenges, such as an increase in fundamental market volatility, which in turn has brought speed and volumes to critical levels. Advanced execution services like direct-market or sponsored access have radically increased speed and volumes for transactions, in an attempt to cope with increasing volatility. Limits to infrastructure capacity nevertheless mean that higher speed and volumes risk generating market disorder and financial instability.

To overcome these challenges, intermediaries and trading venues need to strengthen their own monitoring. A coherent set of emergency procedures in case of market disruptions should be designed in consultation with market participants (e.g. circuit breakers). There are several efficient monitoring systems already in place, which could serve as model systems. Finally, trading rules should be harmonised across markets to avoid instability arising from arbitrage.

Provision of investment services

Business conduct rules and organisational requirements play a crucial role in the provision of investment services, by strengthening investor protection and market integrity across Europe. However, a more harmonised implementation of regulatory actions and supervisory practices by member states should become a priority.

Best execution duties lie at the foundation of the fiduciary relationship between service providers and clients. MiFID tries to grasp all factors influencing the best execution of a financial transaction, and does it in a very general manner. This situation, however, is not necessarily to the detriment of final investors as long as execution policies are properly implemented and data allows sufficient verifiability of execution.

Investors receive information about their execution policies that may be sometimes incomplete. Even with most advanced execution metrics, available data appear insufficient to make a thorough evaluation of execution quality in a fragmented market.

Some market participants argue that best execution policies should be applied 'dynamically' and that simply complying with formal legal requirements is not enough to provide authentic best execution. Other participants however challenge the view that issues with best execution come from execution policies that are MiFID-compliant. Both recognise that those issues emerge from a consistent lack of data on execution quality from trading platforms, which is under discussion in the debate on the new transparency regime.

Although the crisis showed that some of the eligible counterparties (ECPs) were not able to understand risk 'properly', the *client categorisation* regime should not be subject to a major overhaul, other than those changes currently proposed for local authorities. Some market participants suggest that portfolio managers should be entitled to unilaterally require the reclassification as 'retail' clients. They argue that even though portfolio managers are eligible counterparties under MiFID, they manage money on behalf of professional and retail clients and they have the obligation to act in their best interest. Others, however, advocate the inappropriateness of this request since portfolio managers do not simply execute on behalf of their clients, but they would directly gain (commissions on profits) from rules that should theoretically only benefit retail investors.

Investment advice must always be 'suitable' under MiFID. Some market participants claim there should be a thorough review of the mechanisms of incentives to make advice more 'independent'. In particular, they argue that investment advice should be based on a neutral and 'independent' system of remuneration, by only receiving fees from the clients. No commission should be set by product providers.

Other market participants argue that obliging investors to pay for it would increase the access costs to these services and dramatically reduce the use of advisory services, with potential long-term costs for end investors. They suggest keeping the advice fee embedded in the commission, but disclosing whether the advisor is solely remunerated by the client or also by a product provider.

All cost items and remuneration arrangements should be fully disclosed before signing the contract. This would improve the ability of investors to choose the service that best suits their own interest. Changes in MiFID will need to be reconciled with other regulatory initiatives such as Packaged Retail Investment Products, the Insurance Mediation Directive review, and the Prospectus Directive.

The suitability test is crucial in the provision of investment advice and portfolio management services. Views diverge on how to assess the knowledge, financial situation and objectives of investors, and in particular, on how deep the suitability test should look into investor habits and the willingness to take risks. Some regret the lack of harmonisation in the implementation of suitability requirements for discretionary portfolio management. They would welcome action by ESMA to improve legal certainty and reduce barriers to market investment products across the EU. Other market participants, however, do not think any intervention is needed in this regard and are satisfied with the current level of harmonisation, which takes into account the natural market differences among member states.

MiFID foresees a different regime for 'execution-only' services based on the product classification between complex and non-complex financial instruments. Any change should take into account the fact that complexity does not necessarily mean more risk. The objective should be to verify if the product is in line with investors' understanding of the ultimate risk that they are finally going to bear. Regulation should not decide the level of risk investors want to take.

Some market participants believe that certain UCITS (Undertakings for Collective Investments in Transferable Securities) might have become too complex to be easily understood by investors to skip the appropriateness test, at least for retail clients. Others argue that classification, in particular for UCITS, should remain as such, since a change in classification could damage the UCITS brand outside the EU.

MiFID rules on conflicts of interest represent a first step in the introduction of a common approach across Europe for the prevention, identification, management and disclosure of such conflicts. Further initiatives to strengthen the current regime and align supervisory practices would enhance the treatment of these conflicts and benefit financial markets. A harmonised set of sanctions should be combined with enough flexibility for member states to adapt rules and procedures in line with their national contexts.

Organisational requirements play a crucial role in ensuring business continuity, market integrity and investor protection. A proper implementation of the Directive should be ensured by harmonising organisational requirements and supervisory practices across Europe, and by removing ambiguities in the legal text. Ensuring consistency with other upcoming legislation would then avoid inefficiencies. It would also promote a uniform regime of investor protection and market integrity within Europe, which would ultimately increase legal certainty and the attractiveness of investment services.

1. Introduction

This report deals with the regulatory and economic challenges faced by European regulators in the process of reviewing the Markets in Financial Instruments Directive (MiFID). It does not attempt to cover all issues and details raised by the MiFID review. Rather, it focuses on three fundamental areas of the regulation of financial markets and instruments: 1) transparency, 2) market structure and 3) provision of investment services. Within these three areas, the report examines the major trade-offs faced by regulators, industry representatives and investors in the review process. The summary of recommendations merges the findings of this report with an objective and analytical contribution to the regulatory and policy-making process

1.1 The MiFID review

The MiFID review is perceived by some as a way to address pending issues of the original Directive, and by others as a way to reduce imbalances and to level the playing field. Both views converge on the necessity to restore investors' confidence. As a result, the exercise will have a high political visibility as one of the major responses to the recent financial crisis.

Revising a piece of legislation three years after its introduction is a standard but worthwhile procedure. Yet, striking the right balance between potentially conflicting objectives, such as financial stability and market efficiency, is a delicate exercise. The review aims to further harmonise the regulatory framework for investment firms and market infrastructures, while the impact of the wider post-crisis re-regulation in these and other areas remains unclear. It is a consequential piece of legislation, which affects the competitive position of a number of players. It also comes at a delicate moment for Europe's capital markets, where it is necessary to rebuild investors' confidence and to strengthen the internal market. Due to its level of detail, the review of MiFID is a very technical undertaking. Therefore, European regulators need qualitative and quantitative data through the support of private initiatives.

The Directive mandates a review of nine areas:

1) Extension of pre- and post-trade transparency requirements to financial instruments other than shares (Art. 65, MiFID);
2) Removal of obstacles to the consolidation of data (Art. 65, MiFID);
3) Systematic internalisers provisions (Art. 65, MiFID);
4) Tied agents (Art. 65, MiFID);
5) Best execution (information on execution quality; Recital 76, Implementing Directive);
6) Gold-plating;
7) Telephone recording (Arts 51.4 and 51.5, Implementing Directive);
8) Requirements for authorisation (Arts 31 and 32, MiFID); and
9) Commodity derivatives exemption (Art. 65, MiFID).

However, other issues will also be considered, including most of the G20 commitments to increase the safety and stability of the financial system. Amongst the most important categories are the following:

1) Transparency requirements (such as pre-trade transparency issues and waivers, delays on publication time and a new transaction reporting regime);
2) Regulatory boundaries between venues, e.g. levelling the playing field between regulated markets (RMs) and multilateral trading facilities (MTFs);
3) Legal treatment of broker-dealer crossing networks and other platforms currently operated in the over-the-counter (OTC) space for equity and non-equity financial instruments;
4) Issues of financial stability (rules for new trading technologies and implications for financial stability);
5) Investor protection (e.g. selling practices, market access, client and product categorisation) and
6) A special regime for SMEs.

See Table 1.

Table 1. The MiFID review

Mandatory areas	Other areas
Data consolidation	Pre-trade transparency waivers
Systematic internalisers regime	Transparency for non-equity asset classes
Tied agents	Transaction reporting (with MAD)
Commodity derivatives exemption	Trading venues classification and legal treatment
Requirements for authorisation	Disorderly markets
Gold-plating	Selling practices (with PRIPs)
Best execution (data execution quality)	Market access
Telephone recording	Client categorisation
	Product classification (with UCITS Dir.)
	Special regime for SMEs
	Conflicts of interest and inducements
	Organisation requirements
	Investment advice
	Safeguards and asset segregation
	Post-trade transparency delays

Source: European Commission (2010b).

The Committee of European Securities Regulations (CESR) has grouped the issues of the review under three major areas: 1) transaction reporting, 2) equity markets (structure and transparency) and 3) investor protection and intermediaries (CESR, 2010a,b,c). Therefore, this legislative initiative will have to interact with other important initiatives, such as the review of the MAD (Market Abuse Directive),[1] that cover diverse segments of the investment services industry (see Figure 1).

---

[1] Directive 2003/6/EC.

Figure 1. Interaction with main EU regulatory actions

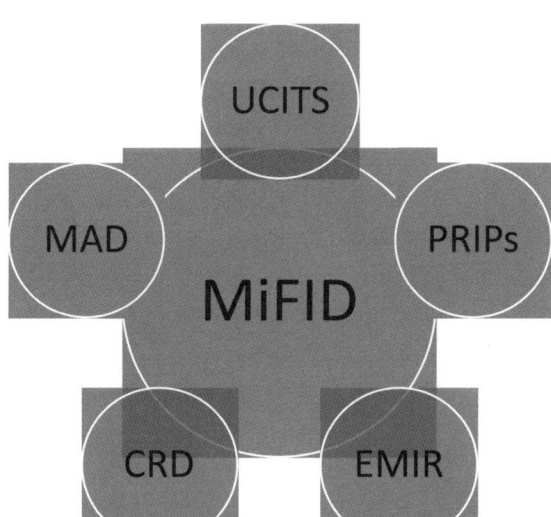

Source: Author

Some outstanding issues regarding MiFID, however, are not related to regulatory gaps, but to the way in which the Directive was implemented and enforced by national authorities. The European Commission and the new European Securities and Markets Authority (ESMA)[2] need to look into the nature of these problems when considering changes to MiFID. Regulators should minimise the risk of adding layers of regulation where failures are rather the result of inadequate supervision or enforcement. Clarifying the intended scope of current regulation may help to create a more harmonised framework of supervisory actions. The revision will affect not only the rules of the business conducted by those providing intermediation as well as trading venue services, but also the interests of investors (both institutional and retail) and issuers.

MiFID came into force in November 2007 (see Figure 2).[3] As cornerstone legislation, it had broad implications for many institutions across sectors, including investment firms, trading venues and regulatory authorities. On the one side, the Directive has unequivocally promoted the

---

[2] Replacing CESR as of January 2011.

[3] For details on the transposition of the Directive across Europe, see http://ec.europa.eu/internal_market/securities/isd/mifid_implementation_en.htm.

creation of a new harmonised framework of rules across Europe that had not existed before (e.g. conduct of business rules and a new pre- and post-trade transparency regime). On the other side, this regulation has promoted a competitive environment for the provision of investment services. However, implementation and supervisory controls were not uniform across member states, creating an uneven playing field among market participants, which the review should solve. There needs to be a better understanding of the impact of MiFID on European financial markets, as the current economic and financial crisis may have distorted the real impact of its implementation. The next sections provide some thoughts and data for assessing the major effects of the Directive.

Finally, as shown in the timeline, the review must follow a strict set of deadlines in order to be approved by 2011 and followed by implementing measures by 2012.

Figure 2. MiFID timeline

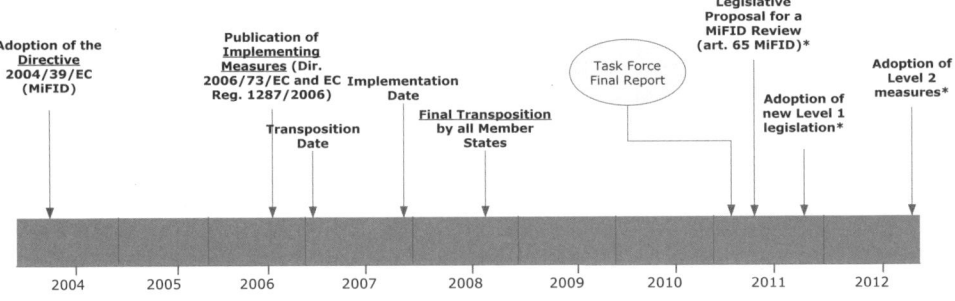

*expected date

Source: European Commission website and rapporteurs.

2. THE MARKETS IN FINANCIAL INSTRUMENTS DIRECTIVE

2.1 The legislative process

The MiFID Directive and its implementing measures are one of the most important components of the Financial Services Action Plan (FSAP). The FSAP represents the follow-up of the 1998 European Council's Conclusions and the Commission's Communication,[4] condensed in the 2000 Lisbon Agenda. The FSAP included 45 measures[5] (originally 42; of which 29 were directives) aimed at developing a single market for financial services, and was renewed by the Europe 2020 agenda (European Commission, 2010a). This plan represents one of the foremost attempts of the European institutions to improve EU financial markets integration[6] and to favour a

---

[4] See European Council, Presidency Conclusions, 15-16 June 1998, Cardiff (http://www.consilium.europa.eu/ueDocs/cms_Data/docs/pressData/en/ec/54315.pdf) and European Commission, Financial Services: Building a Framework for Action, COM 625, 28 October 1998, p. 3 (www.europa.eu).

[5] Originally there were 42 measures, 29 of which were directives (plus the amendment to the 14th Company Law Directive, which was blocked). The Commission then added a Communication on clearing and settlement (COM 312, 2004) and a Regulation on cross-border payments (EC Regulation 2560/2001).

[6] Financial integration of European markets has been on the policy agenda since the 1960s. It was mentioned as early as 1966 in the 'Segré Report' (see Segré, 1966). In May 2007, moreover, the European Council reconfirmed the essential role of integrated financial markets to strengthen the four freedoms of the Internal Market; see Council of the European Union, "Brussels European Council 8/9 March 2007: Presidency Conclusions", 7224/1/07 REV 1, 2 May 2007. A 'new effort' to promote greater financial integration for a European single market has been recently promoted by the 'Monti report' (Monti, 2010), which put economic and financial integration at the top of the EU agenda.

better legislative process for innovative financial regulation. The FSAP aimed at boosting cross-border transactions and financial integration; it remains, however, hard to disentangle the effects of this set of measures from the effects of the Economic and Monetary Union and more recently of the financial crisis. Numerous new pieces of regulation – such as MiFID, MAD, the Prospectus Directive, Transparency Directive, International Accounting Standards (IAS) Regulation, Takeover Bid Directive, Capital Requirements Directive – have provided European financial markets with a common and unique framework of rules for capital markets.

The MiFID, the MAD, the Transparency Directive and the Prospectus Directive have been designed and implemented according to a new legislative process, called the 'Lamfalussy procedure'.[7] This new legislative process entails three levels that represent a combination of regulatory (levels 1 and 2), supervisory (level 3), and enforcement (level 4) actions. It foresees extensive consultations with industry and expert committees (so-called 'comitology'), and strong cooperation between national authorities. Level 1 directives are approved according to the regular co-decision procedure.[8]

The recent financial crisis, however, calls for a deeper analysis of how these measures – and MiFID in particular – performed vis-à-vis the disruption in global financial markets. Nevertheless, the MiFID review occurs in the context of discussions around a new set of directives that make up the European strategy to tackle market failures, restore confidence and promote the internal market and a more open market architecture to favour cross-border transactions. However, economic, legal and social barriers among member states, e.g. taxation, are slowing down the creation of a fully integrated retail and wholesale *pan-European financial market*.

Under the overarching goal of ensuring a single market for financial services, MiFID aimed at establishing a legal framework for integrated securities and derivatives markets in Europe. The Directive attempted to change Europe's capital markets through liberalisation of investment services and more investor protection. MiFID, in effect, was a sophisticated

---

[7] Named after the Chairman of the Committee of Wise Men, Alexandre Lamfalussy, who contributed to defining the terms of this procedure in the *Final report of the Committee of Wise Men on the Regulation of European Securities Markets,* Brussels, 15 February 2001.

[8] Art. 294 (ex Art. 251, ECT) Treaty on the Functioning of the European Union (2010 Consolidated Version; hereinafter, 'TFEU'), *Official Journal of the European Union,* C83/47, 30 March.

and far-reaching attempt of the Commission to provide the European Community with valuable tools for meeting the challenges of the monetary union and reaping the benefits of a single integrated market for financial services. The revision of the legal text aims at solving legal and supervisory divergences across Europe, which hamper market integration, addressing unintended effects of the Directive, extending its coverage and making sure that the benefits of the new competitive environment spread along the value chain and are passed-on to final user, both retail and wholesale.

2.2 The legal structure

MiFID aimed at designing a 'coherent', 'risk-sensitive' and 'comprehensive' regulatory framework for execution of financial instruments to ensure 'high quality of execution' and thus promote investor protection, and the integrity, efficiency and orderly functioning of financial markets (Recital 5, MiFID). By introducing harmonised rules for investment services and securities trading, MiFID has opened up the market to competition. It also provided a unique framework of investor protection rules, as well as stricter rules to preserve market integrity and efficiency.

The Directive replaced the Investment Services Directive (ISD), which was a first attempt to introduce a harmonised regime for investment services in 1993, based more importantly on mutual recognition supported by a European passport. MiFID applies to all financial instruments, excluding commodity derivatives dealt on own account (Art. 2 (i) and (k), MiFID) and other instruments and institutions set in Art. 2. In particular, "the purpose of this Directive is to cover undertakings the regular occupation or business of which is to provide *investment services and/or perform investment activities* on a professional basis. Its scope should not therefore cover any person with a different professional activity" (Recital 7, MiFID). Moreover, the Directive applies not only to MiFID-official trading venues and investment firms providing investment services on a regular basis, but also to credit institutions authorised under Directive 2000/12/EC (not including, for instance, insurance and energy companies) and indirectly to Undertakings for Collective Investments in Transferable Securities (UCITS) companies, even though a formal exemption applies (Art. 2.1 (h), MiFID).[9]

As shown in Figure 3, MiFID aims at reaching two high-level

---

[9] See Box 16.

principles set by the Financial Services Action Plan (FSAP): i) a single market for wholesale financial services and ii) an integrated securities and derivatives market. And this through the implementation of two general goals: investor protection and market efficiency. In the aftermath of the financial crisis, the need to ensure orderly markets and financial stability has gradually become another important objective of the review and so too of the Directive (see Figure 3).

Figure 3. MiFID original principles

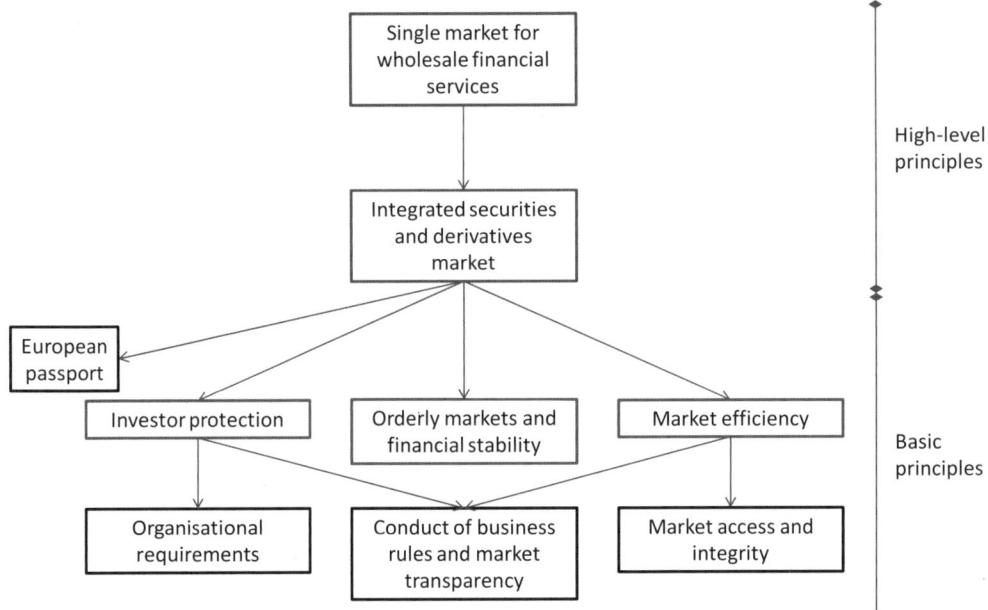

Source: Authors.

MiFID pursues these goals via a set of rules, covering four main areas:
1) European passport (freedom of action across the EEA once received the authorisation in one of the member states);
2) Organisational requirements (compliance officer, outsourcing, internal control systems, record-keeping, conflicts of interests);
3) Conduct of business rules (clients classification, best execution, know-your-customer rules, marketing, information to clients, handling orders rules); and

4) Market structure and transparency (abolition of the concentration rule,[10] detailed transaction reporting, pre- and post-trade transparency, other trading venue requirements).

The comprehensive regulatory regime for investment services and securities trading – as modified by MiFID – had opened up capital markets (in particular, cash equity markets) to competition and produced a new harmonised framework for investor protection, as well as stricter rules to preserve market integrity.

MiFID adopted a functional approach: it regulates the provision of investment services irrespective of the institution carrying out the activity.[11] The Directive applies to all market participants (in particular, credit institutions, investment firms and market operators) acting within its scope, i.e. the investment service activity. For instance, in order to increase investor protection, 'investment advice' – an ancillary service under the ISD – has become a core service under MiFID, thereby obliging all market players providing this service to be compliant with MiFID.

The economic downturn caused by the troubled financial situation, however, has brought pressure to modify this approach towards a more prescriptive one, which aims at ensuring that no areas of financial markets will remain uncovered by the regulation (in line with other forthcoming legislations, e.g. European Market Infrastructure Regulation). Reducing the number of exemptions and extending the scope of the Directive will increase the number of implementing measures to be defined by ESMA and national authorities to make legislation effective. Markets will have almost no space to self-regulate and ongoing supervision will need to keep this broad set of rules up to date with fast-changing market innovation.

In order to foster competition, MiFID promoted two actions: the abolition of concentration rules (for order execution services) and the

---

[10] Before MiFID, countries applied the 'concentration rule' (Art. 14(3) of the 1993 Investment Services Directive). This rule stated that member states had the right to concentrate all orders on a regulated market. In practice, some member states exercised this right either by restricting all trading or all but the largest orders to be executed on the primary exchanges. Some member states did not exercise this right.

[11] A contrasting approach to regulation is the 'institutional' one, which tends to regulate market operators directly, by virtue of their status as 'institution' or legal entity (as defined by the legal text).

extension of the ISD European passport regime (for other investment services). Firstly, by abolishing national concentration rules (pushing trading on few regulated trading venues, i.e. stock exchanges, when member states deemed it necessary for an efficient interaction of orders), MiFID established a new regulatory structure in which all trading venues, whether run by exchanges or other market participants, compete for trade execution services on a level playing field. Secondly, the single authorisation for investment firms and the right to access national infrastructures on a non-discriminatory basis increased cross-border competition between investment firms. In other words, competition under MiFID has two dimensions: competition among trading venues (which might be operated by market operators or investment firms, but must follow the same rules when conducting the same activity) and competition among investment firms when conducting intermediation business.

In parallel to opening up the market for trading venues and investment firms, MiFID sought to harmonise and strengthen market integrity and investor protection – retail, in particular – for the cross-border provision of investment services, through the use of three sets of tools:

i. **'Conduct of business' rules**

The Directive regulates the relationship between retail clients and service providers through: best execution duties (Arts 19.1 and 21, MiFID), conflicts of interest rules (Arts 13.3 and 18, MiFID) and suitability and appropriateness tests (so-called 'know-your-customer rules', Arts 19.4 and 19.5 MiFID). Other relevant requirements are related to: information to clients,[12] client agreements,[13] orders handling[14] and marketing rules.[15] Finally, specific rules define exemptions for eligible counterparties (Art. 24, MiFID) and help client classification.[16] Overall, these regulatory

---

[12] Art. 19.8, MiFID and Arts 40-43 Implementing Directive.
[13] Art. 19.7, MiFID and Arts 14.3 and 39 Implementing Directive.
[14] Art. 22, MiFID and Arts 47-49 Implementing Directive.
[15] Art. 19.2, MiFID and Arts 24 and 27, Implementing Directive.
[16] See also Implementing Directive, Arts 28 and 50. For non-complex instruments, clients can opt out of these safeguards (appropriateness test), asking for 'execution-only' service. For a definition of 'non-complex instruments', see Art. 38, Implementing Directive, or Casey & Lannoo (2009, p. 51). CESR is looking into the definition of 'complex' vs 'non-complex' financial instruments. For instance, they might exclude from the group of 'non-complex' financial instruments all the instruments that embed a derivative and shares in non-UCITS. UCITS may also be split into two groups consistent with their trading strategies, but the proposal may come back at a later stage. See CESR (2010c, pp. 25-26).

requirements address typical issues in a fiduciary relationship between service provider and client.

ii. **Organisational requirements for investment firms and trading venues**

These consist of a range of broad obligations: a general duty to comply with MiFID rules (Art. 13.2 MiFID); creation of internal mechanisms of control (e.g. independent internal audit, IT, etc.; Arts 13.4-13.5, MiFID); outsourcing (to be limited to non-core operational services; Art. 13.5, MiFID); recordkeeping and safeguarding of clients' financial assets (Arts 6-8, MiFID). Other important requirements are: the appointment of a compliance officer (objective and independent), rules on personal transactions and effective procedures for risk assessment. In addition, MiFID also includes specific requirements for trading venues, such as order execution, access and surveillance.

iii. **Transparency regime (pre- and post-trade; see also chapter 1)**

While the first two sets of tools mainly apply to investment firms, the third also applies to both investment firms and execution venues. Legal requirements impose pre- and post-trade transparency for trades in shares, while only an optional extension may be exercised by member states for financial instruments other than shares. The MiFID transparency regime points at multiple objectives, such as investor protection, market integrity, market surveillance and market efficiency.

Post-trading infrastructures. Finally, MiFID recognises a general principle that trading platforms need to provide users with free access to post-trading infrastructures, for both clearing and settlement (Art. 34, MiFID). The purpose of this rule is to preserve competition, avoid bottlenecks along the value chain and avoid cross-subsidisation based on anti-competitive practices. The Directive thus urges member states to push regulated markets (RMs) to open up their infrastructure. It also recognises that building of cross-border links between trading venues and post-trade infrastructures will further favour the creation of a pan-European market (Art. 35, MiFID). The right of investment firms to decide their clearing and settlement infrastructure should apply whether or not the transaction has been executed on a regulated market. In effect, MiFID asks RMs (Art. 34.2) to make these links available, since they were the sole providers in the provision of execution services when the Directive came into force.

3. THE IMPACT OF MiFID ON EUROPEAN MARKETS: SOME EVIDENCE FROM CASH EQUITY MARKETS

3.1 Introduction

MiFID is widely recognised as a major regulatory initiative of the European Union in the financial services sector. It is an overhaul of the European securities market, aimed at introducing a new, harmonised and competitive design for the industry. Under the two high-level principles mentioned above and diagrammed in Figure 3, the main objectives of the Directive were market efficiency and investor protection.

It is difficult to disentangle the effects (positive or negative) of the implementation from the impact of the recent financial crisis, which – next to the competitive pressure from newcomers – has shrunk the business volumes of the incumbent provider of execution services (see Figure 4). Most notably, the reduction of frictional costs for trading and the following increase in volumes may have been masked by the general cyclical downturn brought about by the financial crisis. The crisis makes the overall long-run effects of the Directive on the EU GDP difficult to grasp, but they are estimated at 0.7% and 0.8% (London Economics, 2010).

However, the number of trades has been increasing, and volumes seem to be moving to pre-crisis levels in 2010.

In terms of regulation, more needs to be done to fine-tune the current legal texts with recent market developments and to avoid regulatory gaps.

Hitherto, MiFID has promoted a number of key changes:

1) Greater competition and market fragmentation,
2) Very significant investments in technology for trading and platforms,
3) Growth of dark pools and broker-dealer crossing systems (in line

with market fragmentation),
4) Wider scope of transparency regime and
5) Greater investor protection through a harmonised framework of organisational and conduct-of-business (CoB) rules.

Figure 4. Impact of the crisis on EEA equity turnover and volumes (lit & dark)

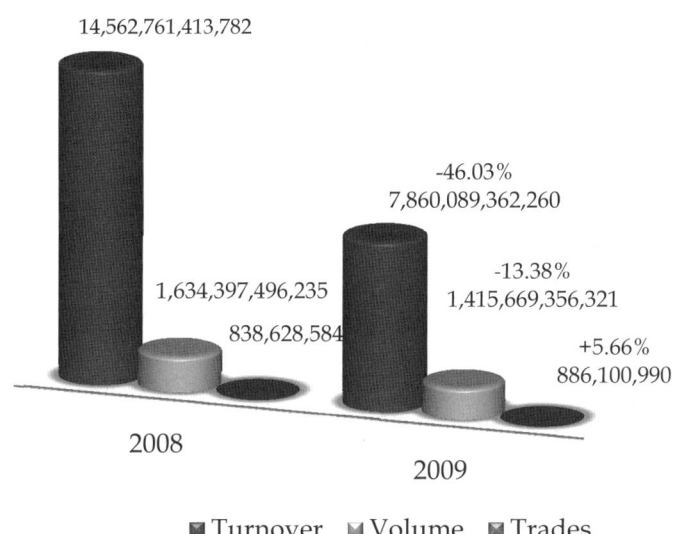

Source: Thomson Reuters, FESE.

The impact on price formation and market integrity remains highly controversial and with no definitive answer. Similar changes in the US seem to have brought some beneficial effects too, in particular in terms of lower implicit and explicit trading costs[17] and greater liquidity (Angel et al., 2010).

---

[17] Explicit costs of trading are those costs fully disclosed, such as trading fees, which are usually known before the investor enters into a deal. Implicit costs of trading are those that may not be fully visible to investors before the transaction, such as opportunity costs of executing an order on another platform that may offer higher explicit costs, but lower implicit costs in terms of market impact.

3.2 A more competitive environment

Despite the original scepticism of the industry, the legislation has proven successful in increasing market competition and efficiency, driving down direct trading and post-trading costs, even though these benefits have not been completely passed-on to end investors. As a result, competition has been concentrating on prices (spreads between official trading venues have increased) and execution services (provided by investment firms in competition between them, brokers and some official MiFID trading venues).[18]

MiFID therefore unleashed competition between:

- Trading venues (by abolishing concentration rules and allowing alternative trading venues),[19]
- Investment firms (by extending the coverage of the European Passport to other services and promoting tied agents),[20] and
- Market infrastructures (by providing the right of choice and access to regulated markets and central counterparties, clearing and settlement systems).[21]

The CESR database has currently registered 243 trading systems, of which 139 are MTFs, 92 RMs and 12 SIs. Concerning the European cash equity market, there are 49 lit[22] markets (27 MTFs and 45 Regulated Markets) and dark markets[23] (9 broker-dealer crossing networks and 23 MTF dark pools) as of June 2010 (Gomber & Pierron, 2010).

---

[18] Official MiFID trading venues are: regulated markets (RMs), multilateral trading facilities (MTFs) and systematic internalisers (SIs).

[19] Arts 4.7, 4.14 and 4.15, MiFID.

[20] Arts 23 and 31, MiFID.

[21] Arts 33, 34, 35, MiFID.

[22] 'Lit markets' are pre-trade displayed limit order book and quotes, in contrast to 'dark books', which are limited order books that do not disclose book and quotes pre-trade. They are only post-trade transparent.

[23] See next Box for a definition.

Figure 5. Registered trading venues in the European Economic Area (EEA) and breakdown for equities

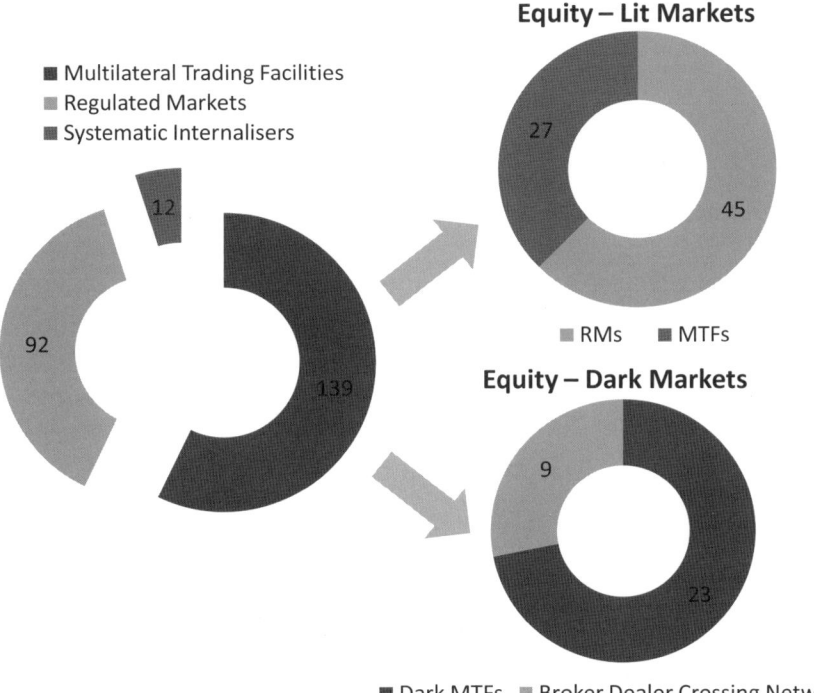

Sources: Authors from CESR and Gomber & Pierron (2010).

Box 1. Defining 'dark' in securities trading

The term 'dark' is often misperceived by the general public, in particular when it comes to be associated with securities trading, and in particular equity trading. Besides any possible pejorative meaning, 'dark' trading is a legal form of trading, foreseen by MiFID, that performs an important economic function in financial markets. It consists of trading with no obligation of pre-trade disclosure of price and volume. Specific conditions to benefit from the so-called 'waivers of pre-trade transparency' apply (see section 4.2.2 below). All other legal requirements – such as post-trade transparency, transaction reporting and market surveillance rules (when trading is done on a MiFID trading venue) – apply in the same way as they do in pre-trade transparent ('lit') markets. 'Dark' venues are generally accessible to non-retail investors who want to protect their trading interests from market impact by not disclosing them before the transaction takes place. 'Market impact' may increase transaction costs and reduce incentives to trade. Other reasons to use dark venues are explored in detail in section 4.2.

> As the report illustrates, dark trading may be only damaging when it becomes such a relevant part of the market that it de facto impedes the smooth functioning of price discovery and formation processes on lit markets.
>
> As used in this report, 'dark liquidity' usually refers to all trading executed in financial markets done with no pre-trade transparency, either under the MiFID exemptions (waivers) or under the MiFID definition of over-the-counter trade.[24] 'Dark trading venues' or 'dark markets', however, refer to a sub-category of dark liquidity, which includes 'dark pools' and broker-dealer crossing systems (see section 5.4). 'Dark pools' are trading venues classified as MTFs (so-called 'dark MTFs'). Those venues refer to neutral trading platforms where trades find their market-clearing price with no obligation of pre-trade disclosure of investors' trading interests.

On the one side, a more competitive environment produced positive effects, as the reduction of direct trading (and post-trading) costs, with no direct detrimental effects for price formation (CFA, 2009). Oxera investigated trading and post-trading costs between 2006 and 2008 and confirmed a relevant downward trend (Oxera, 2009). This trend was also acknowledged by respondents to a 2009 CESR report (CESR, 2009a).

More controversial is the discussion on the reduction of implicit trading costs (e.g. bid/ask spreads). In 2009, spreads have been higher than pre-MiFID (London Economics, 2010), but moving down fast. It is hard to disentangle the effects of the crisis (the stock indexes reached their bottom level in February-March 2009) from the ones brought about by MiFID. However, the latest data from 2010 seems to show a gradual decline of spreads below pre-MiFID levels, in line with the stabilisation of financial markets after the crisis (see Figure 6). Moreover, incumbents and newcomers have been massively investing in infrastructure and new technologies in order to reduce costs of execution and increase speed and quality of execution services.

---

[24] As explained in section 5.4.1, OTC trades may not qualify as 'dark' trade if they meet the requirements set in Recital 53, MiFID.

Figure 6. Bid/ask average spread and implicit volatility on EuroSTOXX, FTSE100 and CAC40

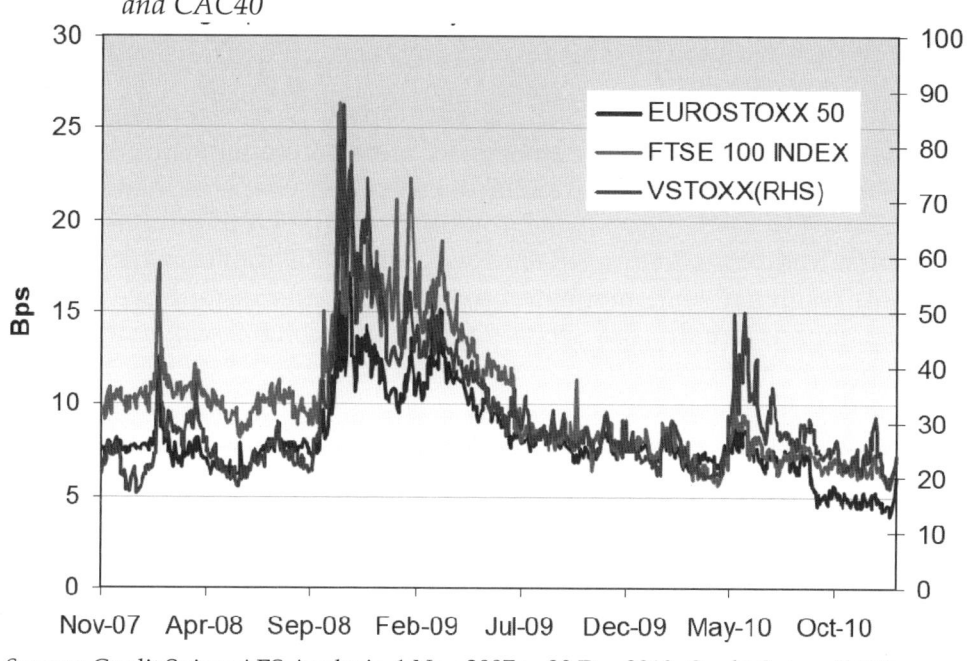

Sources: Credit Suisse AES Analysis, 1 Nov 2007 to 30 Dec 2010; Credit Suisse (2011).

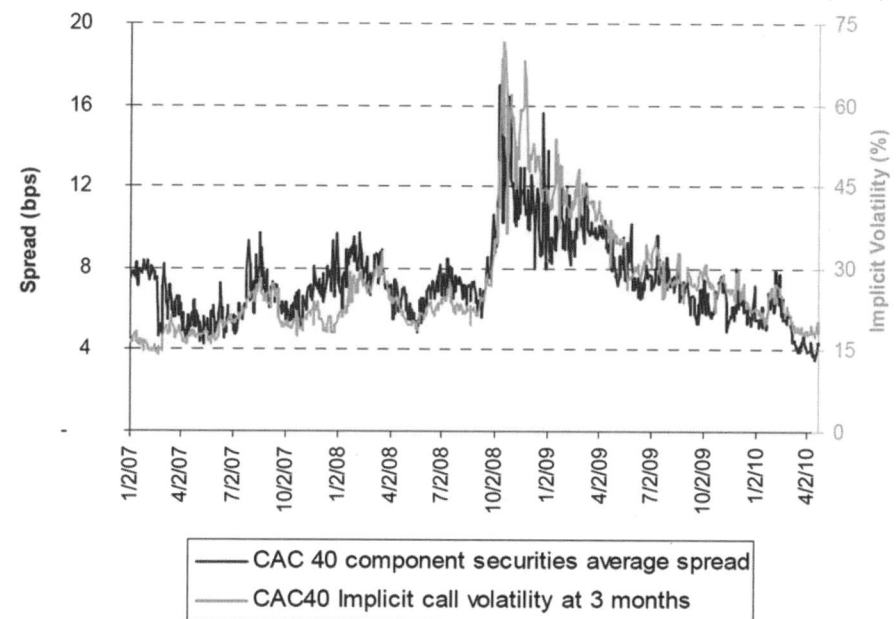

Source: NYSE Euronext (Response to CESR Consultation; CESR, 2010d).

On the other side, the growing number of trading venues has boosted market fragmentation,[25] thus increasing the search costs to source liquidity and potentially also the market impact. Nevertheless, new technologies seem to counterbalance this negative effect, delivering better order management strategies with lower market impact. New technologies and consolidated data solutions have drastically reduced the influence of 'depth in the market of reference' on trading decisions. In effect, estimates show that the impact of market depth and volatility on implicit trading costs, and therefore on trading decisions, is very low post-MiFID (London Economics, 2010). This result can be generally ascribed to the offer of multiple trading venues to source liquidity on secondary markets for the same stock at a reasonable price and cost.

Pan-European platforms. Fiercer competition, moreover, resulted in a loss of market shares for national regulated markets and in the emergence of new pan-European trading platforms (see Figure 7).

Figure 7. EEA equity markets – 2010 pan-European market shares

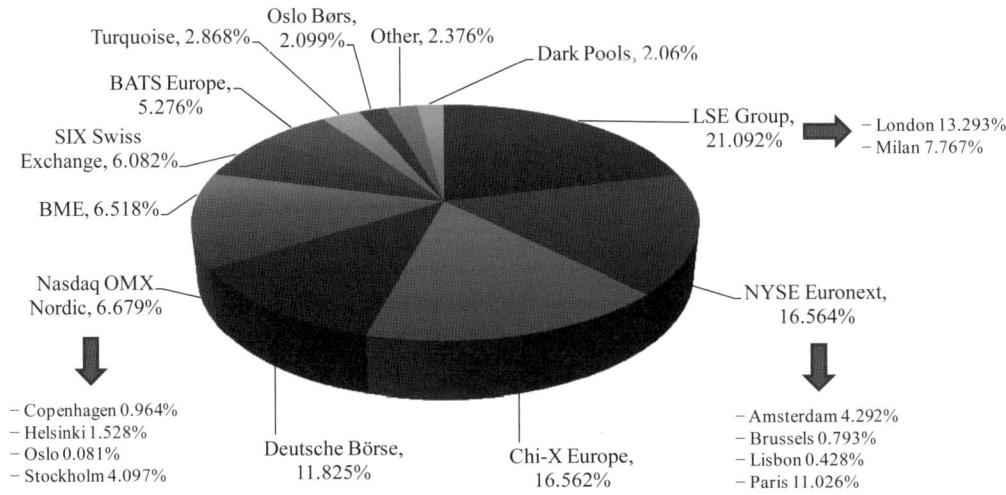

Sources: BATS Europe, Thomson Reuters, FESE (Jan-Dec 2010; % total turnover, lit, auction, and dark order books and hidden orders). For an overview of the main financial indicators for equity and non-equity markets, please see Annex I.

---

[25] See, more generally, chapter 1.

These new trading platforms are gradually increasing their market shares to the detriment of the incumbents through the offer of pan-European lit and dark order books for the secondary markets of most liquid European shares.

Market shares. The pan-European competition is reflected in the fragmentation of the most liquid shares in their national markets (see Figure 8).

Figure 8. Most liquid EU shares by execution venue

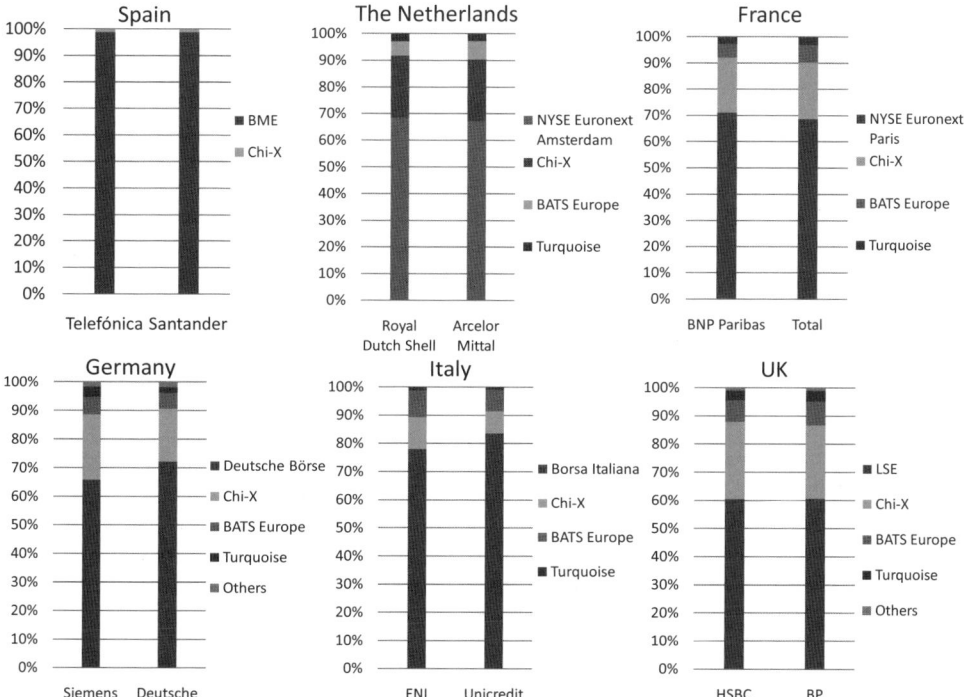

Note: This graph includes the two most liquid shares (as ranked by CESR, by average daily turnover) for the six biggest European equity markets.
Sources: CESR database and Fidessa's Fragulator (% of volumes, YTD, 30 November 2010).

As shown below, market shares of incumbent-regulated markets have consistently shrunk in the last two years. The most liquid shares in their respective national markets have gradually been traded on new, alternative pan-European platforms competing on execution and related services, especially on cost of execution and access to services that allow full exploitation of new trading technologies.

As a result of fierce competition, trading venues are struggling to reach economies of scale, cutting costs and diversifying sources of revenues. This may paradoxically induce the market – in the medium to long term – to reconsolidate around a few operators offering pan-European baskets of execution and related services for the most liquid shares in the secondary markets. It is not clear what effect this final equilibrium will have on European capital markets, since the benefits of network effects and economies of scale, as a result of further integration, may need to be balanced against a less competitive environment. However, competition is usually measured through the level of market barriers to entry and exit, rather than the number of competitors. Hence, the process should be guided by principles of fair competition underpinning the MiFID text.

3.3 The introduction of new technologies

In the last decade, European equity markets have experienced evolutionary changes in their infrastructure and trading methodologies. The introduction of new technologies and greater competition has led trading venues to cater for automated trading and investment firms to invest in algorithmic trading and high-frequency trading (HFT) technologies.[26] These developments stimulated new investments in market infrastructures (in particular, new trading platforms). Speed and likelihood of execution have become increasingly key aspects for professional investors, seeking to reduce the market impact of their orders. As a result, new trading methodologies and technologies have entered the scene and they seem to be here to stay.[27]

High-frequency trading. Currently, more than a third of the transactions executed on the UK FTSE 100 are made through HFT systems (see Table 2) and much more through algorithmic trading. In the US, this number was between 40% and 60% of the average daily volume in 2009 (Celent, 2009) and is set to be above 70% in 2010, as estimated in a recent survey by Aite Group. Trading venues and broker-dealers have invested massively in technology to accelerate and improve trade execution through the use of sophisticated algorithms and to improve capacity. The NYSE's

---

[26] HFT is a form of high-speed automated trading that it is often use by arbitrageurs and by professional investors in order to improve their trading strategies, often supported by complex algorithms.

[27] For a more detailed analysis about the link between new technologies and current market structure, see section 5.5.2.

speed of execution for small, immediately executable orders was 10.1 seconds in January 2005, compared to 0.7 of a second in October 2009 (SEC, 2010a, p. 6). NYSE Euronext Paris is going to move its servers to London to reduce latency and to be closer to the main trading community in Europe, while the LSE Group – after the acquisition of the IT firm Millennium – has launched an infrastructure called 'Millennium Exchange', to which Turquoise has recently migrated, while the main markets and third parties' markets – such as Oslo Børs – will migrate in 2011.

Table 2. Share of HFT by trading venue (shares of order books)

Trading venue	High-Frequency Trading[a]
Chi-X	40%
London Stock Exchange	32%
BME	25-30%[b]
NYSE Euronext	23%
Borsa Italiana	20%
Turquoise	19%[b]
Nasdaq OMX	13%[b]

[a] As a share of total trading value.
[b] As a share of total trading volumes.
Source: CESR responses to consultation paper on micro-structural issues in CESR (2010d).

HFT strategies. A report prepared by a Working Group chaired by Pierre Fleuriot and commissioned by the French Minister for the Economy, Industry and Employment has listed the main trading strategies that can be pursued through HFT systems (Fleuriot, 2010):
- Market-making (orders sent to capture the spread),
- Arbitrage (instantaneous or statistical) and
- Speculation (event-driven strategies to predict future price movements).

This set of strategies falls under those typical functions served by dealers and informed traders in financial markets (Harris, 2002). On the one side, algorithmic trading (AT) and more specifically HFT systems generally allow a faster and more efficient flow of information into prices, with potential price discovery and gains in spreads (Hendershott, Jones &

Menkveld, 2008; Brogaard, 2010). AT also seems to continue after market shocks and benefit from price reversal (Brogaard, 2010), and somehow from asset volatility without necessarily adding up to a generally highly volatile scenario. HFT is concentrated on most liquid stocks (Nasdaq OMX, 2010). On the other side, these systems could put trading platforms under severe stress by increasing volumes and speed to critical levels. Its use is expected to grow substantially in the coming years, as technologies become more widely available to investors. Only the effects of their widespread diffusion will clarify the real benefits and costs of technological developments. However – as with any other trading tool in financial markets – HFT systems may be used beyond their general purposes. In this sense, some market participants may want to pursue more aggressive trading strategies such as quote stuffing.[28] Regulators should therefore constantly supervise the actual use of these complex tools, set common technical standards and define legal boundaries.

New trading technologies. AT and HFT systems, in fact, are often erroneously seen as trading strategies, while they are only tools that allow high-speed computation of orders and new and more efficient trading strategies. However, AT and HFT have boosted new trading strategies, such as statistical arbitrage, which have now become an essential aspect of end investors' trading decisions.[29] Banks are continuously developing and fine-tuning their order-routing systems to remain competitive. Quantitative automated trading strategies, such as smart order routing through algorithmic trading, have become mainstream in trade execution and minimise the risks of sourcing liquidity to reduce market impact. Quantitative strategies based on high-frequency trading tools are now a more significant component of the market, and the success of this technological progress has actually encouraged more entrants. In effect, these sophisticated algorithms ought to slice big orders into small ones (so-called, 'child orders') and spread their execution in a set time frame and price range during the trading day. This substantially reduces risks of

---

[28] Quote stuffing is a manipulative practice pursued through high-frequency trading systems consisting of the introduction and instantaneous cancellation of a huge amount of orders in order to slow down the competitors' systems, gain processing time and deceive the market.

[29] Using data from listed firms, Hendershott & Riordan (2009) found that almost 50% of liquidity on Deutsche Börse comes from algorithmic trading. On Nordic markets, 40% is algorithmic trading and only 7% is 'pure' HFT (Nasdaq OMX, 2010).

market impact. Overall, algorithmic trading seems to consume liquidity when it is cheap, and supply liquidity when it is expensive, that is, when spreads widen. This beneficial outcome does not seem to increase volatility either (Hendershott & Riordan, 2009).

Market access. Moreover, trading platforms offer services to financial institutions in order to install their servers close to their data mainframe and reduce their latency. Other services to reduce latency, such as Direct Market Access (DMA) and Sponsored Access (SA),[30] allow entities to directly or indirectly access a trading platform with different levels of responsibility and controls over their actions (see section 5.5.2). These new access and low-latency services are critical for certain advanced trading strategies and seem to be a source of competitive advantage for trading venues. In addition to them, other access services – such as unfiltered access[31] – may be important for high-frequency trading systems. However, they bring new risks for the infrastructure, which need to predispose adequate systems and controls to monitor and manage potential misbehaviours or human errors (so-called 'fat fingers').

In conclusion, despite the indirect benefits of the availability of new technologies in financial markets (lower trading costs), retail investors remain only partially able to access technologies that facilitate their access to multiple trading venues (e.g. lack of consolidated data solutions). In effect, these technologies may benefit retail investors as long as they are used to promote easier and cheaper access to pan-European markets. Nevertheless, retail investors may have benefited from a modest downward trend of trading costs, as a consequence of an increasingly competitive environment.

3.4 Evolution in market microstructure and brokerage services

The introduction of new technologies and the new trading environment brought about by MiFID[32] have accelerated the evolutionary process in market microstructure and brokerage services.

---

[30] See Section 5.5.2.
[31] Unfiltered access is a sort of 'naked' sponsored access, in which the members' client can place an order on the trading platform that flows directly into the markets without a first screening of broker-dealer systems.
[32] Smith (2010) has found evidence that links latest developments in market microstructure (e.g. increased use of HFT and automated trading) with implementation of RegNMS in the US.

Concerning market microstructure, there are two relevant changes: 1) the decline of dealer quote-driven markets in favour of limit order books (dark and lit), even in the OTC space (Broker-dealer Crossing Systems, BCSs); and 2) the growth of dark pools volumes.[33]

Limit order books. Firstly, the general request for more transparency in trading instruments and infrastructures, and trading continuity – plus the evolution of technologies and trading systems – have favoured the use of limit order books. The use of smart order routing systems and other sophisticated automated trading systems advocates the crucial role of transparent limit order books (order-driven), which ensure more efficient and less costly trading continuity than dealer markets as long as there is a sufficient liquidity in the pool. MiFID has undoubtedly promoted a wider regime of transparency and investments in new trading technologies. However, on limit order books the market impact is potentially higher than in quote-driven markets, since dealers have the knowledge of the order before setting the price. Therefore, limit order books are usually characterised by greater ability to absorb small orders than big ones (Malinova & Park, 2008).

Secondly, the abovementioned change in market microstructure and the increased fragmentation of liquidity have increased the requests from market operators to deal with institutional orders on non-displayed limit order books (or so-called, *'dark pools'*) in order to reduce market impact. In effect, the public knowledge of an institutional order hitting the order book may provoke 'front-running' by parasitic traders aimed at using this information to exploit the expected price movement at the expense of the institutional orders, which may not find enough liquidity if prices move away from the target (so-called 'exposure risk'; Harris, 1997).

As a result, Table 3 suggests a growth of dark order book volumes in the 3Q of 2010, in comparison with 2009. Specifically, the use of dark pools of liquidity increased by more than three times last year, although it still remains a small fraction of total volumes (1.72%). From three main dark books in January 2009, this number was 11 at the beginning of 2010, and new entrants (both MTFs and RMs) are increasingly offering similar execution platforms.[34] New systems that allow automated trading activity also offer better reporting and clarity on volumes than before.

---

[33] For a more detailed discussion, see section 5.5.
[34] Section 4.2 will discuss the impact of dark order books on price formation and discovery.

Table 3. EEA trading venues' volumes (thousands of shares; by order book)

	2008 total volume	% Tot.	2009 total volume	% Tot.	2010 total volume	% Tot.	Δ '09/'10
Lit order book*	1,071,687,579	88.03	1,067,998,138	89.28	1,191,073,305	87.17	+11.52%
Order book - auction	143,871,002	11.82	116,440,019	9.73	146,209,746	10.7	+25.57%
Dark order venues	1,916,249	0.16	11,785,681	0.99	29,083,060	2.13	+146.77%
Total	1,217,474,830		1,196,223,839		1,366,366,110		+14.22%

* Including hidden orders.
Source: Authors from Thomson Reuters.

Finally, brokerage service providers are experiencing a strong consolidation phase as the proliferation of technologies and the need for advanced execution services allow a more sophisticated offer through centralised platforms. These platforms can thus exploit increasing economies of scale and scope (network effects). Cheaper trading costs for high-volume traders and institutional investors give an opportunity to dealers to enter this market and combine advanced *brokerage with execution services*, in order to minimise both market impact and risks, and to source liquidity in a fragmented market. Broker-dealer crossing networks (BCNs)[35] are the result of this evolutionary process, as they provide execution services with best execution, on a discretionary basis.[36]

3.5 A more comprehensive transparency regime

MiFID recognises the role of transparency in financial markets as a means

---

[35] BCNs represent linked groups of broker-dealer crossing systems (or BCSs) designed to form one pool of liquidity and reach a critical mass to cross orders. Matching of orders typically takes place with no pre-trade transparency and supported by best execution duties. For the sake of simplicity, we will use these two terms (BCN and BCS) interchangeably in the present text, as we are interested in the function they serve more than in the modality by which they perform those services.

[36] For a more detailed discussion of the economic and regulatory implications of BCNs, please see section 5.4.

to enhance liquidity and increase investor protection.[37] The Directive extended the *coverage* and scope of the transparency regime to all equity trading venues. However, the extension to non-equity markets was left to the discretion of member states. Only two countries (Sweden and Italy) decided to apply this transparency regime to fixed-income.

The *scope* of the transparency regime is fairly wide. Legal obligations require the disclosure of pre-trade information (quotes) by the abovementioned trading venues and post-trade information by investment firms (directly or indirectly through a third party) wherever the shares (admitted to trading on a regulated market) are actually traded. The post-trade transparency regime applies not only to equity orders executed on regulated markets, but also on alternative platforms and over-the-counter crossing systems. Information, through different reports, is disclosed to the market (trade reporting) and to regulators (transaction reporting)[38] with different requirements and granularity. Pre-trade transparency, however, can be waived in some specific cases and in order to serve specific market needs.

Despite the greater scope and the stricter requirements of the MiFID transparency regime, the implementation has produced inconsistencies in the quality of market data and the reporting methodology. Data for over-the-counter transactions lack quality, including duplicate reporting, and create uncertainty about its relevance in Europe's capital markets.

3.6 Greater investor protection

Another important achievement of MiFID is in the area of investor protection, through the harmonisation of a meaningful set of business conduct rules and organisational requirements. Investor protection has been levelled across Europe. Among the most important measures, the introduction of conflict of interest rules, best execution and know-your-customer rules (e.g. suitability and appropriateness tests), which specify the general duty of the agent 'to act in the principal's best interest' (Art. 19.1, MiFID).

Main measures. The parallel introduction of 'know-your-customer rules' and best execution for all orders (and all financial instruments,[39]

---

[37] See chapter 1.
[38] See Arts 27-30, 44 and 45, MiFID.
[39] But not all kinds of investors (e.g. eligible counterparties).

except spot foreign exchange products) has promoted a stronger relationship with clients. This is true in particular between retail clients and investment firms in the provision of specific services (such as order execution services). These two rules have made the European and US financial markets regulation closer than ever before. Exemptions for professional investors (or eligible counterparties) or dilution effects foreseen by the legal text allow them to 'contract around' or 'opt-out' of the standard rules (e.g. best execution), in order to minimise transaction costs. Moreover, the Directive has harmonised the framework of rules on conflicts of interest, which previously fell under the principle of the home country control.

Finally, concerns have been raised about the implementation of these rules. Implementing measures are often adopted to reflect only the minimum legal requirements without assessing the quality of execution and the actual level of investor protection.

4. A 'RENEWED' TRANSPARENCY REGIME

4.1 The role of transparency in financial markets

Transparency is the possibility by market participants to see the market mechanisms, in particular information on market price of a security and its determinants (order flow). It has gradually become a crucial aspect of financial markets, in parallel with the evolution in market microstructure and new technologies. In effect, with full information asymmetry there is no price equilibrium and no exchange will take place (Madhavan, 1992), due to strong adverse selection and moral hazard problems.[40] Therefore, the primary objective of transparency – in its many dimensions – is to reduce information asymmetry and transaction costs in order to make the exchange between buyers and sellers happen, thus reducing search costs and promoting more efficient price formation. In other words, appropriate transparency promotes price discovery in order to find the market-clearing price (price formation) of a financial instrument.

---

[40] 'Adverse selection' is an informational problem that arises when products of a different quality (e.g. lemons and good cars; junk and good bonds and so on) are sold at a single price because of asymmetric information (inability of the buyer to understand the actual quality/risk of the cars/financial product or borrower), so that too much of the low-quality product and too little of the high-quality product are sold. The equilibrium will result in a market price (due to this inability of the buyer to understand *ex ante* the quality of the product) a bit higher than the real value of low-quality products and consistently lower than the real value of high-quality products. Hence, the market equilibrium, in the mid-term, will determine that only low-quality products are sold in the market. This fundamental issue can freeze markets, thereby justifying mechanisms for quality signals, such as neutral third-party informational tools (rating agencies, etc.) or regulatory actions to increase transparency or simply pre-sale services. See, in general, Akerlof (1970) and Kraakman (1986). 'Moral hazard' is an informational problem created by the opportunistic behaviour of the more informed party, who tries to exploit the informational advantage and the scarce ability of the less informed party to monitor his/her activity. See, in general, Holmstrom (1979) and Milgrom & Roberts (1992).

What information? The general problem typically is what kind of information should be published and who should be entitled to receive it (O'Hara, 1995). The implementation of a transparency regime is a complex exercise. The kind of information that should be disclosed needs to be carefully assessed, since full disclosure in some cases may have unintended consequences. Therefore, the type of published information is strictly related to the market microstructure (e.g. asset classes, trading organisation) that underpins financial markets.[41]

The rapid increase of volumes in the last decade has boosted the use of limit order books (auction markets), which have pushed down transaction costs (explicit and implicit costs) and ensured continuous trading as requested by new technologies (automated trading services). Secondary markets, in particular for equity, have gradually moved from more opaque quote-driven dealerships to auction markets (limit order books). Limit order books need a certain degree of transparency. To ensure that the order flow is transparent in a meaningful way, there are generally two levels of data that may in some instances need to be disclosed: 1) pre-trade data (quote) and 2) post-trade data (trade disclosure). Such data finally need to be provided with sufficient depth, breadth and quality in order to benefit markets.

To whom? The appropriate flow of information generally benefits uninformed investors,[42] as they increase their knowledge of the market. However, as shown in the next sections, disclosing information may be harmful for some types of uninformed traders and markets that are not based on auctions. Therefore, the general goal to protect uninformed traders – who are not necessarily retail – may need to be carefully balanced against the risks to market efficiency coming from a fully transparent market setting.

---

[41] The main empirical literature on market transparency comes from research and empirical studies on equities or financial instruments traded on organised trading platforms through order-driven markets or quote-driven dealer markets. Studies in financial instruments traded OTC are very limited since there is almost no publicly available information and their market share was quite limited until the beginning of the new century. There is currently no regime of trade reporting (public disclosure) and transaction reporting (disclosure to regulators). For a discussion on market microstructure, see section 5.5.

[42] 'Uninformed investors' are those who trade with no private information, "but know that prices will reflect the information of the informed traders" (Dow & Gorton, 2006).

Objectives. It is in the market's interest to have a certain level of transparency. However, incentives may not be in line with public policies,[43] so regulators may need to push market operators to disclose more information. In effect, transparency requirements under MiFID (Arts 27-30, 44 and 45, MiFID) serve two public policy purposes:
i) Price efficiency
ii) Investor protection

Price efficiency. Public disclosure requirements (or trade reporting)[44] to the public should be proportional to the market mechanisms that shape investor behaviour and through which securities are generally traded. For sake of simplicity, this report splits the available market mechanisms in open limit-order books (or 'order-driven'; hereinafter, OLOB)[45] and 'quote-driven' dealer markets,[46] both ensuring continuity of trading.[47] Both systems currently support automated trading. In general, public disclosure of the order flow improves the flow of information into prices and can enhance liquidity[48] because it lowers search costs (more efficient price

---

[43] Transparency is something that everyone benefits from but very few would be willing to provide information about their trades without explicit requirements. Therefore, the level of transparency with no regulatory intervention may be sub-optimal. See also ESME (2009b).

[44] The report distinguishes between trade reporting – public disclosure pre-trade or post-trade requirements – from transaction reporting, which is a publication system for trade reports to regulators.

[45] OLOBs is a system in which submitted limit orders continuously receive immediate execution against the book. Orders are submitted by public investors and dealers. It operates as an auction because the price is formed through a continuous multilateral matching of orders. A quote-driven continuous dealer market is a market in which investors immediately execute their orders against the quotes provided by competing market-makers. Bid/ask quotations typically depend on the size of orders. See, in particular, Madhavan (1992).

[46] Quote-driven markets are trading systems whose public quotes are the result of competing quotations offered by market-makers and dealers for a certain amount of a specific financial instrument. Main quote-driven markets are fixed income and derivatives markets, whose trading activities can be done 'on exchange' or 'over-the-counter'.

[47] Trading may be also done through periodic auctions, batch or transparent (Pagano-Roëll, 1996). In fact, periodic auctions that involve the submission of buy and sell limit orders – which are matched at a price/quantity set by the market or the dealer (batch auction) or all crossed at a common price (transparent auction) – are typically part of the opening call auction, that is to form prices when there is a low level of liquidity.

[48] Liquidity is a multi-faceted concept and it is difficult to find a definition that can perfectly fit all dimensions of securities trading. A market is liquid when it "is almost infinitely tight, which is not infinitely deep, and […] resilient enough so that prices eventually tend to their

discovery). It also minimises adverse selection effects for uninformed traders, with positive effects on opening spreads especially for dealer markets (Pagano & Roëll, 1996; Flood et al., 1999). OLOBs may benefit from greater transparency, as enhances liquidity; reduces volatility; and increases price efficiency (Giraud & D'Hondt, 2006). Prices are converging faster to fundamental values in a more transparent market setting. For instance, cash equity markets are so large and involve so many uninformed investors that greater transparency requirements (as defined by MiFID) seem beneficial, since they reduce volatility and improve market quality. In 'thinner' markets, with insufficient noise trading, volatility will increase with market disclosure (Madhavan, 1996).

Competition. In addition, efficient information transmission between markets may help to keep competition in the market between market-makers and trading venues, and mitigates risks of fragmentation (Madhavan, 1995). Artificially fragmented market settings may harm the market with side effects on the cost of capital and the economy.[49]

However, wide trade disclosure – principally for dealer markets (and potentially for liquidity providers in OLOBs) – may reduce transactional efficiency in those markets, since disclosure of private information can reduce market-makers' incentive to compete on spreads (Bloomfield & O'Hara, 1999). In a nutshell – by increasing transparency – an important trade-off emerges. Regulators thus should look at striking the right balance between overall benefits for uninformed traders and negative effects upon informed traders (including dealers), who will not be able to benefit from their informational advantage (market knowledge) if a wider transparency regime applies. In some markets, the informational gap may be the only incentive for dealers to deal with illiquid products, and thereby create a market where none hitherto existed. A trade-off emerges in particular when dealers play a more relevant role in the market, as in quote-driven

---

underlying value" (Kyle, 1985, p. 1317). Three aspects emerge from this definition: i) tightness (which is the possibility to turn over a position at the fastest speed technically possible, when needed); ii) depth (which refers to the ability of the market to absorb quantities without having a large effect on price; it is usually not constant over time in some asset classes); and iii) resiliency (which is the speed at which prices return to their fundamental value after a move due to regular trading or – with more intensity – to external shocks).

[49] See chapter 1.

markets for instance. Therefore, two factors must be considered when imposing transparency requirements (Kumar et al., 2009):

1) The active role of informed traders in the market (e.g. a market consisting of only institutional investors) and
2) The active commitment and participation of liquidity suppliers (e.g. quote-driven illiquid markets).

The presence of these two factors may sensibly reduce the beneficial effects of greater public disclosure, pre- and post-trade.

Moreover, the direct exposure of some types of orders (i.e. big size orders) to OLOBs can generate market impact and thus push liquidity out of the market (implicit transaction costs; Harris, 1997). Non-calibrated transparency requirements may indeed harm liquidity, hence widening spreads in quote-driven markets or reducing book depth[50] in order-driven markets and making markets 'thinner'. In order to address these potential trade-offs between transparency and market quality and efficiency, MiFID has already set in the original text a list of exemptions from disclosure and delayed publications in cash equity markets.

In non-equity markets,[51] where trading mechanisms are mainly facilitated by dealers, the transparency regime needs to be defined and calibrated in a different way, since those markets have a fundamentally different market microstructure from cash equity markets.

Investor protection. A transparent market may also generate reputational capital, as an efficient transparency system can stimulate surveillance by other traders and provide more control over insiders (less moral hazard; Chowdhry & Nanda, 1991). It also gives more information to investors in order to make more informed decisions for their investments, as well as a more effective assessment on how intermediaries are complying with their best execution policy. Moreover, greater disclosure for investor protection purposes is also ensured through an ad hoc transaction reporting system to regulators, which improves market surveillance, market integrity and enforcement of current legislation. A market subject to manipulation will infuse loss of confidence in the efficient market functioning and raise problems of moral hazard.

---

[50] Market depth is a measure of liquidity that represents the ability to absorb order flows without large changes in prices (Glosten, 1994); it represents the volume required to generate a market unit price change (Kyle, 1985).
[51] This report will generally refer to 'non-equity markets' as markets that are not primary or secondary cash equity.

> **Conclusion # 1**
>
> *Transparency plays a crucial role for the smooth functioning of financial markets and the monitoring of systemic risk. It also ensures the correct functioning of the price formation process through efficient price discovery mechanisms. However, regulatory actions in certain areas are needed, not only as a result of the recent financial crisis but also from the experience gained since the transposition of the Directive. Interventions should be proportional to the market structure through which investors' orders find the market-clearing price. Disproportionate transparency requirements would harm market efficiency in some illiquid markets with no increase of investor protection or reduction of systemic risk, as the market would become less-liquid and more subject to manipulation and eventually to market crashes.*

4.2 Pre-trade transparency for cash equities: Benefits and costs

In order to preserve the abovementioned objectives, MiFID designed a two-level regime of transparency for cash equities, pre-trade and post-trade. This structure seems to be well-designed, in particular for OLOBs, which are continuous auction markets and inherently more transparent than other forms of markets (Pagano & Roëll, 1996).

Definition. Pre-trade transparency concerns the public disclosure of quotes and trading interests. Appropriate and effective pre-trade transparency requirements ought to serve investor protection and price efficiency supporting price discovery (through real-time quote disclosure) and best execution (through smart order routers). These transparency requirements mainly apply to the official trading venues under MiFID (RMs, MTFs and SIs; Arts 22.2, 27, 29 and 44, MiFID). In an integrated market, more pre-trade transparency tends to even levels of information between market participants. Overall – as shown below – evidence seems to confirm that pre-trade transparency may be beneficial if the market is 'large enough' (as defined by Madhavan, 1996 and Baruch, 2005), i.e. benefits for uninformed investors (liquidity demanders) are higher than costs for informed ones (liquidity suppliers). Therefore, price discovery seems still to be rewarding, since there is sufficient noise trading and space for arbitrage (there is still private information that can be rewarded).

Benefits. The literature found conflicting evidence on the benefits of pre-trade transparency, and the results seem to be different in relation to the trading mechanisms that underpin the market structure.[52] In OLOBs, disclosure of quotes and order flow provide uninformed investors and the entire markets with visibility of best prices and a part of the order flow (usually first five best quotes) on real-time. If market players are able to consolidate quotes across trading venues, the positive effects of these requirements may offset the potential negative effects of liquidity fragmentation (Glosten, 1994, Madhavan, 1995 and O'Hara & Ye, 2009). Bohemer et al. (2005) found the opening-up of a limit order book to pre-trade transparency to be beneficial. As a consequence, the new transparency settings impacted on trading strategies: traders manage exposure of orders with less market impact (higher cancellation rate and shorter time-to-cancellation rate) and there are overall fewer specialists in the market (informed traders). These changes improved market quality and more specifically ameliorated:

i) Informational efficiency (smaller deviations of transaction prices from efficient price) and
ii) Liquidity (increase of depth and decline in effective spreads).

The case study of Island in the US (Hendershott & Jones, 2005) shows that reducing pre-trade transparency may have negative effects on the trading venue. In effect, after Island decided to go dark, it lost half of the market share, while effective and realized spreads went up drastically. Other lit markets saw their market share increasing and spreads going down, with unclear net overall effects. In 2003, Island redisplayed quotes, but market share and spreads did not go back to the previous levels (at least not in the short/medium term). Other evidence from Eom & Park (2007) suggest that market quality increases with the level of pre-trade transparency up to a point, after which the quality decreases, in line with the characteristics of a concave function (see figure below). Traders adjust their preferences about the real value of the share as quote disclosure changes or as other traders' behaviour changes. However, market quality – measured through six parameters[53] – would improve up to a certain level, where an inflection point signals the reversal of the trend.

---

[52] For an overview of literature on market transparency, see Sabatini & Tarola (2002).

[53] Spread and relative spread; market depth (bid/ask spreads and limit orders size); transitory volatility (from liquidity provision); market-to-limit order ratio; full information trade cost (FITC); and 2 components of the trade execution costs, implied spread (adverse selection and transitory cost). Eom & Park (2007, p. 323).

Figure 9. Pre-trade transparency and market quality

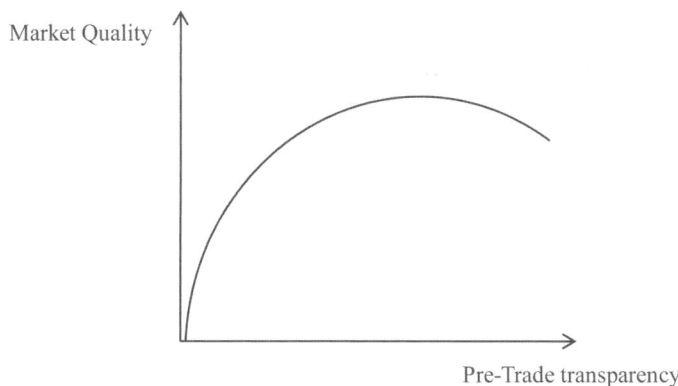

Source: Author from EOM & Park (2007).

This pattern has also been suggested by recent studies on OTC equity trading. There is no strong evidence of a positive relation between the size of OTC trading and market depth (Gresse, 2010). However, Buti et al. (2010b) find – on a sample of US stocks – that dark markets[54] (non pre-trade transparent venues) are not detrimental to market quality, although their introduction pushed quoted spreads down until those venues reached a certain market share.[55] This intuition seems to be confirmed by an ongoing study (Degryse, 2010), which tries to find hard evidence of a positive relationship between market depth and size of over-the-counter trading.[56]

---

[54] In the EU, the terms may only include MTFs or RMs applying pre-trade transparency waivers. In this specific case, authors refer to all trading venues with no pre-trade transparency (including broker-dealer matching systems).

[55] Authors identify this share at between 8% and 10%. However, they doubt the validity of this threshold and warn that the causal relationship between dark pool and market quality needs to be further investigated.

[56] Over-the-counter trading in these studies reflects a number that may be altered by double counting and does not include all dark liquidity, as the report describes in the next sections in more detail. However, it may include useful information on the impact of non pre-trade transparent liquidity on market quality.

Figure 10. Market depth and OTC activity

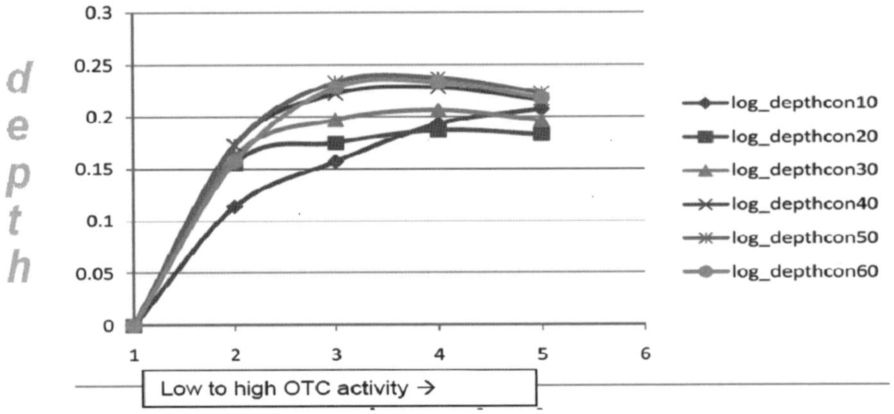

[Chart showing depth on y-axis (0 to 0.3) vs "Low to high OTC activity →" on x-axis (1 to 6), with six curves: log_depthcon10, log_depthcon20, log_depthcon30, log_depthcon40, log_depthcon50, log_depthcon60]

Source: Degryse et al. (2010).

A preview of the results – showed to our Task Force – suggests that OTC trading is beneficial to market depth until it reaches a certain market share (see Figure 10). The authors computed the depth of visible market for different potential price movements (10 to 60 bps). They regressed daily measures of logarithmic depth with controls (time dummy variables, etc.) and five OTC activity buckets (<1%; 1-5%; 5-12%; 12-27%; >27%).[57] As a consequence, the existence of non pre-trade transparent liquidity – below a certain amount – seems to benefit the whole market. This outcome appears to be the result of increased competitive pressure by dark venues not only on handling large trades but also on price improvements in comparison to those of other trading venues. With inter-market competition, pre-trade transparency in the main market allows 'free-riding' and creates new markets. Price discovery should be informative and rewarding, so dark pools can free-ride on information about prices due to noise trading, i.e. there are still different kinds of traders operating in this market (and most of them uninformed).

Costs. However, as previously stated, pre-trade transparency may not be always beneficial. Madhavan et al. (2005) found evidence on the Toronto Stock Exchange that opening up floor and CATS (Computerised

---

[57] This exercise showed that the threshold of actual trading that seems tolerable is between 12% and 27%. Also in this case, authors (such as Buti et al., 2010), warn that this threshold may not be accurate and that more and better data should be made available to the market in order to further investigate these issues.

Automated Trading System) markets' pre-trade transparency to the public (for members it was already available) may be harmful, in particular for markets with specialists (floor trading). In effect, the results of this action increased gaming risks around the opening price, spreads and volatility, and lowered market depth (in particular for floor trading). The rationale behind this case study relies on the assumption that limit orders can be seen as an option at a specified price. Therefore, when limit orders are forced to interact with market orders on the same pre-trade information level, liquidity providers (informed traders) are less willing to provide 'free options' to market orders. This situation increases adverse selection effects. As a consequence, liquidity decreases, spreads widen and price volatility soars. However, levelling the amount of information available to traders should also attract new investors to the table.

Exposure risk. Revealing specific trading interests to the public on the limit order book may expose traders to unforeseen costs (exposure risk and market impact; Madhavan, 1995; Harris, 1997, 2002). Order exposure may be costly if the exposure (Harris, 1997):

1) Reveals traders' motives,
2) Reveals the potential price impact of future trades or
3) Reveals valuable trading options.

Firstly, by revealing trader's motives they will lose proprietary information on the real value of the share, so reducing time for defensive measures and exposing the trader to squeezers, who will be able to control the order flow.

Secondly, orders exposure may attract parasitic traders,[58] who profit by anticipating large impact orders and taking liquidity on the order book before the large order is executed (front-running).[59] In this way, large traders pay more for providing liquidity (they will buy at a higher price).

Thirdly, private information on exposure on the order book may lead traders to set limit orders just above the limit price of the big trader, in order to use it as stop loss if prices go down instead of up (they will sell to the large trader). The large trader therefore gives a 'free' valuable option to

---

[58] Parasitic traders are a category of reactive traders (Harris, 1997), i.e. those who reply with trading in response to trading opportunities given by other traders.

[59] This practice is illegal if done by brokers on orders held on own account, in line with Recital 19, Directive 2006/6/EC on market abuse (MAD).

other traders (with some risk for the last ones, though). In addition, decreasing tick sizes may have led more orders to be hidden due to higher exposure risk, since orders may be more easily subject to legal front-running through smaller price unit changes.

In conclusion, pre-trade disclosure of information on highly illiquid products may affect the price formation process of other related financial instruments, or disclose private information that parties do not want to disclose as part of private negotiations.

> *Conclusion # 2*
>
> *Pre-trade transparency is fundamental for trading venues and their trading structure, as well as for an efficient price discovery and a better implementation of best execution policies. It is also important to exempt some trading interests (e.g. block trades) from pre-trade transparency requirements, because – as mentioned above – this situation may otherwise have a negative impact on the market. The breadth of these exemptions is under debate and conflicting views emerge on several aspects, as explained in the following sections.*

> *Box 2. Defensive strategies*
>
> In order to manage exposure risks and aside from the illegality of some of these practices, Harris (1997) categorised the potential defensive strategies that traders can pursue to reduce adverse effects of exposing trading interests. These strategies may be summarised as:
>
> a. evasive (retaining information),
> b. deceptive (confusing through the use of misleading information) and
> c. offensive (counter-attacking with opposite orders).
>
> Evasive strategies may use: i) multiple brokers, ii) anonymous/dark trading, iii) counterparty selection strategies (by the trader or the venue where the trader executes his/her orders), iv) slice and dice strategies (slicing orders), v) internal matching systems, vi) indications of interests (IoIs),[60] or vii) waiting strategies.
>
> Secondly, traders may disseminate inaccurate information through legal mechanisms such as: i) trading in the opposite direction of the big order that

---

[60] An indication of interest (IoI) "is the name commonly used to refer to a message sent between investment firms to convey information about available trading interest. IOIs are also used by dark pools to attract order flow and to maximise trading opportunities by enabling investors to find the contra-side of orders. The information provided in an IOI can include the symbol of the security, the side (i.e. buy or sell) and volume/price of trading interest" (CESR, 2010b).

> he/she tries to execute, ii) trading on a related market in order to divert market attention, iii) introducing and cancelling orders in order to create uncertainty around their trading interest or iv) introducing orders with lower size in order to create different expectations and get better terms.
>
> Finally, traders may reduce their exposure by adopting offensive strategies to attack front-runners, by trading in the opposite direction and then removing the interest.

4.2.1 Dark liquidity

Exposure risks and market depth (as above) may require the use of liquidity that is not-pre-trade transparent (dark liquidity).[61] In general, all trades are important for price formation as they form liquidity, even if they are not displayed. Dark liquidity – below a still unclear market share – may bring some beneficial effects to the whole market. Recent findings on hidden orders show that some opacity in the market improves liquidity in a centralised limit order book with no fragmentation (Moinas, 2010). It can be justified by the strong incentive for informed traders to sniff out where hidden liquidity sits on the lit book (De Winne & D'Hondt, 2007). Hidden orders stimulate informed traders to search for liquidity. In addition, if you expose those orders, you may generate the effect of withdrawing liquidity from the market, thereby making it more vulnerable to manipulation because of its much lower thickness and depth ('thinner'). The presence of hidden orders, therefore, stimulates greater activity for liquidity demanders in order to find trading opportunities within the book. This is a major difference between stand-alone dark pools, which do not have direct liquidity links, and lit books (they do not hit the displayed limit order book).

Purposes. Traders' motivation to engage in dark trading have been already implicitly or explicitly mentioned, but the IOSCO (2010c) has recently listed the reasons in a consultation paper. They can be summarised as:

1) avoiding private (or proprietary trading) information leakage,
2) minimising market impact costs (information leakage and/or insufficient market depth),
3) ensuring better order management (lowering the risk of being

---

[61] This term includes dark pools, hidden orders and BCNs.

'picked-off'),
4) avoiding also hidden orders as they may be sniffed out by sophisticated software,
5) taking advantage of a price improvement and
6) minimising transaction costs.

The *size* of non-pre-trade transparent liquidity is constantly growing across Europe (see Table 3) and currently represents 6.76% of total EEA trading (off and on-order book; see Table 4) and 10.86% of EEA trading on RMs, MTFs and broker-dealer crossing systems (BCSs).

Table 4. Dark liquidity in the EU (% of total EEA trading)*

	2009				2010
	Q1	Q2	Q3	Q4	Q1
Dark pools and hidden orders**	4.71%	5.68%	5.6%	6.11%	5.26%^
Broker-dealer crossing systems	0.9%	0.9%	0.9%	1.4%	1.5%
	5.61%	6.58%	6.5%	7.51%	6.76%

* Trading under waivers, % of EEA total trading.
** Estimated market share as % of EEA total trading, assuming a constant average market share of OTC trading of 38% in 2009 and Q1 2010 (CESR 2010b).
^ Does not include Poland.
Source: Authors' calculation from CESR (2010b).

Table 5. Dark liquidity in the EU (% of EEA RMs, MTFs and BCNs trading)*

	2009				2010
	Q1	Q2	Q3	Q4	Q1
Dark pools and hidden orders	7.6%	9.2%	9.0%	9.8%	8.5%^
Broker-dealer crossing systems**	1.43%	1.43%	1.43%	2.21%	2.36%
	9.03%	10.63%	10.43%	12.01%	10.86%

* Trading under waivers, % of total EEA trading on RMs and MTFs.
** Estimated market share as % of total EEA trading on RMs, MTFs and BCNs, assuming a constant average market share of OTC trading of 38% over time (CESR, 2010b).
^ Does not include Poland.
Source: Authors' calculation from CESR (2010b).

Externalities. Different views emerge on where dark liquidity might be concentrated. Some authors argue that stocks with high volumes, high market depth and low volatility are mainly traded 'dark' (Degryse et al., 2008; Buti et al., 2010b). Others (Ready, 2009) suggest that dark liquidity trading would be converging on stocks with high spreads, in order to find a better deal on other venues. In effect, the idea is that – although high liquid shares may receive easy execution on dark pools – liquid shares will receive low execution costs on other venues as well, so the opportunity costs of trading on lit pools are very small. There are few incentives to look to other venues. With large spreads on lit books, instead, traders may search for other venues giving price improvements (Cheuvreux, 2010). In the EU, this should be even truer as traders get at least the mid-point (but also a volume weighted average price, VWAP)[62] from dark pools applying the reference price waiver,[63] while lit trading venues may offer very high bid/ask spreads on that specific product. Ready (2009) also suggests that institutional investors with big average positions and less turnover make more use of dark liquidity, in line with the theoretical framework.

Dark liquidity may also generate negative externalities, in terms of liquidity fragmentation and order migration. In effect, adding a dark pool to a liquid market with OLOBs may lead orders to migrate towards this new pool ('cream skimming'), which stimulates the arrival of new orders (with liquidity-externality effects). The new environment seems to benefit institutional investors, but it may decrease the price discovery ability of retail ones, as they will not be able to see a part of the market (less efficient price discovery, Buti et al., 2010a). Analysts find that overall the total welfare increases, but the distributional effects remain. Moreover, the abovementioned studies – even though with limited evidence – seem to concur that an excessive volume of dark liquidity may generate negative effects and market operators would not have incentives to reduce those effects once they materialised. In effect, high network externalities and effects on revenues may push players to act out the 'prisoner's dilemma' (bad equilibrium). There may be no incentive to cooperate when a damaging threshold is reached, even though the final outcome may not benefit any of the pools in the market. Therefore, regulators may need to

---

[62] See CESR (2010e, p. 3).

[63] This venue uses prices formed on lit venues, mainly regulated markets.

monitor these liquidity pools to learn when their size begins to undermine market quality (mainly price formation and discovery processes).

IoIs. In order to increase the market quality of the liquidity pool, dark trading venues (dark MTFs/RMs) may adopt a non-binding indication of interest (IoI) messaging system. This system is typically designed to attract liquidity, by giving access to privileged private information on trading interests, including size, price (or a targeted weighted average price), buy or sell, and often the symbol of the security. IoIs are typically sent to some traders on a discriminatory basis. Therefore, those investors may benefit from the network of dark pools without competing for liquidity with other traders.

Some market operators argue that this might be an elegant way to circumvent the public pre-trade disclosure of quotes, discriminating against potential investors who might be interested. At the same time, disclosure of IoIs does not bind the counterparty to conclude the trade. On the one hand, a non-binding IoI messaging system may increase legal uncertainty by stimulating expectations (inefficient commitment) about the stipulation of the contract (trade). On the other hand, MiFID recognises the importance of non-discriminatory access to order information on trading venues (RMs/MTFs) in addition to the overarching objective for organised trading venues (as defined by CESR, 2010g) to comply with pre-trade transparency requirements. Therefore, CESR (2010b) considers the provision of private valuable order information on a discriminatory basis as a violation of MiFID principles (unfair), in conformity with the SEC policy (2009). However, the Committee did recognise the role of IoIs in OTC trading if finalised to find selected counterparties to a large order waiting for execution. This practice was already widely in use before the implementation of MiFID.

OTC trading. Dark liquidity can sit on official trading venues, both MiFID-compliant and over-the counter. MiFID recognises the importance of OTC trading (Recital 53[64]) as part of the general freedom of investors

---

[64] "It is not the intention of this Directive to require the application of pre-trade transparency rules to transactions carried out on an OTC basis, the characteristics of which include that they are ad-hoc and irregular and are carried out with wholesale counterparties and are part of a business relationship which is itself characterised by dealings above standard market size, and where the deals are carried out outside the systems usually used by the firm concerned for its business as a systematic internaliser.", Recital 53, MiFID. For more details about OTC trading venues, see section 5.4.

(shareholders) and legal entities to trade shares privately – if specific circumstances are met. It also acknowledges that OTC trading can promote the smooth operation of financial markets by providing in some instances better investment services outside MiFID official venues. There are conflicting views on the actual size of OTC trading (in terms of price forming trading), which this report will consider in the next sections.[65] CESR estimated OTC trading as 38% of trading in the EEA. However, as CESR itself stated (2010b, p. 35), these data may be inflated by double counting and misreporting; hence a lack of quality and accuracy urges actions to reduce inconsistencies and increase granularity.

4.2.2   Pre-trade transparency waivers: Where do we stand?

Pre-trade transparency obligations are placed on both RMs and MTFs by MiFID for shares listed on regulated markets (for SIs, a specific system of publishing quotes applies).[66] The Directive, however, acknowledges the risk of market impact caused by transparency obligations for certain types of orders and trading venues. In response, regulators have introduced a list of exemptions in specific cases. In particular, MiFID recognises pre-trade transparency waivers for market models and for orders of a certain type or size. However, dark trading may deteriorate market quality if it reaches an undefined overall size. Empirical evidence does not provide a clear answer – either to whether a threshold for dark liquidity and waivers would capture the critical point or where this overall threshold should be placed, whether by regulators or the market. Therefore, waivers of pre-trade transparency should be constantly monitored and updated as soon as market developments make it necessary. CESR (2010b) is thus proposing a more rule-based approach, with ESMA defining binding technical standards and ongoing supervision in line with its new powers as a new European authority.[67]

---

[65] For a more detailed discussion, see section 4.4.

[66] In particular, SIs should publish quotes for liquid shares if executed orders are below the Standard Market Size (SMS); Art. 27, MiFID; Arts 21-25, Implementing Regulation.

[67] Art. 6 (1) (a), (2) (a), Art. 7 and 7e, adopted position at first reading by European Parliament on 22 September 2010 (http://www.europarl.europa.eu/sides/getDoc.do?pubRef=-//EP//TEXT+TA+P7-TA-2010-0339+0+DOC+XML+V0//EN#title3).

According to MiFID,[68] there are four kind of waivers:
i) Reference price[69]
ii) Large in-scale orders (LISOs)[70]
iii) Negotiated trades[71]
iv) Order management facility.[72]

These waivers serve multiple functions:
i) Stimulating price competition (improvements) and containing information leakage (reference price),
ii) Protecting orders from market impact (LISO) and
iii) Ensuring the smooth functioning of capital markets and execution services (negotiated trades and order management facility).

Overall, waivers aim at reducing the exposure risks that may affect market quality and integrity. Well-functioning financial markets allow the efficient allocation of resources and thus the increase of total welfare for all end investors.

Reference price. The reference price waiver applies to RMs and MTFs, given the importance of alternative dark trading venues when it comes to competition on trading costs and potential price improvements. Those venues are typically MTFs that try to offer protection from information leakage and market impact at competing prices, with no price discovery (passive pricing system). European trading under reference price waivers has been estimated around €25 billion in the Q1 of 2010, 5 times more than

---

[68] For a detailed overview of the MiFID waivers (with examples), see CESR (2010e) and Moloney (2008, pp. 826-830).

[69] Art. 18.1 (a), Implementing Regulation. This waiver applies to trades that are crossed at a price generated by another trading venue. In this case, the trading venue uses prices of more liquid pools of liquidity in order to avoid the risk of not reaching the 'critical mass' of liquidity. See CESR (2010e, p. 3).

[70] Art. 20, Implementing Regulation. The waiver applies to orders equal to or above a minimum size specified in Table 2, Annex 2, Implementing Regulation. The calculation of the 'normal market size' should be made using the average daily turnover, which shall be calculated as defined by Art. 33, Implementing Regulation. CESR (2010e, p. 17).

[71] Art. 18.1 (b), Implementing Regulation. Specific conditions apply to negotiated trades that avoid pre-trade market transparency as they are subject to different conditions than those currently offered on public markets. CESR (2010e, p. 11).

[72] Art. 18.2, Implementing Regulation. This waiver applies to orders held in an order management facility (or 'Reserve') run by regulated markets or MTFs, which have the potential to be introduced in the order book to be executed – for instance – against incoming aggressive orders. See CESR (2010e, p. 14).

in the same period of 2009, but only accounting for 1% of total trading on RMs and MTFs (see Figure 11). As mentioned above, the presence of alternative dark venues can improve market quality and stimulates new flows of liquidity with a beneficial impact on investors' choice and competitiveness of trading venues. This waiver is designed for venues willing to offer lower trading costs and potentially price improvements in relation to the 'referenced' venue. Orders should be executed at mid-point of the bid/ask spread of the primary market or at mid-point or best bid or best ask of the European Best Bid and Offer (EBBO), as currently established by CESR (2010e). However, market participants have conflicting views on this issue. They are split between those who would set a specific threshold (individual/aggregated) for the size of orders that use this waiver or capping the volumes regarding trading under waivers), and those who would leave the decision to the market on how many trading venues should use this waiver with the obligation for these venues to provide price improvements in exchange for the waiver.

Market views. The former group, in effect, implicitly proposes to set a threshold (e.g. a percentage of Large-In-Scale Orders;[73] see Fleuriot, 2010) that de facto makes this waiver available only to a type of order (large ones) disregarding the type of trading system (as also pointed out by some CESR members; CESR, 2010b). In their view, MiFID foresaw waivers to limit the market impact of large orders and price hence should be limited to the mid-point as only at that point of the spread would it be justifiable for those orders not to contribute to the price formation process. Against this view, other market participants argued that this waiver was originally designed to favour competition on explicit and implicit trading costs between dark and lit books. In their view, therefore, these venues should be allowed to match orders within the spread of primary markets or EBBO, with the guarantee of a price improvement. It is important to ensure a price improvement when the price comes from another system. A limitation based on size of orders – in their view – would harm the market, as no longer will small or 'child' orders (of large 'parent' orders[74]) be traded 'dark', with no protection from information leakage and so exposure risks.

---

[73] As defined by Table 2, Annex II, MiFID Implementing Regulation; for the purpose of determining the size of large-in-scale orders, the average daily turnover is defined by Art. 33, Implementing Regulation.

[74] As part of 'slice and dice' defensive trading strategies in order to reduce market impact.

In addition, this waiver currently captures only a small fraction of the market (1%).

Figure 11. Current use of waivers

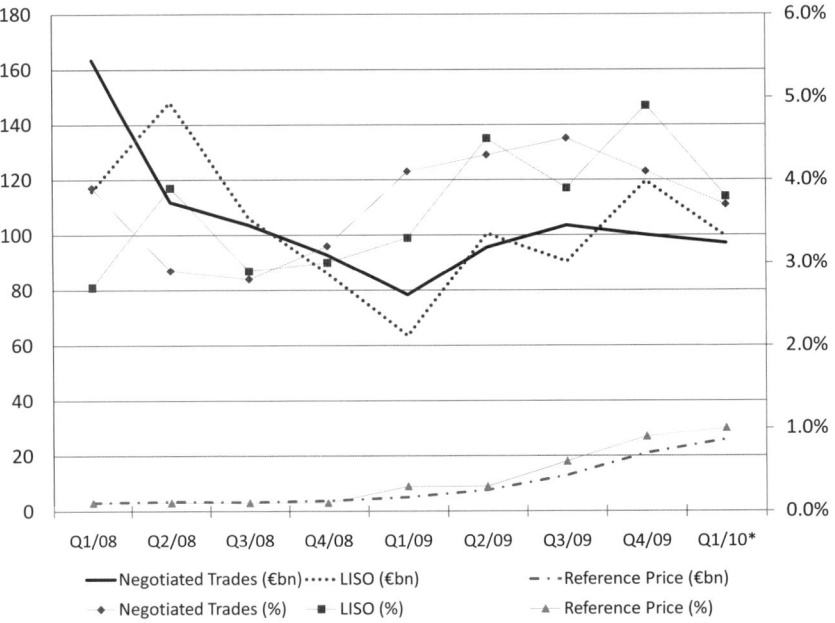

Source: CESR (2010b).

LISO. The large-in-scale order waiver applies to orders that are bigger than special thresholds set by MiFID for each defined liquidity band (average daily order book turnover, 'ADT').[75] It tries to soften the exposure risk of large orders, which may generate market impact. It is largely used by MTFs and RMs (for their hidden orders pools). As suggested by the literature review above, hidden orders increase the quality of lit books as they attract liquidity from large traders and informed traders, who try to act more aggressively in order to capture this new liquidity flow. Therefore, in order to ensure high market quality, the LISO waiver should work properly and be able to capture fundamental liquidity in capital markets.

Market participants' views are here again conflicting, and include those that would reduce the threshold given that the average size of orders

---

[75] See footnote 73.

is constantly dropping[76] and those that fear inflating 'dark markets' to the benefit of a small part of the market that makes large use of this waiver, while eventually deteriorating market quality. The former group claims the importance of applying the waiver in a consistent and efficient manner. As recently estimated in the UK market (LSE Group, 2010), the difference between the standard market size (SMS)[77] and the LISO thresholds is on average 44 times larger (with high volatility within the basket of most liquid stocks). In addition, it emerges from these calculations that by reducing the LISO size on the FTSE 100 by 75% instead of the 25% proposed by CESR, the capacity of the value of orders that may qualify for the LISO waiver would reach almost 2% (circa 17% for the small and mid cap index). Data show how the high variability of the LIS threshold generally depends on the trading venue characteristics and size. This would suggest that deciding the LIS size by liquidity bands may be correct but the current thresholds set by each band may not reflect the changes in the standard market size, which has been gradually going down in recent years (in particular, with the introduction of MiFID). Therefore, this part of the market is asking for a review of the LIS thresholds and a consistent reduction in order to allow lit order books (in particular, those using hidden orders facilities) to compete more efficiently especially with dark MTFs.

The latter group, instead, believes that current thresholds are sufficient and that a reduction would increase the size of non-displayed trading and liquidity fragmentation, ultimately hampering the price discovery process. Small investors claim that the reduction of the average size of orders has been mainly caused by trading methodologies of intermediaries, so a reduction of the LIS may only benefit them, with unclear effects on end investors. In their view, the size of small end investors' orders has not decreased; therefore the way in which intermediaries handle them should not affect in any case the way in which end investors decide their investments.

---

[76] See section 5.5.

[77] Orders above the SMS are typically considered as orders that may deserve 'special treatment' due to their market size, also outside the official trading venues (OTC; Recital 53, MiFID).

CESR also discussed the treatment of residual LIS orders (so-called 'stubs'), with no final answer but a majority of its members agreed that stubs may need to become lit to avoid distorting price formation (CESR, 2010b). In their view, this will not have the same market impact. However, other members of CESR and some market participants have highlighted that the immediate publication of stubs may reveal the original size of the large order or leak private information on the handling of these trades (especially if the execution is not yet completed), leading to stubs not being executed at all. If a stub is modified by the trader, market participants generally agree that the LIS waiver should not apply.

Negotiated trades. The negotiated trade waiver is typically used for transactions bilaterally negotiated with other parties, so not accessible to other members on RMs and MTFs. A protection from pre-trade transparency would here enable intermediaries to provide best execution (CESR, 2010b) and give the opportunity to investors to exercise their contractual power. Applying pre-trade transparency requirements to these trades may deceive price discovery processes since economic terms of the execution are the result of specific conditions that do not reflect current market prices. Moreover, the waiver aims at avoiding some trades from destabilising displayed continuous trading systems due to their systemic importance. In Q1 2010, those trades were 3.7% of EEA trading on RMs and MTFs, with a stable trend from 2008. From an economic and financial standpoint, negotiated trades are very similar to OTC trades, as 'upstairs trading'.[78] The main difference is that an OTC trade carries best execution duties, since it is executed through a broker-dealer (execution on behalf of the client), while negotiated trades do not benefit from best execution duties since they are the result of 'face-to-face' or 'back-to-back' transactions.

Market views. There is widespread agreement that this waiver should be retained. It plays a crucial role in reducing systemic risk of OTC trades that cannot be executed on a central trading mechanism. It is also used when principal transactions (back-to-back) are not subject to current market price but to a principal volume weighted average price (VWAP; CESR, 2010b). Some market participants believe that this waiver should be extended also to RMs and MTFs that do not offer a displayed order book or

---

[78] For instance, in the UK, MiFID gives the possibility to investment firms to report OTC trades either as 'negotiated' or as 'OTC'.

continuous trading.

Turning onto the order management facility waiver, there is widespread agreement that this waiver should be kept without major changes. It allows better management of orders kept in 'reserves' (e.g. iceberg orders) in order to be used whenever the market would be under stress due to several aggressive orders hitting the book at that moment. The waiver therefore allows a more efficient execution service, attracting more liquidity through brokers. CESR (2010b) clarified that differences between RMs/MTFs and brokers applying this waiver should remain, as they perform two different functions in financial markets.

> ***Conclusion # 3***
>
> *Under certain conditions, pre-trade transparency may impair market liquidity. Hence, MiFID introduced waivers, which should be retained. A move towards a more rule-based approach should be balanced with flexible application and ongoing supervision in order to meet market needs. However, conflicting views between stakeholders emerge when discussing the breadth of these exemptions. In effect, thresholds may need to be revised regularly, in line with latest market developments. More specifically, regulators need to carve out a new set of rules that promote the smooth functioning of capital markets and meet investors' needs with no adverse impact on market structure, which may ultimately affect market liquidity, efficiency and investor confidence. Consistent and uniform application across Europe should be ensured.*

4.2.3 A consolidated quote system

The market entry of several trading venues in the last three years raised concerns around the availability of pre-trade transparency data across venues. The difficulty faced by investors, retail in particular, to access pre-trade consolidated data solutions and a pan-European best bid and offer (EBBO) may pose a potential obstacle to the creation of a competitive pan-European market. The provision of consolidated quote solutions would improve investors' choice and increase competition between trading venues on spreads, with the possibility for liquidity providers to compete in a truly transparent environment. In effect, if investors are able to see the best price across trading venues, they may be able to push intermediaries to bridge links with these infrastructures offering better deals. Obstacles to cheaper and more easily accessible consolidated quote solutions are in general the same as currently experienced by the post-trade transparency space (see next section). Once these barriers are removed, markets would be able to offer new data consolidation services and meet investors' needs.

> **Conclusion # 4**
>
> *Despite the importance of a consolidated quotation system, priority should be given to the removal of relevant impediments to widespread use of consolidated post-trade data solutions. In particular, it is important to improve investors' access to both pre- and post-trade data solutions, in order to transform fragmentation into beneficial competition for end investors. Data accessibility to regulated and OTC venues is key for data consolidation.*

4.3 What pre-trade transparency for non-equity instruments?

Recital 46. Under this provision, MiFID, gives the faculty to member states to broaden the transparency regime to financial instruments other than shares. Only two member states have exercised this option and extended this regime to bond markets (Italy and Sweden).

There are two main reasons why this option has not been widely exercised: i) non-equity markets[79] have a different market microstructure from equity markets and trading mechanisms are designed to enhance resilience in case of liquidity issues; ii) A general possibility to opt in may not give enough incentives for member states to exercise the option, thereby pushing them to behave strategically. In effect, the latter represents a typical prisoner's dilemma. Member states have no incentives to 'behave cooperatively'. If they deviate from their current application of MiFID, they may put their markets at a disadvantage, in particular if they impose stricter requirements for non-equity instruments.

Dealer markets. Non-equity markets, moreover, have different trading mechanisms. Trades are typically dealt with a quote-driven dealer system or bilateral negotiations with the support of an intermediary. Most transactions are arranged via a dealer. Trading can be continuous or periodic and dealers typically have an informational advantage over investors as intermediaries. Accordingly, market-makers move first and propose price schedules. Therefore, equilibrium may be found in dealer markets (with one specialist or competing market-makers), since they are more resilient and efficient as long as the market is not too big and the information asymmetry not too large (Glosten, 1989; O'Hara, 1995). Dealer

---

[79] CESR (2010f) has defined as non-equity financial instruments: a) corporate bonds; b) structured finance products (Asset Backed Securities and Collateralised Debt Obligations); c) Credit Default Swaps; d) Interest rate derivatives; e) Equity derivatives; f) Foreign exchange derivatives; g) Commodity derivatives. Other non-equity financial instruments that should be considered are sovereign and local authorities bonds, and equity-like instruments.

markets are hence designed to deal with less-liquid markets, only if this 'low liquidity condition' is verified. Dealer markets, in general, can:
1) Provide stronger protection against exposure risks (Pagano & Roëll, 1993),
2) Reduce information leakage,
3) Reduce costs for uninformed traders (if they have contractual power due to the market illiquidity or competition in the dealer market) and
4) Better price if dealers can exploit private information and investors can control their fair use (Madhavan, 1995).

There are other two specific reasons why most non-equity products, even less complex ones, are currently traded in quote-driven markets, with a strong dealership:
i) Structure of the demand and
ii) Structure of the intermediation.

Firstly, demand for such products comes mainly from institutional investors and other dealers, since retail participation remains highly costly in terms of cost and lack of sufficient knowledge. The nature of clients, and the complexity, heterogeneity and large size of non-equity financial instruments affect market structure and thus the prices of financial instruments. In dealer markets, institutional investors can exploit their contractual power and customise their transactions more than in a non-discriminatory and open market setting (Biais & Green, 2007). Moreover, dealers can have more control of their risk positions when they deal with few market operators and exposures.

Secondly, the structure of the intermediation favours certain market developments. In effect, the amount of capital committed to intermediation by dealers may affect per se the choice of a specific level of transparency. If dealers act as a principal in the transaction, on the one hand, there is more chance to create a market for illiquid products by selling them direct to investors, but – on the other hand – financial products will sit on dealers' balance sheets, with inventory positions that need some protection from market impact through less public disclosure, in order to be still able to act as intermediary. Then, if dealers only act as broker-agents, on the one side, there will be less capital committed and thus less need for protection from market impact and more public disclosure. But, on the other side, illiquid products may not receive execution due to insufficient demand. The complex nature of modern financial markets and economies requires intermediaries to provide clients with more tailored and sophisticated products and services, which may often be traded only in specific market settings and with limited public disclosure. The use of electronic multi-dealer platforms has surely increased competition between dealers, who compete with executable quotes, and extended market accessibility to a wider set of investors who qualify as 'members' (typically only brokers or institutional investors). A strong push towards pre-trade public disclosure may require a rethinking of current market structure and intermediation of less-liquid asset classes (such as some categories of bonds, OTC derivatives and structured products), which may anyway lack price transparency since they are typically based on proprietary valuation models (CESR, 2009).

Benefits and costs. Greater pre-trade transparency can indeed reduce search costs and enhance price discovery processes as long as all relevant investors can easily access these markets and dealers are not damaged by information revelation. Flood et al. (1999) found that in a dealer market opening spreads would be wider and trading volume lower, but price discovery should be faster since traders would behave more aggressively in order to find liquidity. Other authors therefore find a negative trade-off between liquidity and price efficiency if transparency varies. Bloomfield and O'Hara (1999) did not find any relevant impact of pre-trade transparency requirements on dealer markets. Greater transparency, on the one side, may reduce the informational advantage that dealers exploit in exchange for the provision of liquidity and introduce uncertainty in bilateral negotiations. The nature of the counterparty, for instance, is usually included in the calculation of the price offered by dealers, which cannot usually be estimated without an explicit request from the client. On the other hand, however, the absence of pre-trade information may keep the price discovery process for non-equity products very costly and therefore inefficient, and it may promote a market setting with low competition.

For all these reasons, a pre-trade transparency regime for non-equity financial instruments should be designed in a different way from auction order-driven markets or quote-driven dealer markets (duly adapted and proportionate). In this regard, MiFID pre-trade transparency requirements cannot be transposed as they now stand in order to prevent unintended consequences on the incentives of dealers to provide liquidity through the use of private information. In effect, pre-trade transparency may improve search liquidity, since pre-trade information is asset-specific and helps to reduce search costs and uncertainty around them, even in dealer markets (Laganá et al., 2006). However, a pre-trade transparency regime could be effective, depending on the number of potential counterparties that can offer that tailored product and on the level of exposure of dealers' inventory positions to the market, since trade size is typically far higher than the retail one. This leads dealers to offer executable quotes only on electronic platforms where liquidity is selected and accessible to members meeting certain requirements. On platforms where traded products are commonly accessed by retail investors, it would be easier to implement general pre-trade transparency requirements as long as the demand is very high, which may not be the case for complex non-equity products. Current market microstructure makes public disclosure of executable quotes difficult and costly (Biais et al., 2006). Also, many non-equity products are highly customised, so pre-trade transparency might be of little help. The greater concern is liquidity, which is to find a dealer that can tailor a transaction around the client's needs. If transparency requirements reduce market makers' returns, they may ultimately confine their activities to those products that are inherently more liquid, exiting markets for less-liquid ones. Pre-trade transparency for complex non-equity products could only work by changing the way how these instruments are actually traded towards open limit order books. To achieve this, the nature of the demand needs to be constant and sufficiently high over time.

New proposals. The Commission (2010b, p. 28) has finally proposed that investment firms willing to quote or receive a request for quote (RFQ, probably run on organised trading facilities) would be requested to publish price and volume available to the public, and eventually commit to it for sizes below a certain threshold (retail size). The threshold will be specified per asset class.

Conclusion # 5

A strong push towards more pre-trade public disclosure would require, in some cases, a rethink of the current market structure for less-liquid asset classes, and a shift from its mainly institutional demand to a more retail and smaller professional one. Conflicting views in this area emerge around what should be the most efficient market structure for these products. Liquidity in non-equity markets, such as markets for bonds, derivatives and structured products, is currently handled through quote-driven auction markets, inter-dealer platforms or bilateral negotiations led by dealers' capital commitment.

For auction markets, whether led by dealers/market-makers (quote-driven) or directly by demand (order-driven), pre-trade transparency is urgently needed. For inter-dealer platforms (request-for-quotes model) or bilateral negotiations, where dealers commit capital by being non-neutral counterparty, less pre-trade transparency than order-driven ones (e.g. equity) is needed to function properly. Executable prices might thus not always be consistently available. The alternative to a shift in market structure and in demand, which may not necessarily occur, is to design a different transparency regime from the one applied to equities. In general, pre-trade transparency may not be of any help to the market if it does not serve price discovery of investors. For markets in which the demand is more retail-driven, the need to have greater pre-trade transparency will be higher as it will noticeably reduce search costs. However, an appropriate level of pre-trade transparency may be beneficial for non-auction markets as well, as it may reduce investors' search costs and promote greater competition between dealers. Some market participants consider that currently available pre-trade data is sufficient and legal requirements are not needed, since non-equity markets do not necessarily function as equity markets and current transparency have not limited participation to these markets.[80] Others instead (and CESR, 2010f) believe, however, that an ad hoc pre-trade transparency regime (with waivers) should apply for non-equity products (in particular, bonds) listed on RMs or MTFs. Access to this information should be made easier for retail investors.

Conflicting views also emerge as to how to design the transparency regime. Many believe that preference should be given to the nature of the market rather than the nature of investors (retail versus wholesale). For financial instruments mainly traded over-the-counter on a bilateral basis, the introduction of any pre-trade transparency regime must prioritise the avoidance of adverse liquidity consequences for involved counterparties and systemic risk.

4.4 Post-trade transparency regime: Fixing 'bugs' and extending scope

Definition. Transparency may take on different forms and dimensions, according to the mechanisms underpinning market microstructure and investors' needs. In conjunction with a pre-trade transparency regime, MiFID established a regime of post-trade transparency, which applies to all shares admitted to trading on a regulated market, wherever they are actually traded.

Benefits. Post-trade transparency is particularly important to preserve market integrity through the indirect control of market participants upon competing investors (discouraging insider trading). The regime also supports price formation processes since it reduces informational gaps and investors' search costs, with overall price efficiency gains, also for quote-

---

[80] For instance, AFME's www.investinginbondseurope.org provides pre-trade non-executable price on more than 1,500 bonds (government, sub-government and corporate), which may help end-investors find the best price for the financial product they are willing to purchase. Regarding OTC derivatives, Markit publishes intraday indicative CDS prices for instance (http://www.markit.com/cds/cds-page.html) and Bloomberg, Reuters, and TradeWeb provide pre-trade information on interest rate derivatives.

driven markets (Flood et al., 1997; Bloomfield & O'Hara, 1999). Accordingly, trade disclosure may reduce adverse selection and increase the market's reputational capital, as the market will be less open to manipulation (Chowdry & Nanda, 1991). Market participants may thus develop better services and provide best execution at a lower transaction cost, in particular

Costs. However, while transparency is certainly instrumental to promoting liquidity in order-driven markets (e.g. cash equities) if calibrated with delays for large transactions, quote-driven and dealership markets may suffer from a strict trade disclosure regime (e.g. OTC derivatives). Dealers may no longer benefit from their informational advantage and may thus be subject to exposure risks[81] and inventory risks,[82] since they need to manage large amounts of their own capital in related instruments. Therefore, they may commit less capital to the market and reduce their willingness to bear risk, thereby reducing liquidity (Madhavan, 1995, 1996; Hendershott et al., 2007). Increased exposure risk also means that uninformed investors may benefit from greater transparency, with potential effects on market liquidity, however (Pagano & Roëll, 1996). Moreover, the disclosure of trade information (e.g. price) under specific bilateral agreements may deceive the price formation mechanisms and asset price valuation, as the price is the result of non-replicable market conditions. Finally, Kovtunenko (2002) argues that – with full post-trade transparency, that is signalling the size of the uninformed demand and observing other dealers' quotes – dealers can act strategically to control the level of spreads as the size of uninformed demand varies, and punish those who deviate from a collusive equilibrium (through a price war).

Microstructure. Overall, transparency does not necessarily smooth liquidity issues away, especially in quote-driven markets. Strict transparency requirements may create a shift in market microstructure towards a trading mechanism with less active participation of dealers and without necessarily setting off a more active participation of other investors. In effect, the literature has tried to shed light on the role of

---

[81] As illustrated in Section 4.2.

[82] The risk coming from unforeseen price changes on assets held for market-making purposes.

transparency in micro-structural processes, but without success. For instance, there is no clear answer as to the cause of past changes in the bond market microstructure; it is uncertain whether lower transparency was the cause or the effect of that structural change (Biais & Green, 2007). In coming years, aware of potential side effects, policy-makers will need to decide whether they want stricter transparency requirements to promote access by small professional and retail investors or more complex (not necessarily riskier) financial instruments. There is a trade-off between enhancing investor confidence and disclosure costs. Changes here may modify the market structure, not always with beneficial effects.

Systemic risk. The recent financial crisis has added a further dimension to transparency, which refers to monitoring and controlling macro-prudential risks by competent authorities in specific markets for financial stability purposes (e.g. OTC derivatives) through the use of aggregate data on exposures in single or multiple financial instruments (FSB, 2010). These data are increasingly available, typically through the establishment of dedicated trade repositories per asset class. The need to control systemic risk (and minimise spill-over effects) by macro regulators has exercised some pressure to increase the overall transparency of financial markets. This has occurred even in segments where transparency was previously limited, due to a microstructure based on the role of dealers and bilateral over-the-counter transactions.

Box 3. Transaction reporting: Current regime and CESR's proposals

Post-trade disclosure enables regulators to preserve market integrity and surveillance across several trading venues by detecting transactions that may breach market abuse rules, or represent other breaches of MiFID requirements. MiFID introduced a regime of transaction reporting (Art. 25)[83] and cooperation between major financial authorities (Art. 58) that allows regulators to confidentially access information concerning transactions executed in any financial instrument admitted to trading on regulated markets. Both CESR and the Commission proposed to extend the scope to also cover financial instruments admitted to trading only on MTFs and organised trading facilities (OTFs; Commission, 2010b, p. 46). The report can be sent to the competent authority by the investment firms, by a third party on their behalf, by an approved trade-reporting system or by the regulated market or MTF; and it shall be delivered by

---

[83] In conjunction with Art. 9-16, Implementing Regulation.

the close of business the following day. The competent authority may request additional requirements in 'exceptional circumstances'.[84] Data on transactions should be stored for at least five years and ongoing reporting should meet specific criteria, including details on names, dates, times, quantity, prices and codes to identify parties and venues.[85] Reports should be sent to the competent authority no later than the following working day after the execution of the transaction. Transaction refers to 'any agreement concluded with a counterparty to buy or sell one or more financial instruments' (EU COM, 2010b, p. 47).

CESR has currently proposed amendments to the transaction reporting regime.[86] First, the Committee has proposed to add a third trading capacity to transaction reports (in addition to 'principal on own account' and 'agent'), the so-called 'risk-less principal', which consists of the investment firm acting on its own account and on behalf of the client (client facilitator). This scenario would simplify the harmonisation of current transaction reporting standards across Europe.[87] The immediate implementation of this proposal raises some concerns since automated reporting systems would need to be changed accordingly. Secondly, CESR advanced a proposal to mandate the collection of client identifiers by competent authorities, increase their standardisation, and include client IDs when investment firms transmit orders for execution.[88]

On the latter, the Directive requires reporting of executed transactions, which may not necessarily require the disclosure of the clients' ID if the order is executed by an investment firm other than the one that received the order execution.[89]

The Committee then suggested extending transaction reporting to members of RMs, MTFs and OTFs that are not authorised as investment firms (e.g. market-makers) since they fall outside MiFID (assuming they do not provide investment services). Trading activities of non-members also contribute to price formation, and leaving them out of the sight of regulators may undermine the

---

[84] Art. 4, Implementing Directive.

[85] Art. 13 & Table 1 Annex I, Implementing Directive.

[86] See, in general, CESR (2010a).

[87] For instance, in some countries (such as the UK) the category of riskless principal is already present in the transaction reporting regime.

[88] CESR (2010a, pp. 9-16).

[89] Following Art. 5, Implementing Regulation - for the purpose of the transaction regime – 'transaction' represents "the purchase securities financing transactions, the exercise of options or of covered warrants, and primary market transactions (such as issuance, allotment or subscription) in financial instruments falling within Article 4(1)(18)(a) and (b) of Directive 2004/39/EC."

market monitoring function of national competent authorities. Alternatively, transaction reporting obligations could be imposed on RMs, MTFs or OTFs which have admitted these firms as a member, but these obligations would just shift the reporting responsibility to entities that do not directly control this confidential information. Reporting may thus be inaccurate for supervisory purposes.

In conclusion, the Commission (2010b, p. 49) to modify the reporting channels as defined by MiFID, in line with the CESR advice. In particular, the Commission will assess: 1) the viability of a consolidated European reporting mechanism to which investment firms will report directly and competent authorities will have direct access; 2) third party reporting firm should be approved as 'Approved Reporting Mechanisms' (ARM); 3) waiving reporting transactions if they have already been reported to trade repositories or approved by a competent authority, such as ARM. In line with the trade reporting system of consolidation, the proposal would establish a European consolidator run most probably by ESMA, which will work across asset classes. For trade reporting (public disclosure), instead, the system of data consolidation will need to treat different asset classes with separate tapes. Investors, therefore, will be able to subscribe to the data solution that fits their needs at competitive costs.

Conclusion # 6

Overall, post-trade transparency serves various important functions in financial markets, such as improving price formation and market integrity. In effect, trade disclosure may stimulate self-designed market surveillance and increase visibility at the same time as market liquidity, thus increasing investors' confidence and promoting price discovery. However – as illustrated in the following sections – there is a need for regulatory actions in certain areas, not only as a result of the recent financial crisis but also of the experience gained since the transposition of the Directive. Transparency is not panacea for market failure, though, and interventions should be proportional to the market structure and dynamics through which investors' orders find their market-clearing price. Ill-defined transparency requirements would harm market efficiency in less-liquid markets with no increase of investor protection or reduction of systemic risk, as the market would become less-liquid and more volatile.

Finally – in order to reduce the risk of manipulation on less-liquid 'thinner' markets and improve market integrity and surveillance – it would be appropriate to extend the scope of the transaction reporting regime run by regulators to all financial instruments admitted to trading on MiFID-official venues, with no distinction between instruments listed on regulated markets, multilateral trading facilities or organised trading facilities. Nevertheless, this work needs to be coordinated with other initiatives at EU level, such as the review of the Market Abuse Directive, and with a thorough cost-benefit analysis. In effect, the extension would help the harmonisation of transaction reporting regimes and supervisory practices across Europe.

4.4.1 The trade reporting regime for shares

MiFID set out a trade disclosure regime (Arts 28-30 and 45, MiFID) that covers all shares admitted to trading on RMs, irrespective of where those shares are actually traded (in RMs themselves, MTFs, SIs or OTC). Therefore, MiFID extended post-trade transparency requirements to shares traded on new trading platforms and for the first time over-the-counter. Some member states had no transparency requirements for OTC trades in shares before the Directive came into force (e.g. Germany). In terms of scope, while for 'equity-like' instruments an extension of the current regime for shares is broadly favoured, the picture is less clear for instruments other than shares (CESR, 2010b).

Reports of completed trades should include information on trading day, time, instrument identification, price, quantity and venue.[90] Publication should be made "as close to real time as possible", but "in any case within three minutes of the relevant transaction".[91] Deferral to official time publication can be granted for large transactions,[92] as a waiver to pre-trade transparency, in particular to afford liquidity providers enough time to unwind inventory positions before investors become aware of them. In this regard, CESR has proposed to raise the thresholds for delayed publication and reduce the maximum granted delay to the end of the trading day. The latter is currently set to three trading days after the trade execution (Table 4, Annex II, Impl. Reg.).[93]

> **Conclusion # 7**
>
> *The extension of public disclosure requirements (trade reporting) to equity-like instruments and to shares admitted to trading only on MTFs or organised trading facilities would help harmonise requirements among financial instruments that serve similar purposes. For financial instruments other than shares and equity-like instruments, the mere extension would most likely generate inconsistencies with the very nature of these financial instruments (see following sections).*

---

[90] Art. 27, Annex I Table 1, Implementing Regulation.

[91] Art. 29, Implementing Regulation. The three-minute buffer, however, should be only used if it is not technically possible to publish this data in real time. See Recital 18, Implementing regulation. CESR has recently proposed to reduce this buffer to 1 minute.

[92] Art. 28 and Table 4 in Annex II, Implementing Regulation.

[93] CESR (2010b), 'Consultation Paper...Equity Markets', op. cit., p. 18.

> *In terms of time limits for trade reporting, new technologies can help reduce delays. The industry is working to make all market data that are not subject to delays freely available after 15 minutes, in line with ESMA's recommendation. However, reducing the maximum allowed delay from three minutes to one may prove immaterial since this delay cannot be exploited by trading platforms in favour of their members. In addition, trades may be affected by technical delays (latency issues) that ultimately affect all market participants. In any case, the legal obligation is to report 'as close to real time as possible' and should be duly enforced. Delays should be allowed in specific circumstances, with appropriate calibration for trades done at the end of the day. Current proposals should be further evaluated since they may affect risk positions, with potential adverse consequences on the market.*[94]

4.4.2 Challenges with data consolidation

New trading venues have entered the market to offer execution services on shares across Europe, increasing market fragmentation. MiFID's strategy for achieving a truly pan-European equity market lies in stimulating a more competitive environment. However, this strategy currently strives to deliver. Despite the industry's commitment to make consolidated data solutions more accessible (both tape and quote)[95] and provide data on a non-discriminatory basis, data remain costly, in particular for retail and small professional investors. In addition, quality and granularity of trade reports (e.g. OTC) is sometimes insufficient to generate cost-effective consolidation.

Pre and post-trade data on equity can be consolidated in two ways:[96]
1) Through direct access to market sources[97] and
2) Through solutions offered by data vendors.[98]

---

[94] The LSE Group (2010) has calculated that – for off-book securities admitted to trading in their regulated market and traded under their rules – reducing the deferred publication time to the end of the day (with no exception) would mean that 27.2% of overall trade value in that market (1.4% as number of trades) would be pushed to disclose positions by the end of the day. This may create unforeseen consequences and push liquidity providers to reduce the amount of capital committed to these markets.

[95] A consolidated tape solution refers to the aggregation in one virtual basket of all post-trade data of competing trading platforms in a specific market (in this case, the European Economic Area, EEA). A consolidated quote solution should potentially offer pre-trade data of all EEA trading platforms.

[96] For an overview of the market for market data, please see ESME (2009a).

[97] Market sources are regulated markets, MTFs and SIs that provide static pre- and post-trade data of shares admitted to trading on their systems, or investment firms publishing data with proprietary arrangements.

Market data sources offer real-time information for shares traded on their systems. These data have been typically offered by incumbents (RMs) with different levels of granularity[99] at a cost to final users, while new comers (MTFs) currently offer this service for free as part of their strategy to increase market share. Fees vary according to the type of user and the use they make of these data. There are currently three types of fees that are flexibly applied by trading venues (ESME, 2009a):

i) License distribution fee,
ii) License non-display fee and
iii) Data fee.

The first type of fee is designed for data vendors that resell data with special features or together with data on other asset classes. The second one refers to the fee typically charged to investment banks and buy-side firms that directly access the market feed for their own use, typically associated with other services (co-location,[100] etc.). Those fees are designed in particular for algorithmic traders or investment firms that systematically use high-frequency trading tools. Finally, data fees are those charged to retail or small professional investors to access pre and/or post-trade data directly from their computers. If not freely accessible in real-time, post-trade data are typically offered for free with a delay of 15 minutes, in line with CESR's recommendation (CESR, 2010b). Despite the fact that the average fee charged by regulated markets has partially decreased,[101] the

---

[98] Data vendors are providers of data that typically collect a vast amount of information from several market sources and rearrange them in order to make them more easily accessible to retail and professional final users.

[99] There are in general two levels of granularity: level 1 (which only includes the 'touch price') and level 2 (which gives a view over the order book, typically the first five best and bid offers).

[100] Co-location services allow members of the trading platform to install their desks close to the central data storage of the platform in order to reduce latency and receive data at the lowest time physically possible.

[101] The fee for the 'last trade' price charged by major exchanges (95% of EEA lit books current volumes, but not as % of listed shares) is currently €75 per month. The full cost to access a consolidated tape and quote solution in the US is roughly €70 per month. However, the US data solution does not only offer 'last trade' prices, but complete pre- and post-trade data (levels 1 and 2), including the Best and Bid Offer (BBO), and covers 100% of listed shares. To have only the level 1 pre- and post-trade data service in Europe for all EEA markets, the price is around €409 per month (Atradia, 2010).

full cost (including data vendors fees and IT costs, where applicable) of access to pre- and post-trade data (full level 1 data only) remains fairly high (CESR, 2010b), in particular for small professional and retail investors. However, regulated markets freely distribute post-trade data after 15 minutes. Moreover, CESR has also recommended the full unbundling of pre- and post-trade data transparency information, which exchanges have partially implemented in recent months by splitting post-trade from pre-trade data.[102] Revenues from market data are an important item of the total revenues of exchanges (see Box 7). A drastic cut of fees might not be manageable for them in the short term, since the collection and disclosure of data is a service that normally comes at cost for market sources.

The second way to access consolidated post- or pre-trade data is through data vendors, which pay distribution fees to exchanges and resell data in a consolidated fashion. Since the costs of accessing several trading venues are high, end investors may opt for one-stop-shop solution, even though it may not offer the same depth and quality as the direct market feed. However, the costs of one-stop data vending solution seem to be high as well. Unbundling of services in this market may substantially reduce costs for end users, however. In effect, a right to access single offered services on a non-discriminatory basis may reduce costs for non-sophisticated end users and allow data vendors to generate significant economies of scale and scope by aggregating data from several asset classes. This change would stimulate further competition[103] and potentially drive overall costs down further over the long term. In effect, concentration is rather high in the current market setting. Two players, Bloomberg and Thomson Reuters, capture two-thirds of the demand taking into account the whole market, including data from asset classes other than equity (see Figure 12). The market share of these two players is higher if only equity market data is considered. The whole market for equity data sales and trading is roughly $4.45 billion, of which $1.8 billion in Europe (Burton-Taylor, 2010). Also in this market, the offer is typically done through cross-selling practices (bundling or tying),[104] which allow partial market

---

[102] See FESE press release (http://www.fese.be/en/?inc=news&id=141).

[103] Bundling increases the specificity of the product, reducing its homogeneity. Competitors will ultimately find it more difficult to compete with a bundle of several data services, with no possibility to compete with single data services.

[104] Tying is a widespread business practice that occurs when two or more products are sold together in a package and at least one of these products is not sold separately. In this case,

segmentation. In addition, a lack of standardisation of data formats between data vendors impedes interaction and does not allow users to access separate services of data providers from the same IT platform.

Figure 12. Data vendors' market shares (all asset classes)

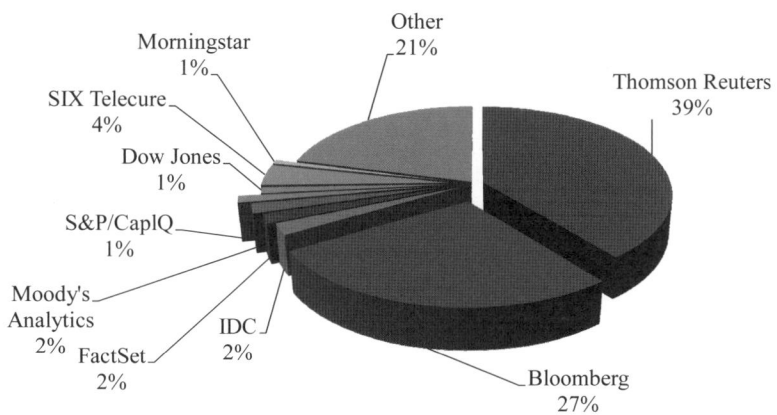

Source: Atradia (2010).

The combined effects of unbundling data services and fees for exchanges and data vendors may reduce overall costs for final users that seek pan-European consolidated data solutions.

Quality of market data. Although MiFID harmonised transparency requirements among member states, the quality of market data has partially deteriorated in some areas, mainly due to the combined effect of market fragmentation and incomplete specification and implementation of reporting requirements (CESR, 2010b; see Box 10). Several aspects, however, affect the quality of data and its eligibility for consolidation

---

the end user would be able to buy the tied product alone, but not the tying product without the tied one. Bundling occurs when none of the components of the package is sold separately, and components are offered in fixed proportions. It is the simultaneous sale of two or more products as a package, with no possibility to purchase both or one of them individually. For a more detailed analysis, see CEPS and Van Djik Consultants (2009), "Tying and other potentially unfair commercial practices in the retail financial service sector", a study submitted to the European Commission, 24 November (http://ec.europa.eu/internal_market/consultations/docs/2010/tying/report_en.pdf).

(ESME, 2009a):

1) Quotes should be executable and not indicative only,
2) Data should be delivered on real-time, with no delay (except where waivers and calibration apply),
3) Data should refer to liquid markets and
4) Data formats and flags should be sufficiently standardised.

In particular, the use of diverse trade flags[105] does not allow an easy consolidation of data. The objective should be the reduction of flags to less than 10 across all European trading venues. Moreover, on the one hand, the insufficient granularity and monitoring of OTC reporting increases the risk of misreporting and the uncertainty around quality of price formation and of best execution (see section 5.4.1). On the other hand, trade reporting obligations under MiFID create a serious issue of duplicative reporting (see example in 0), which impedes an assessment of the actual size and shape of the market.

APAs. In order to improve data accessibility and reliability, CESR proposed to publish post-trade information through Approved Publication Arrangements (APAs), which can be RMs, MTFs, organised trading facilities (OTFs) or other operators (but not an investment firm itself). In this way, trading venues would compete with data vendors for the provision of market data to consolidators.[106] In order to facilitate data consolidation, APAs should define stricter requirements, approved and monitored by competent authorities. However, it is fundamental that APAs are designed around harmonised standards[107] in order to reduce

---

[105] A 'flag' is a code attached to the information on a trade that signals its status and/or the venue where the trade has been executed. This report will refer to 'flags' more simply as codes for venue identification.

[106] NYSE Euronext has recently announced the intention to introduce a consolidated tape with real-time post-trade data of all regulated markets, MTFs and OTC markets. See http://www.euronext.com/news/press_release/press_release-1731-FR.html?docid=929763.

[107] In order to reduce inconsistencies in trade and transaction reporting across asset classes, free international open (i.e, non-proprietary) industry standards – such as those developed by the industry in line with the ISO 20022 standard (Universal financial industry message scheme) – may offer a high degree of reliability, transparency and standardisation to ultimately enable data comparability and analysis by authorities with the possibility – if needed – to adapt them to the characteristics of the market. Moreover, the introduction of universal standards may reduce the risk of market segmentation and ensure a more competitive and harmonised environment. CESR (2010g) has proposed the introduction of ISO standards for post-trade publication fields.

differences in the definition and implementation of APAs across the EEA. These requirements should minimise issues of double-counting and misreporting. The Commission (2010b, pp. 31-32) proposed to introduce criteria such as: high data security standards; access to data at a 'reasonable' cost and on a non-discriminatory basis; procedures to identify erroneous trade reports; adequate resources and contingency arrangements; and conflicts of interest procedures.

In addition, CESR (2010g) proposed two options:

i) To prescribe only standards that data sources (RMs, MTFs, APAs) would need to use to disseminate post-trade data to end users and

ii) To prescribe not only those standards, but also a common message protocol for the transfer of post-trade data by RMs, MTFs and APAs.

The second option carries higher costs for data sources, which may need to be further assessed. In any case, full harmonisation would make data consolidation easier, since there would be "no requirement for data consolidators to map the data they receive into their own standard" (CESR, 2010g, p. 6).

EU Mandatory Consolidated Tape. Whether or not a new APA regime is effectively implemented, CESR believes that a set of requirements should be inserted in MiFID in order to provide easily accessible and less costly consolidated market data solutions in the EEA. This proposal is called 'EU Mandatory Consolidated Tape' (MCT). Consolidated tapes should be designed by the industry and disclose post-trade information on shares admitted to trading on RMs or MTFs in the EEA, wherever the execution of the trade takes place. All information should come from RMs, MTFs or APA real-time and fully unbundled. Data will be then consolidated and sold at a 'competitive price' by a given operator, who will meet strict requirements and be responsible for the detection of multiple publications (double reporting or counting). Only if the industry does not deliver this solution by itself, should ESMA adopt the necessary arrangements to set a US-style consolidated tape in the EU, run by a non-profit entity. MiFID should give enough powers to ESMA to act accordingly. The Commission (2010b, p. 34) proposed that a European MCT could be structured in different ways, under variable degrees of regulatory intervention. The proposal favours the creation of a consolidated tape for all financial instruments – instead of only equities – admitted to trading in the EEA, wherever the execution takes place. It should be noted however that building a tape for assets other than shares would be difficult to achieve in the short term, since a consistent and harmonised regime of post-trade transparency for non-equity financial instruments does not exist yet. MiFID should ensure that data consolidators would be able to collect all tapes and provide one access point to end investors. A market-led solution would probably be the least costly and most efficient option (Option C). Competition among data providers would be the best way to spur the creation of consolidated data solutions outside equity markets. The Commission is concerned about the cost of data, which it wants to keep under 'reasonable' bounds.

However, what constitutes reasonable pricing is difficult, if not impossible, to define in practice. Instead, the Commission should aim at ensuring 'competitive' pricing. Only real competition between data providers would keep costs at a 'reasonable' level. The Commission's attempt (2010b, p. 34) to impose a single no-profit or for-profit entity (Options A and B) for the provision of the consolidated tape would not lead to 'competitive' pricing, but would only impose a risky price regulation. Rather, it would ultimately define costs for end investors by splitting revenues among trading platforms and APAs, which could create inefficiencies and distort trading incentives (as showed by the US experience, see Box 4 below). Furthermore, the Commission's proposal to require APA's to be expressly authorised for the provision of consolidated tapes would slow down the whole process and ultimately reduce incentives to compete. In sum, achieving minimum consistency though industry cooperation would probably be more efficient than strong regulatory intervention. In this regard, ESMA should rather support current industry-led initiatives to major impediments to cheaper and more efficient solutions. However, either the Commission or ESMA should be able to impose consistency if commercial initiatives do not lead to a satisfactory solution in a reasonable time frame.

Box 4. The US consolidated tape and quote system

The US consolidated tape system was officially created in 1976 by the National Market System in an effort to promote economic efficiency and allow brokers to deliver best execution (Caglio & Mayhew, 2009). Three networks (A, B and C) - respectively run by NYSE, AMEX and NASDAQ – display real-time trade reports (Consolidated Tape System) and market quotes (Consolidated Quotation System). The published information refers to securities traded on all exchanges, regional markets, electronic crossing networks (ECNs) and broker-dealer crossing networks and collected through three different networks by dividing shares listed on national and regional exchanges (Networks A and B) and NASDAQ National

Market and Small Cap (Network C). Networks A and B are governed by the Consolidated Tape Association Plan (CTA) and the Consolidated Quotation Plan (CQ), while network C is governed by the OTC/UTP Plan. These plans collect fees charged for the access to the consolidated tape and quotation and distribute them across all primary markets, in line with a defined allocation formula.

Prior to 2007, at least half of the revenues from Networks A and B were distributed in proportion to the number of reported trades, while Network C redistributed half of its revenues in relation to the number of trades and half as a proportion of the volume of trades in those shares. The allocation formula boosted a widespread rebate programme through which exchanges pushed their members to split their orders even though there was no risk of market impact. In effect, this system created strong incentives to generate volumes, to print trades.

The implementation of RegNMS[108] in April 2007 modified this allocation formula by splitting revenues as follows: 25% depending on the number of shares, 25% on the number of trades, and 50% on quote aggressiveness, i.e. frequently displaying better prices and thereby helping to narrow quoted spreads, while distinguishing manually displayed quotation systems. The introduction of this formula was followed by the SEC requesting the exchanges to adopt a rule against tape shredding.[109] Both these policies have helped to partially increase the average trade size (Caglio & Mayhew, 2009), which proves that the allocation formula does influence current trading activities and raises a trade-off between control over data consolidation and indirect incentives on trading. Moreover, since the introduction of this formula, the average number of quotes displayed every minute has constantly increased (see figure below). Soaring trading volumes and algorithmic trading (Angel et. al., 2010) may not be the only explanation for this later effect. Hence, the impact of this new allocation rule deserves further investigation.

In addition to these networks, – in March 2007 – the SEC established Trade Reporting Facilities (TRF), which report directly to the consolidated tape any trades executed on venues other than national and regional exchanges.

---

[108] Securities and Exchange Commission (SEC), Release No. 34-51808; File No. S7-10-04, April 2007, Rule 601 and 603.

[109] Members of exchanges can break up their customers' orders into smaller trades only for compliance with best execution obligation (best price).

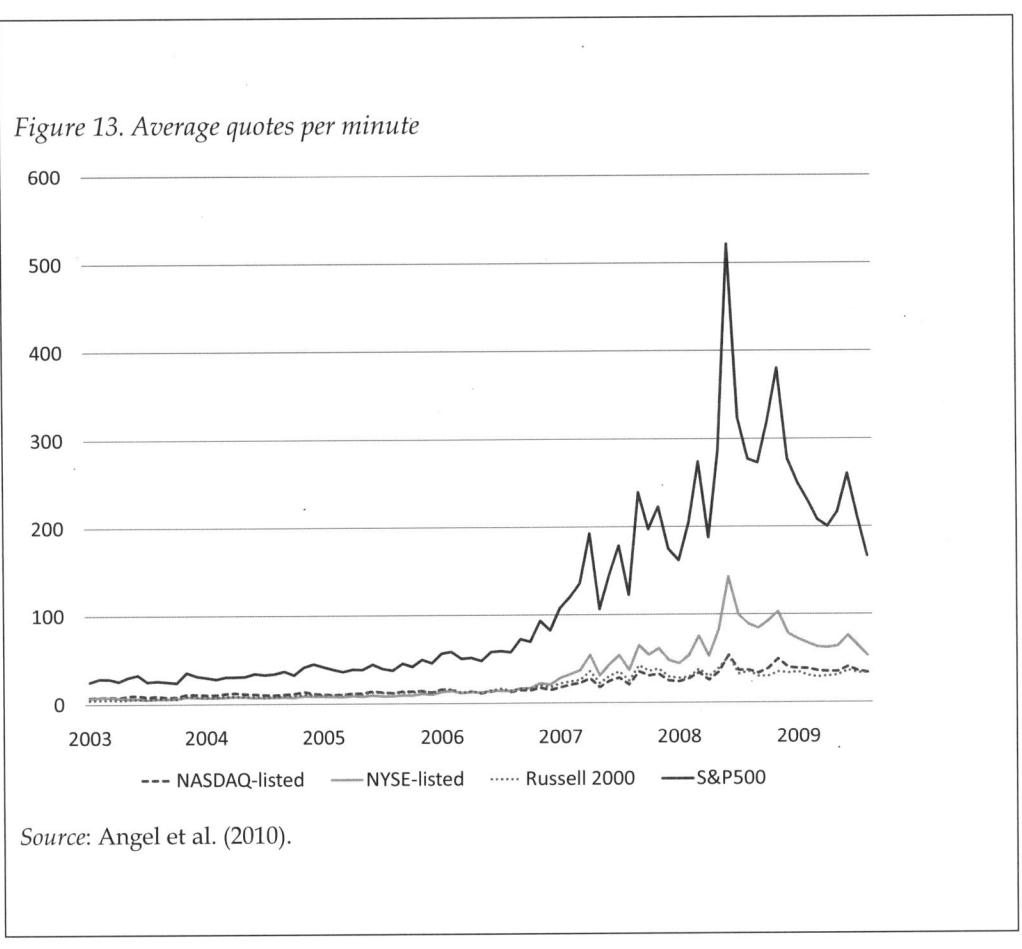

Figure 13. Average quotes per minute

Source: Angel et al. (2010).

Conclusion # 8

In the post-MiFID era, several aspects have reduced the quality of data and hindered consolidation. In order to improve this situation, the MiFID review should look both at the standardisation of data formats (code identifiers, etc.) and data granularity through flags. The relevance of trade flags comes from the support they offer to liquidity discovery mechanisms across trading venues. Market initiatives should reduce the number of trade flags, currently around 50, to fewer than 10 across Europe. On the proliferation of data formats, sources and vendors are working to reduce their number and bridge inconsistencies. Achieving minimum consistency though industry cooperation would probably be more efficient than strong regulatory intervention. In this regard, ESMA should rather support current industry-led initiatives on standardisation. However, either the Commission or ESMA should be able to impose consistency if commercial initiatives do not lead to a satisfactory solution in a reasonable time frame.

Consolidated data solutions promote best execution and help to mitigate the potentially negative effects of liquidity fragmentation. More accessible consolidated data

> solutions should be delivered, in particular to retail and small professional investors. Formats would need to be standardised and granularity increased, which would curb costs for users and increase accessibility. Already some market participants have committed to reduce costs for final users by unbundling fees for pre- and post-trade data; a step in the right direction that data vendors and distributors should follow. When lower data collection costs are realised, they should be passed on to final users. Regulators and competition authorities should draw attention to potentially unfair market practices and anticompetitive market conditions that impede markets from offering data solutions at a 'reasonable' cost, rather than attempting to define when a cost is actually 'reasonable'.
>
> The US experience with the unintended consequences of a consolidated tape run by a public entity should suggest alternative solutions. Consolidated tapes can be designed and offered by competing data operators (so-called Approved Public Arrangements or APAs), once the rules of the game have been clearly defined and duly enforced. These tapes could cover not only shares but also other financial instruments admitted to trading on RMs, MTFs or organised trading facilities, as long as a sound regime has been put in place.
>
> Regulators should set the conditions to facilitate the consolidation and timely delivery of data to investors in real time and fully unbundled through APAs. Operators would have to meet strict requirements and be responsible for the detection of multiple publications (misreporting or double-counting). Only if the industry does not deliver with these conditions, should ESMA adopt the necessary arrangements to set a single consolidated tape in the EU.

4.4.3 Bond markets

Public trade disclosure of financial instruments other than shares has been typically left to the market, in particular given the different market structures that shape trading mechanisms for corporate and sovereign bonds. In recent years, certain initiatives have been taken to offer public access to partial pre-trade and post-trade data, such as non-executable prices available through AFME[110] and Xtraker.[111] Despite initial scepticism about post-trade transparency for bonds (CESR, 2008; EU COM, 2008), problems posed by liquidity during the financial crisis – for instance the evaluation of illiquid products – have led regulators to claim a post-trade transparency regime, even though no other significant market failures have been detected (CESR, 2009b). Moreover, the growing interest of retail investors in these markets (IOSCO, 2004) has drawn the regulators' attention to allowing their needs to coexist with those of wholesale and

---

[110] See: www.investinginbondseurope.org
[111] See: http://BondMarketPrices.com

institutional investors.

Bond markets (corporate, sovereign and other public bonds)[112] are typically quote-driven markets or OTC bilateral negotiations, in which intermediation plays a critical role. On the buy-side, the demand for these financial instruments is overwhelmingly institutional, with very limited retail participation (CESR, 2008). The vast majority of bonds are listed on regulated markets, and, if traded there, they are typically pre- and post-trade transparent, like shares. However, this situation refers to a very limited number of securities; only those where there is enough liquidity to allow trading on a regulated market. Typically, opacity prevails as intermediaries are rewarded by their informational advantage in less-liquid products. Portes et al. (2006) listed the characteristics of bond markets, which explains their typical low liquidity. In effect, bonds (Biais & Declerk, 2007):

1) Attract long-term investors (hold and buy strategies),
2) Are difficult to short sell (at least in the same market) and so to manage inventory risks,
3) Have few differences between each other (predictable returns) and
4) Are less concentrated than stocks (each issuer have several bond issuances outstanding).

In addition, transaction costs for bonds usually decrease with high ratings, short maturity and size (Edwards et al., 2007). Investing in short maturity and bigger sizes may only provide incentives for a part of the demand, which may ultimately affect liquidity in the market.

These characteristics have boosted institutional demand, which has reciprocally influenced market microstructure. For instance, bond markets in the US were typically order-driven markets with strong retail participation in the 1920s. In a few years – without relevant changes in the role of bonds in financing the economy – the weight of institutions reached a turning point in which small trades were led towards a market equilibrium designed for large investors (Biais & Green, 2007). Where dealers commit capital on illiquid products, they will only do this in exchange of less disclosure, since this is the equilibrium that rewards their

---

[112] This report considers sovereign bonds as part of the wider 'public bonds category', which has been defined by CESR (2010f), p. 12. In particular, it includes bonds issued by governments, governmental authorities and national/international organisations financed by governments.

informational advantage (Madhavan, 1995). The use of big amounts of capital to maintain and develop trading activities implies high fixed costs (especially, opportunity costs), which requires a proper system of incentives for the firms committing those resources.

Proposals to increase transparency in dealer markets usually generate conflicting views in terms of their benefits and costs. Legislative proposals will need to strike the right balance of requirements concerning public disclosure. On the one hand, transparency is a public good and its optimal level may not emerge spontaneously in the market. On the other hand, opacity is not a market failure in itself and, to a certain extent, should be well calibrated, especially when it comes to dealer markets.

A transparent market setting may improve price formation and investor protection by reducing information asymmetries and thus adverse selection and moral hazard. A more transparent (post-trade) market setting can promote:

i) A more efficient price formation process by reducing search costs for end investors (Bloomfield & O'Hara, 1999; Edwards et al., 2007);
ii) Greater competition among dealers and market-makers on risk-sharing (Naik et al., 1999) and
iii) A fairer environment as long as information is publicly available to all to increase their knowledge about the market (level playing field; Casey, 2006).

Box 5. Investing in bonds

Bonds are usually associated with the idea of a 'safe' investment since they are meant to provide stable payoffs (fixed interest/income) until maturity. In effect, bonds are products that can be considered 'safer' than more 'aggressive' instruments (such as equity and some derivatives), in particular when investors buy them at issuance and hold the product until maturity. This strategy is mostly followed through plain 'vanilla' bonds, which typically give no options for the issuer and can be designed as 'straight' ('zero coupon', 'bullet'; interest is paid at maturity) or 'coupon' (interest is paid in each specified period), linked or not to the inflation rate. In this case, risks would be limited to:

- Default or restructuring risks (the probability that the institution will default or restructure its own debt);
- Inflation rate risks (the probability that the inflation rate is higher at maturity than at the time of purchase, which reduces the cash flow value);
- Exchange rate risk (when payments are made in another currency, the

probability that the exchange rate makes the value of the cash flow lower in comparison to the original investment); and
- Exogenous risks (the probability that external unforeseeable events would delay payments of interests, principal, or lead to a debt restructuring).

However, where investors dispose of a bond before maturity the level of risk dramatically increases. In this scenario, the final outcome of the transaction (specifically, the bond price on the secondary market) can be affected by these additional factors (Fabozzi, 2007):
- Interest rate risk (the probability that the bondholder will bear opportunity costs– and expressed in the decline of the bond price – when the official market interest rate increases);
- Floating rate risk (the probability that the interest rate paid to the bondholder would be lower than the prevailing fixed interest rate paid for bullet bonds);
- Yield curve risk (the probability of a shift in the long-term yield curve due to changes of the general market conditions);
- Reinvestment risk (for bonds that periodically pay interest and principal, which may need to be reinvested at least with the same return);
- Downgrade risk (as mentioned above, the probability that the rating on the issuer's credit risk worsens, making the bond price decline);
- Credit spread risk (the probability that the premium over a default-free benchmark – typically 10y US Treasury or 10y German Bund – can increase due to movements in related markets, as credit default swaps);
- Liquidity risk (the probability that the market does not have enough liquidity to price bonds at their theoretical level);
- Volatility risk (the probability that the yield would follow an unexpected and highly volatile pattern);
- Call and prepayment risk (where the bond – in exchange for a higher return – includes a provision that allows the issuer to call back the bond before the maturity date by repurchasing it at market price or an pre-established one);
- Sovereign risk (where the issuer is a government or government-funded institution, the probability that the government exercises the sovereign powers to unilaterally decide to default or restructure its debt).

As a result, investing in bonds may involve a high level of complexity, which ultimately requires a carefully designed transparency regime. Ill-defined transparency requirements may have unintended consequences for market liquidity and investors' participation in the bond market.

A more competitive environment – due to more willingness to take on risk, knowing the position of other dealers (risk-sharing) – may reduce informational advantages and ultimately lower transaction costs and bid/ask spreads (Goldstein et al., 2007). Lower search costs may stimulate efficient pricing, greater use of electronic multi-dealer platforms to diffuse quotes, and more interconnection between current venues. This may push inter-dealer platforms to expand their reach towards small professional investors or small intermediaries that struggle to receive best execution with the current regulatory gap, including retail investors (Ferrarini, 2009). Moreover, bond prices are often used to calculate default probabilities and as a benchmark for the valuation of illiquid bonds or other illiquid instruments/assets (e.g. pricing matrix). Efficient pricing mechanisms engender positive liquidity externalities (Amihud et al., 1997; Bessembinder et al., 2006; Cici et al., 2008), which spread benefits to the whole market. Finally, aggregate disclosure of bond holdings may increase systemic liquidity[113] (Laganá et al., 2006), reducing uncertainty around exposure in times of uncertainty.

In terms of costs, in a multi-stage transaction process, Naik et al. (1999) have showed that big inventory positions may suffer price revision risk, despite greater transparency reducing information asymmetries between dealers and hence improving inventory risk-sharing. In effect, in following periods, prices will reflect private information fully, minimising the informational advantage and reducing the capital committed to a sub-optimal level. Therefore, the commitment of dealers may be affected in the first place. In effect, it would become more costly to manage inventories given the potential opportunistic behaviours of a typical prisoner's dilemma.[114] Opportunistic behaviours may be also pursued through parallel exploitative actions in linked markets (such as swap or CDS). Excessive transparency can also damage liquidity, as informed traders will act knowing their competitors' positions and vice versa. Strict transparency

---

[113] Systemic liquidity is the market liquidity in 'stressed times', when liquidity is typically driven by the homogeneous herd behaviours of investors (e.g. 'panic' or 'euphoria'). It is specifically related to market participants' behaviour. It is the opposite of 'search liquidity', which is the liquidity in 'normal times' when liquidity is typically driven by search costs for end investors. See, Laganá et al. (2006).

[114] The prisoner's dilemma is a situation in which parties behave opportunistically in order to maximise their outcome. By acting uncooperatively, parties will end up in a worse position than if they had coordinated their actions.

requirements may give them enough information to be able to enforce the artificial price of the oligopolistic market equilibrium (Kovtunenko, 2003). Disproportionate information about securities' payoffs may reduce informational advantages for informed investors with respect to dealers, thus pushing part of this liquidity out of the market.

Trade disclosure. Finally, greater trade disclosure may also have an unclear impact on systemic liquidity by increasing homogeneity of valuation and risk management tools on the one hand, which may be put under critical pressure when market conditions in the linked market worsen (cascade effects), and, on the other hand improving asset valuation tools.

Due to the reasons mentioned above, speed, breadth (granularity) and depth of information should be designed around 'dynamic' liquidity measures, which may apply to some related asset classes (such as liquid structured products and CDSs). Post-trade information that is useful for price discovery purposes[115] is generally information about the characteristics of the bond (price, volume and identifiers), frequency of trading, credit ratings at the issue, and whether bonds are listed and/or traded off-exchange (flags). Data should be consolidated across trading platforms wherever possible (IOSCO, 2004). To preserve systemic liquidity and to monitor systemic risk, some aggregate information about notional value and current holdings should be provided to regulators, even on a confidential basis.

Transparency requirements. The Commission confirmed that, while transparency requirements will be differentiated by asset class, the new regime will cover all bonds with a prospectus or admitted to trading on a RM or MTF (even if traded OTC; EU COM, 2010b, p. 27). The extension does not cover bonds that may be traded only OTC, as a result of a private placement. CESR (2010f), proposed the introduction of a post-trade transparency regime for corporate and 'public' bonds, which are defined as "transferable debt securities [...] with a maturity of at least 12 months". However, both CESR and the Commission only took into account the size of transactions as a valid liquidity measure to set thresholds and delays for post-trade transparency. Liquidity measures typically encompass a wide array of measures (not only size) that may need to be considered

---

[115] The report does not consider information requested for transaction reporting purposes at this stage, which is covered by current MiFID text and in the earlier section of the report.

altogether. CESR did not consider the frequency of trades to set the threshold but the possibility to delay publication by 15 minutes in exceptional circumstances can eventually help where products are infrequently traded. To give an example, on Xtrakter,[116] almost 75% of the 43,000 corporate bond issuances are traded mainly wholesale and less than 10 times a month (orders can be up to 15% of all the bond issuance). In October 2010, the highest average daily number of trades for a single bond was 129 times. Moreover, while 80% of government bonds are traded electronically (50-60% of volumes), only roughly 30% of corporate bonds is traded on electronic platforms. This setting may drastically affect the level of data that can be obtained in the 15 minutes buffer defined by CESR and the Commission.

However, bonds infrequently traded may need some protection from full or partial post-trade transparency, especially when traded in big 'wholesale' sizes. In effect, full disclosure of these trades may stimulate actions against the holder in other related markets (as CDS market), in order to exploit the private information. Nevertheless, this issue may be tackled with a specific scheme of delays (as done for equities). This scheme could also take into account the frequency of trades. Delays calibrated by the initial issuance, the frequency of transactions and their size may be indispensable for these markets to function well. It would also play a key role in winding up and unwinding big inventory positions.

Finally, it is fundamental to make sure that standards of publication (e.g. identifiers, condition codes, transaction definition, etc) are clearly defined and implemented across trading venues. This would eventually stimulate data consolidation, which may be difficult to implement where publicly available quotes are not executable. In any case, even partial coverage would increase the attractiveness of these markets and,

---

[116] As mentioned above, Xtrakter publishes some information about bonds, available on www.bondmarketprices.com. Xtrakter runs an approved reporting mechanism to the FSA in London, which has processed 578 million transactions in 2009. It offers bid/offer quotations and transaction reporting (through TRAX) for equities, fixed income securities (a vast majority) and OTC derivatives. Xtrakter produces bond liquidity data on a monthly basis that includes 28,000 to 35,000 securities per month; its database contains nearly 400,000 documents. Published data is only on fixed income securities. Overall, Xtrakter already captures at least one leg of 60-70% of all fixed income market (at least one leg transacted in London).

potentially, overall liquidity.

> **Box 6. The TRACE experience**
>
> With the introduction of a Trade Reporting And Compliance Engine (TRACE), on 1st July 2002, the US officially introduced a trade reporting system for corporate bonds, a 'big-bang' for US corporate bond markets which covers agency debt from March 2010 and asset-backed securities since 2011. This system reports post-trade information – within 15 minutes – of transactions below $5 million at par value. It consolidates the time of execution, price, yield and volume for 100% of OTC transactions in over 43,000 securities, representing 99% of the corporate bond and agency debt market activity.
>
> Despite concerns of the industry due to the loose protection of inventory positions and large trades, regulators have implemented this solution in a relatively short timeframe for the entire market. On the one side, it is extremely difficult to measure any unintended long-term effects of TRACE on liquidity and market innovation. In particular, it is unclear whether lower costs are not offset at the expense of promoting sub-optimal market equilibrium in the long term, by impairing dealers' capital commitment. However, some academic studies have provided empirical evidence on the effects of TRACE. The system has:
>
> - Reduced trade execution costs (Bessembinder et al., 2006; Edwards et al., 2007),
> - Reduced spreads on more liquid bonds (Goldstein et al., 2007) and
> - Improved corporate bond valuation (Cici et al., 2008).
>
> These studies suggest that the impact of TRACE has been very positive on trading costs and corporate bond valuation, while less so on liquidity over the long term.
>
> Finally, the nature of the US system – where dealers operate rather as broker-agents, with low capital commitment – makes the implementation of a regime such as TRACE easier than in Europe. In effect, in Europe dealers typically act as principals to the transaction, competing with other dealers to buy bonds that may sit on their balance sheets afterwards. Bonds are then sold to investors by offering executable prices on a platform or bilaterally. In this respect, in order to keep liquidity in the market, the introduction of a transparency regime should be gradual, to preserve large trades and relevant inventory positions in the market. Moreover, European and US bond markets also have other differences (Biais & Declerk, 2007):
>
> - European markets are more competitive, since national banks compete with dealers to offer bonds to wholesale and retail investors.
> - Frequency of trades is higher in Europe than the US.
> - Effective spreads post-TRACE are not lower than European ones.
>
> This situation does not imply that TRACE has not generated positive effects in the US and it does not preclude a similar regime in Europe from having a positive

impact on European markets as well. A more competitive market setting plays a crucial role in reducing or increasing these differences.

> *Conclusion # 9*
>
> *A transparency regime for bond markets should provide meaningful information to stimulate price discovery. The speed, breadth, and depth of information should be designed around 'dynamic' liquidity measures. Since there is not a single measure of liquidity readily available, transparency requirements should be developed on an instrument-by-instrument basis. This task should rather be left to secondary legislation, such as Level 2 implementing measures or binding technical standards.*
>
> *Liquidity is a dynamic aspect, which may take different forms according to the characteristics of the financial instrument and the trading mechanism. This reality should be taken into account where allowing exemptions or deferred publication in order to preserve an efficient and sound price formation process. Dynamic measures of liquidity can be designed around aspects such as frequency of trades, overall turnover or prospective liquidity, product standardisation, or transaction size. Finally, since data is fragmented, data formats and flags may need to be further standardised for the purpose of pre-trade transparency.*
>
> *Promoting structural market changes in non-equity markets to give easier access to retail investors may raise conflicting issues. For some market participants, the market for fixed income securities should remain wholesale dealer-driven. In their view – even though a commendable objective – direct retail access to non-equity instruments may destabilise dealer-driven markets, as it may generate higher volatility with no liquidity enhancements.*
>
> *These effects would ultimately heighten risks for retail investors, given the increasing complexity of fixed income securities. Other stakeholders, however, firmly support the opening of bond markets to retail investors. Greater transparency may be a liquidity driver for these markets. Under proper delays and exemptions, the impact of retail trading activities would be fairly limited.*

4.4.4 Structured financial products

Structured financial products (SFPs) are securities whose cash flow payments come from a pool of assets. Securities are typically issued by an independent legal entity, so-called 'special purpose vehicle' (SPV). Credit enhancements, which are different levels of credit seniority, give them the possibility to reach a wide range of investors (retail and institutional). SFPs can be divided into three major categories (CESR, 2008):

i) Asset-backed securities (ABSs),
ii) Collateralised debt obligations (CDOs) and
iii) Asset-backed commercial paper (ABCPs).

ABSs are securities issued and financed by the sale of specific assets. In effect, there are several sub-categories, named after the underlying asset.

Some of them are: residential mortgage backed securities (RMBSs); commercial mortgage backed securities (CMBSs); and other securities backed by other assets/receivables (as loans, auto loans, etc.).

CDOs are securities typically 'collateralised' with a portfolio of other fixed income securities. The income generated by these securities actually feeds the cash flows generated by CDOs over time.

ABCPs are commercial notes collateralised by other assets that have a short maturity (180 days maximum).

SFPs often are very illiquid, in particular during times of financial distress. In effect, the size of the SFPs market was drastically reduced as a result of the crisis. Banks heavily involved in securitisation and SFPs issuances suffered important losses and, in extreme cases, defaulted. The crisis highlighted relevant market failures, such as distorted system of incentives and lack of reliable information in the market. While the demand for these products gradually recovers, 90% of new issuances are still done only for 'repo' purposes (with no private placement). It is highly unlikely that the market will revert to 2006-7 levels, at least in the short term. As fixed income securities, SFPs have many similarities with bonds and in theory are designed to reproduce a similar payoff structure. However, the financial design of SFPs is often more complicated and is in general not directly linked to the credit risk of a legal entity, but to a pool of assets whose information may not be publicly available or not meaningful for investment purposes. Limited information about SFPs can be accessed by a limited number of investors. This information suffers from a lack of completeness and dispersion in memoranda (a sort of prospectus), rating agency reports, issuer's presentations, and pool reports. The complexity of these documents often makes it difficult to extract meaningful information for investment purposes (IOSCO, 2009b).

CESR (2010f) and the Commission (2010b, p. 27) have finally opined that the transparency regime for structured products should cover all asset-backed securities (ABS) and collateralised debt obligations (CDOs) for which a prospectus has been published (i.e. including all ABS and CDOs admitted to trading on EEA RMs) or which are admitted to trading on an MTF. Due to the perceived illiquidity of these markets, CESR suggested a phased approach for a post-trade transparency regime. Any extension of a post-transparency regime to non-equity markets needs to be properly calibrated. The Commission's consultation report on MiFID also takes stock of the CESR advice (European Commission, 2010b, p. 28), which will apply the approach to other non-equity products too. A crucial role will be played by trade repositories (see next section).

4.4.5 Over-the-counter derivatives

OTC Derivatives. Derivatives are "financial instruments whose value (price of the contract) is derived from the value of an underlying asset (e.g. equity, bond, or commodity) or market variable (e.g. interest rate, credit risk, exchange rate, or stock index)" (Valiante, 2010, p. 1). Almost all transactions (around 84%)[117] are executed OTC, i.e. bilaterally negotiated or through inter-dealer platforms that display to their members executable quotes collected from a group of dealers with a limited role for regulated markets and official alternative trading platforms.[118] These instruments are regularly used for hedging, funding, speculation and arbitrage. The frequency of trades is very low. The figure below shows the daily number of trades per currency and maturity that are executed in the OTC interest rate swap (IRS) market, which represents almost 75% of the global OTC derivatives markets (measured in notional value).[119]

Figure 14. Average daily number of IRS trades by currency

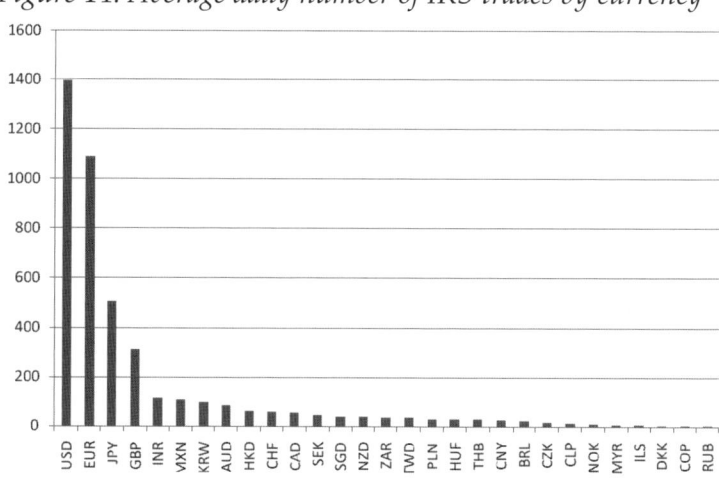

---

[117] Updated figure from BIS, by comparing notional amount of average daily turnover of OTC and exchange-traded derivatives; see http://www.bis.org/publ/rpfx10.pdf?noframes=1, and http://www.bis.org/statistics/otcder/dt1920a.pdf.

[118] For a more detailed discussion on the nature of these products and markets, see in general Valiante (2010).

[119] The notional value (or simply 'notional') consists of the face value of the OTC derivatives contracts.

Source: TriOptima.

Figure 15. Average daily number of new IRS trades by maturity

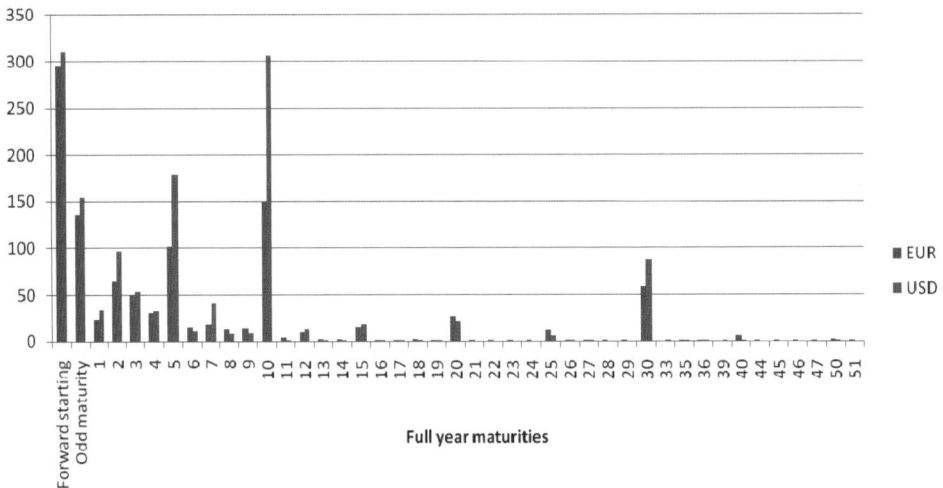

Source: TriOptima.

Credit default swaps. Another important class of OTC derivatives is credit default swaps (CDSs). These contracts allow a counterparty to get full protection over an exposure held by the subscriber with a third party. The protection seller periodically receives a premium in exchange for paying the difference between the face value of the obligation (e.g. securities) covered by the CDS contract and the current market value, when a 'credit event' occurs. Alternatively, the insurer can pay the face value and take the obligation in exchange. The CDS is 'triggered' when a specific 'credit event' occurs. In addition to a default, a CDS contract can be also triggered by other events, such as a debt restructuring or moratorium (ISDA, 2003).

Credit derivatives have played a crucial role by providing a source of pricing for some corporate bonds. They also offer protection for inventory positions in bond markets since CDS markets allow going long on bonds with no need to provide high cash payments as collateral. Furthermore, bonds covered by CDS contracts are regularly accepted for repo transactions, which give a strong incentive to deal with illiquid products. Recent evidences (Shim & Zhu, 2010) support this statement and show that CDS trading actually has boosted liquidity in Asian bond markets. This self-reinforcing relationship between CDS and bond markets has fostered credit derivatives markets in the last decade. Despite quick growth, however, CDS single-name contracts are still very illiquid, with over 99% of trades occurring fewer than 10 times a day from December 2009 to June 2010 (DTCC, CDS Data Warehouse). CDS index contracts, however, have a more liquid market but only 20% of trades are actually traded more than 10 times a day and 10% more than 50 times a day from March 2010 to September 2010 according to DTCC CDS Data Warehouse. CDS indexed contracts are also highly standardised (ISDA, 2003) and electronically traded. Aggregated data are periodically published by DTCC Deriv/Serv, although no data are provided on net exposures of systemically important financial institutions.

Trade disclosure. A post-trade transparency regime for SFPs and OTC derivatives may be designed around requirements similar to the ones adopted for bonds. However, since transactions are mainly OTC bilateral negotiations with very low frequency and high size, information may be not only meaningless but eventually harmful, especially if the financial instrument acts as a benchmark for evaluating similar products. Therefore, exemptions and delays for these financial instruments should be on average wider than for bonds and primarily based on the size and frequency of trades. Nevertheless, SFPs and OTC derivatives typically lack price transparency, given the use of proprietary valuation models to price complex products (CESR, 2009b). In this case, aggregate price indexes should be publicly available in real time, whenever possible. In effect, given the low number of transactions in these products, a continuous flow of information may not necessarily be available to support the pricing of these products by competing binding indication of interests from end investors (as OLOBs). Therefore, proprietary pricing models become indispensable tools.

Aggregate data. Securitisation and OTC derivatives may be formidable tools to free capital back to the real economy and promote better allocation of risk and resources. They contribute to transfer credit risk and spread it in the markets to those who are more able to bear it. However, the experience of the financial crisis has taught us that spreading risk among many counterparties through complex financial instruments does not ultimately cancel it. Information about the underlying assets and net exposures should always be publicly available in order to monitor systemic risk. Competent regulators should have access to data via reporting, especially through *trade repositories*. During stress time, aggregated information on net exposures could help contain herd behaviours set off by market opacity. It is thought that this form of transparency can improve systemic liquidity (Lagana et al., 2006). Investment firms would have to provide this information, which would subsequently be aggregated by trade repositories (TRs), with sufficient skills and capabilities to collect and aggregate this information (European Commission, 2010b, p. 13). However, aggregated information on net exposures might not be readily available; hence financial institutions could explore the possibility to modify their data management system in order to collect information on net exposures in a way that does not compromise the confidentiality of sensitive information. Trade repositories would then be able to aggregate this information and offer a global picture. Trade repositories would therefore play a double function: a) disclosing aggregate data on net exposures (trade reporting); and b) providing specific data on transactions to regulators on a confidential basis (transaction reporting). The transparency regime should cover all derivatives centrally cleared and those reported to trade repositories (Art. 6.1, EMIR).

Conclusion # 10

A post-trade transparency regime for derivatives and structured products should be more detailed and tailored to the nature of these products. Where listed on RMs and/or MTFs, the regime could be designed with the same methodology employed for bonds, but its implementation should follow a phased approach.

Exemptions and due calibrations should be allowed in order to preserve efficient price formation and guarantee the effective monitoring of systemic risk. Calibrations should take into account the nature of these markets and of each financial instrument, rather than a division into broader categories (e.g. by asset classes). A mere application of post-trade transparency to a general list of instruments would definitely hamper market liquidity. As for bond markets, measurements of liquidity should be taken into account with due care to avoid adverse consequences in terms of liquidity for wholesale participants.

The extension of trade and transaction reporting to non-equity markets can be facilitated by current infrastructures, thereby reducing costs.

Finally, harmonising the scope of 'eligibility' for clearing purposes with the legal duty to be pre- and post-trade transparent would leave big gaps in the actual implementation of the transparency regime. In addition, it may also distort trading activities and redirect them towards non-centrally cleared products, since – on top of the costs of centralised clearing – firms would bear the risk coming from pre- and post-trade transparency with no assessment of size and frequency of transactions. Extension of post-trade and transaction reporting to non-equity markets can be facilitated by current infrastructures (reducing costs) but it is critical that transparency requirements remain independent from trading and clearing eligibility requirements. In effect, the requirements to access a central counterparty clearing (CCP) are not only based on liquidity itself but also on the standardisation of technical and legal aspects, and therefore the mere eligibility for clearing of an instrument should not be considered to be a proper test of liquidity and frequency of trading for transparency purposes.

MiFID 2.0: Casting New Light on Europe's Capital Markets | 99

> For instance, as shown above, CDS contracts are quite standardised and over 75% of trades are confirmed on the same day. Dealers expect as much as 90% of these contracts to be cleared on CCPs.[120] While expectation about eligibility to central clearing are high, this choice does not necessarily consider market liquidity, which remains still very low with less than 20% of CDS contracts traded more than 10 times a day and less than once for the vast majority of them. Potential delays and issues affecting the process of centralisation of clearing on CCPs may ultimately affect the implementation of disclosure requirements in these markets.

---

[120] See http://www.finextra.com/news/fullstory.aspx?newsitemid=20458.

5. RESHAPING MARKET STRUCTURE

5.1 Introduction

The structure of financial markets changed dramatically over the last decade. New trading technologies and growing volumes have generated important network externalities, which have ultimately reshaped the original market design based on natural monopolies. These developments, together with innovative policy decisions, have also favoured changes in three areas: competition and market fragmentation micro-structure and infrastructure. In this framework, MiFID has managed to provide a comprehensive regulatory framework that boosted the aforementioned developments and minimised potential unintended consequences for market quality and investor protection. This report does not address the issue of what market structure works best. For this question, there is, in principle, no final answer. The best market structure is the one "in which a market-clearing price can always be found" (O'Hara, 1995, p. 269).

5.2 Securities markets as network industry

Definition. A network is a market setting in which the output is the result of the interaction of several inputs (so-called 'nodes') that generate externalities when combined in a certain way. Three aspects characterise a network industry (Economides, 1993): complementarity, compatibility and coordination.

The output of a network infrastructure is typically a composite good, which 'mixes and matches' inputs that are complementary.[121] For instance, a phone call is the result of a network that links the caller with the receiver.

---

[121] A and B are two complementary products when an increase in the price of A also reduces the quantity of B.

The link between the caller and the adapter/switch is complementary to the link between the adapter or switch and the receiver, which at the end compose a phone call. For the formation of the composite output of the network, the relationship among the nodes, their complementarity and their compatibility, is essential. In this sense, complementarity only exists if the inputs composing the final good are compatible, i.e. both follow the same standards and appear coordinated in time and space.

Network externalities. The network output can generate two kinds of externalities: i) direct and ii) indirect. An externality is 'direct', when any additional customer/node increases the size of the whole network by $2*n$ potential new goods. The overall number of complementary goods is $n*(n-1)$. This externality is also called production externality and is generated by the economies of scope produced by an additional node. An externality is 'indirect', when an extra customer does not necessarily represent $2*n$ potential goods, but only increases the size of the network and the possibility of finding a good matching. It is also called consumption externality or size externality, i.e. the value of a unit of the good increases with the 'expected' number of units sold (Economides, 1996). This kind of externality relies upon the presence of economies of scale and represents the inverse of the 'classic' law of the demand since the value of the good increases with the number of units sold (or produced).

Network settings. Networks can have two 'basic' market settings or a combined one: one-way, two-way and mixed.

A one-way network (e.g. TV broadcasting) is a network where the output is function of n consumers and m developers/suppliers of products. Producers develop the product and make it available through the 'grid'. This generates indirect network externalities: more users will increase the number of developers and vice-versa. However, there is no strict complementarity between consumer and developer. One extra customer does not necessarily add $2*n$ potential complementary goods, but it will 'indirectly' increase the overall value of the network since it will be more likely that an exchange will take place at its best value (consumption or size externality).

A two-way network is a network where n consumers interact with $n-1$ other consumers over the 'switch', that is the product that allow consumers to access different suppliers. This network setting generates direct network externalities: one additional consumer equals n new combined products or $2*n$ complementary nodes (due to its different nature). As mentioned above, a market for local or international phone calls is a typical two-way network setting. The externality effect of having one more customer 'directly' affects the utility function of the other consumers/investors (direct or production externality).

Finally, the two 'basic' settings may interact according to the level of complementarity between groups of users/platforms/goods. Interactions allow for combinations of goods or consumers/investors whose willingness to trade generate both one-way and two-way network externalities. This network setting will occur more frequently in multi-sided markets, whereby the interaction of types of users/goods/platforms takes place.

5.2.1 Markets Multi-sidedness and Securities Markets

Multi-sided markets. Networks can be classified according to their pricing structure, i.e. the possibility that platforms can charge different prices to different groups of users. The market would be considered as 'two-sided' or more generally 'multi-sided' when the pricing structure of respectively one or multiple platforms is based on:

i) The interaction of groups of users-only (Rochet & Tirole, 2003) in which n receivers interact with m senders through a platform; often the platform subsidizes the entrance of n receivers on the one-side with the interest of m to get in contact with n on the other side;[122] and

ii) The interaction of both groups of users and platforms (Armstrong, 2006) n users can interact with m other users; the value of the network is the possibility that you can interact through different platforms, so-called 'multi-homing'[123]).

---

[122] The videogame industry (e.g. Microsoft Xbox 360, Sony Playstation, etc.) epitomises a good example of a two-sided market, in which the value of the network will increase by stimulating the interaction between users of the platform (gamers) and developers of game software. The platform will therefore charge a more modest fee to developers (typically free access or sometimes even paying them) in order to attract more users and generate size externalities. The balance between the two fees (price distortions) will change as the platform gains more users and increases its value or from the potential intensity of network externalities that attracting a group of user may generate.

[123] B2B exchanges (e.g. Alibaba.com, etc.) are platforms that link business buyers and sellers. Sellers are charged for posting their products, while buyers typically access those platforms for free. The possibility to offer the content in multi-homing – i.e. on multiple platforms – increases the value of the overall network as it increases the potential reach of sellers' proposals, whether or not both sides of users are both multi-home. Users wish to reap the

Both interactions may generate direct or indirect externalities as characteristic of one-way or two-way networks.

Securities markets can be considered as 'networks', whose output is the exchange of the financial instrument at the 'best' available terms (a combination of complementary goods, i.e. investors' bid and offer). The structure of markets for financial instruments is a combination of different network settings that allow the interaction of liquidity demanders and suppliers through buying and selling securities. Through this interaction of bids and offers, resources will have more chances to find their best allocation in the economy. In effect, transaction costs would be prohibitive in a world with no exchange platforms; investors or issuers would have to bear the full cost of finding the counterparty who best values their securities, which would ultimately lead to resources being inefficiently allocated. Markets can reduce transaction costs (by facilitating transactions on agreeable terms) and allow more efficient allocation of resources, but not all market designs reduce costs to the same extent (Coase, 1960; Demsetz, 1968).

Primary markets. Securities markets (in particular for shares) can be divided into primary and secondary markets.[124] Although they both match liquidity demand and supply, their network settings may be different since they might be based on the interaction of groups of users, on multiple platforms or both. In primary markets, securities are sold by issuers for the first time, as a combination of issuers' offer and a set of buyers' bids. These markets may be extremely volatile before the security is sold at the market-clearing price. Volatility occurs at the time where the security is proposed to potential buyers at a theoretical value, which will change according to their willingness to buy (the number of offers).

---

benefits of network externalities in an environment of non-interconnected platforms (Rochet & Tirole, 2006).

[124] The report discusses the interaction of investors' interests in trading platforms. Little attention is actually given to the network settings of the post-trade industry, which typically take a different shape from the one of trading platforms.

Figure 16. Primary securities markets

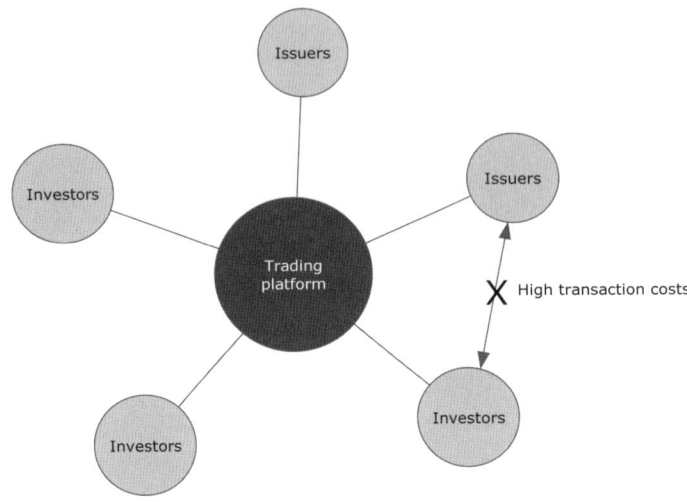

Source: Authors.

As shown in the figure above, primary markets gather investors and issuers in the same place. It is a single-home market, since issuers list their shares in the market of their choice, which typically coincides with the main national regulated market for both legal (official listing) and economic reasons (most liquid primary markets). In this case, the national regulated market will be the only place where buyers can purchase those shares when the issue begins. Cross-border listing is possible but generally occurs at different terms. The pricing structure of primary markets is two-sided; issuers are willing to pay for accessing the platform (listing fees), while members of the market get access to those executable quotes at more favourable terms (or within the membership access fee they actually pays) when the security is issued. The platform subsidizes the interaction of n investors with the interest of m issuers to offer them their securities (Rochet & Tirole, 2003). For listing of SMEs – which typically represent a less mature market with lower liquidity (so size externalities) – issuers may get more favourable terms to access the trading platform to place their instruments.

Figure 17. Secondary securities markets

[Figure 17: Diagram showing secondary securities markets structure with Investors' offers at top flowing through Intermediaries (with Membership/Access Fee and Execution Fee) via DMA/SA to nine Trading Platforms (A through I), then flowing back through Intermediaries to Investors' bids at the bottom.]

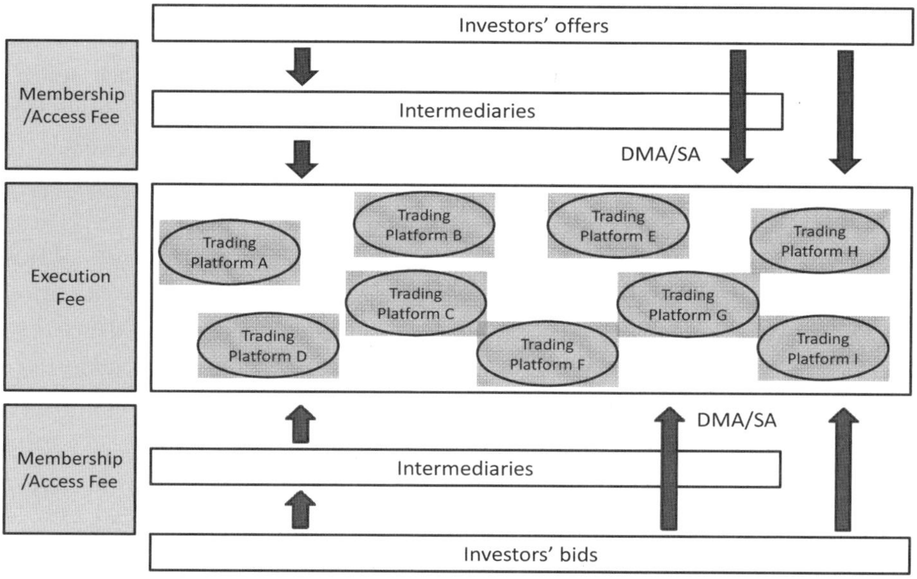

Source: Authors' own elaboration.

Secondary markets allow the interaction between investors' bids and offers (the 'complementary goods') in order to achieve the exchange of a financial instrument (liquidity). Investors can access the platform through a switch (intermediaries, e.g. brokers or dealers) or directly through Direct Market Access (DMA) if the firm has enough expertise, but under the supervision of an intermediary.

Two pricing structures are usually charged in this network industry setting. Firstly, both bids and offers pay a fee for every executed order, which is generally the same for bids and offers. Commissions typically vary according to the number and size of orders, thereby promoting more volumes and revenues, to increase the value of the entire network (Economides, 1993) and reach the critical mass through size externalities (Pagano, 1989). The nature and pricing structure of the network at this stage is thus one-sided with 'indirect' size externalities (as a one-way network). In addition, access fees are passed on to final investors by intermediaries (spreads) if the investor does not directly access the market.

Two-sided markets. Secondly, trading platforms generally charge a membership fee to grant access to the venue (see Figure 17). For investors who do not meet the admission criteria, fees are embedded in the intermediaries' executable bid/ask spread (e.g. retail investors). The same occurs for investors who prefer to access markets through intermediaries (brokers/dealers) because they deal with several trading venues and find it inconvenient to pay multiple membership fees. In effect, there are several categories of traders/investors, who may need to access multiple platforms to execute their orders to get best execution (Harris, 2002). Markets with automated continuous auction systems (called 'broker-dealer crossing networks') have a pricing structure that is typically two-sided ('non-neutrality' of access fees[125]). This pricing also exists in markets where dealers commit own capital or provide crossing services with or without fiduciary duties (or quote-driven dealer markets). Fees in these two markets are designed to stimulate the interaction between uninformed and informed investors, thus generating strong network externalities (of the indirect type).

In effect, four conditions help us to define secondary securities markets as 'two-sided':
1) Both groups of users (bids and offers) gain from accessing the platform.
2) Too high transaction costs would not allow private bilateral agreements on how to deal with externalities (Coase, 1960).
3) Users pay access fees.
4) Access fees are 'non-neutral'.

Despite strong size externalities (economies of scale), securities markets – here two-sided markets – have shown the ability to support competing trading venues ('multi-homing'; Armstrong, 2006) where at least one group of users needs to access multiple platforms, as a reflection of the diverse needs of market participants beyond simple price factors. Advanced technologies (smart order routing systems, etc.) have provided investors with tools to exploit direct network externalities (economies of scope) coming from the interaction of competing (trading) platforms, in particular if complementary (Van Cayseele & Reynaerts, 2010).[126] The value

---

[125] The 'non-neutrality' of access fees is the primary condition of two-sided markets (Rochet & Tirole, 2004). This means that the overall volume of transactions depends on the allocation of fees between groups of users. The platform can influence the overall number of transactions by modifying the membership for a group of users, keeping the other fees constant. In effect, members acting in different capacities may get (in relative terms) a lower fee (as they bring uninformed and low-risk investors to the market) than a firm requesting membership in its own capacity only.

[126] The role of economies of scale and scope in the post-trading infrastructure have been

of the network derives not only from its size externality and its ability to reach a 'critical mass' of liquidity – as originally perceived by markets and policy-makers. It also comes from the interaction of competing trading venues with different market designs to meet multi-faceted investors' needs. In effect, today an investor can pursue different strategies (e.g. price improvements and speed) by executing simultaneously two different orders on multiple platforms.

> *Conclusion # 11*
>
> *Today's markets benefit from the interaction of groups of users and platforms, as well as competition/interaction between platforms (including dealers' networks). As a vital part of the network, competition strives if markets are contestable, not only from a technological standpoint (sunk costs), but also in terms of fair market practices and an evenly applied market regulation (dynamic view). This implies the need to abate barriers to entry and exit and monitor adopted market practices. Competition authorities should play an increasingly important role in this regard.*

5.3 Competition and fragmentation

Concentration rules. The structure of financial markets has remarkably evolved in the last decade. Most notably, equity markets have experienced unprecedented changes that have redefined the interaction between investors and trading platforms. The tension between reaching 'critical mass' (with its self-reinforcing network effects) and meeting investors' need for diversified execution services (as a result of their multi-form

---

discussed at length, in particular for settlement services. Some recent studies (Schmiedel, 2002; Schmiedel et al., 2006; Van Cayseele & Wuyts, 2006) suggest that there are potentially strong economies of scale in the EU post-trading landscape, which may lead to further alliances and mergers between incumbents. Divergent views arise around the policy implications that these authors suggest. On the one hand, some authors (Schmiedel et al., 2006) argue that to fully exploit the economies of scale of network infrastructures, mergers and further integration in the post-trade industry should be promoted. On these theoretical rationales, for instance, the ECB decided to go ahead with Target2Securities (T2S), which is a project to create a pan-European platform for securities settlement accounts in central bank money. On the other side, others (Van Cayseele & Wuyts, 2007; Van Cayseele & Reynaerts, 2010) noted that economies of scale are limited and are typically exhausted before the pan-European scale is achieved. In addition, 'bridges' and multi-homing services suggest that economies of scope may be significant. Hence, they suggest that regulators should carry on further investigation before unbundling services or creating monopolies in any part of the value chain.

nature; Harris 2002) has generated a conflict between consolidation and fragmentation. Prior to the introduction of MiFID, stock exchanges benefited from the application of concentration rules, which forced intermediaries and investors to carry out any transactions in listed shares on their main national market. The aim was to preserve price formation and market integrity by concentrating trading activities in one consolidated limit order book, even though the primary economic objective and nature of a trading network is the reduction of transaction costs to increase volumes. Infrastructures for order execution (exchanges) have been widely considered as a natural monopoly until the widespread diffusion of new technologies and internet. This conception was based on two premises, firstly, that amassing liquidity in one place would generate positive externalities and, secondly, that liquidity would gravitate around the most liquid market (Pagano, 1989). However, technology has transformed securities markets into networks where users and platforms interact. Interaction reduces transaction costs (marginal costs[127]) close to zero by generating positive externalities, given economies of scale and scope. In effect, the rationale of a natural monopoly lies in the basic condition that only one firm can produce the output (here the exchange of financial instruments) at the lowest marginal costs and at the minimum efficient scale (Varian, 2006). Under this assumption, costs would be declining with a growing number of users (size externalities, see Figure 18 A below) as opposed to an ordinary cost structure (Figure 18 B). Regulation must set prices equal to marginal cost (that is the price of a perfectly competitive market). Otherwise, the monopolist would produce or generate a sub-optimal volume of trading. However, defining the price of perfect competition (price equal to marginal costs) notably is not a perfect science.

---

[127] The marginal cost is the cost of producing one additional unit of the final output.

Figure 18. Cost structures with (A) and without (B) size externalities

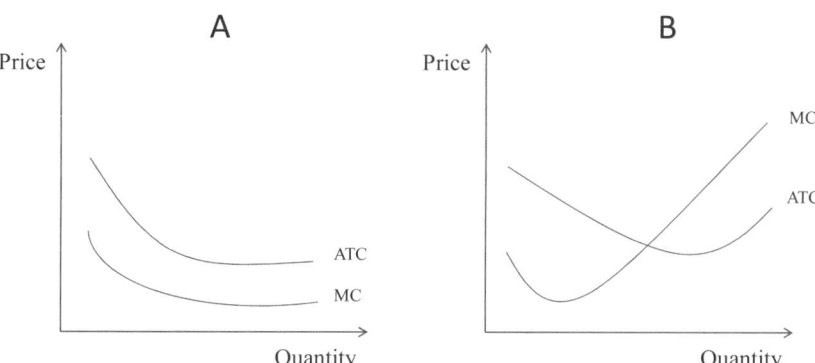

Note: MC = Marginal Costs) and ATC = Average Total Costs.
Source: Authors.

If at least one market participant could replicate the cost structure of the monopolist (A), the market should no longer be considered a natural monopoly (it would not be naturally designed for one market participant since a monopolistic equilibrium would be sub-optimal in terms of prices and volumes). As shown below, many studies in the last two decades suggest that competition between trading venues is possible and somehow beneficial, thereby discarding the presence of a natural monopoly in the market for securities (for a review, see Lee, 2002, amongst others, and Economides, 1996).

In effect, transaction costs (implicit and explicit) have plummeted across European and US markets after the abolition of the concentration rule in both jurisdictions, which has contributed to fragment the trading landscape (Lannoo & Valiante, 2010). In Europe, the abolition de facto took place in 2007-08 when member states fully transposed MiFID rules in their national legal systems, while in the US Rule 390 had been already abolished by the New York Stock Exchange (NYSE) in December 1999.

Contestability and fragmentation. The contestability[128] of financial markets has been increasing since the 1980s, when automation of trading

---

[128] A perfectly contestable market is a market in which barriers to entry and exit are low enough to give newcomers enough incentives to enter the market and compete with the incumbents (Baumol, 1982).

(and computers) has gradually become widespread, allowing the dematerialisation of securities and new forms of trading for investors as well as higher speed and capacity for trading venues. Technology made the dematerialisation of securities possible, together with new forms of trading for investors and higher speed and capacity for trading venues. Automation of trading, in effect, has drastically reduced entry barriers in terms of sunk (fixed) costs since technologies have become commoditised and easy to customise (Domowitz & Steil, 1999). However, only with the commercial diffusion of the internet in the mid-1990s, securities markets became widely contestable, given the abating of geographical barriers. Floor trading specialists have been replaced by sophisticated algorithms executed from only a few locations around the globe, as they are more able to deal with market impact (Domowitz, 1990). Nowadays, retail investors can potentially access every market in the world from their home PC. Hence, in the last decade new demand for securities has flowed into financial markets and volumes have been constantly increasing across the planet (see regional and global indicators in Annex I). The number of uninformed investors has grown and become less rare than it used to be. Overall, soaring volumes have promoted important changes in the structure of the market, and as a result open limit order books (OLOBs) have become a stable institution (Glosten, 1994).

Increased contestability means more possibilities for newcomers to enter the market for order execution and matching services. Market fragmentation – to be distinguished from liquidity fragmentation[129] – became a recurring aspect across European and US markets after the abolition of concentration rules. Incumbent exchanges have been demutualised by becoming for-profit firms (for a review, Levin, 2003) and put in competition with alternative trading platforms (so-called 'Multilateral Trading Facilities'[130]), internalisers and crossing networks run by brokers/dealers (see next section).

Benefits and costs. Fragmentation has positive and negative implications, due to two potential effects:

---

[129] Market fragmentation concerns the co-existence of several trading platforms in the same marketplace. This does not necessarily mean that this market setting favours the fragmentation of liquidity by reducing interconnection and thus hampering price discovery processes and market quality. This report uses the terms 'fragmentation' and 'market fragmentation' interchangeably.

[130] Art. 4, MiFID.

1) Order creation
2) Order diversion.

The interaction between these forces determine the impact of co-existing trading systems and the optimal degree of transparency, in particular for a dealer market setting with low probabilities of trade execution and experiencing the potential entry of a competing venue (Degryse et al., 2009).

On the one hand, fragmentation fosters competition between trading venues on access and execution fees (or bid/ask spreads), as well as competition on execution services between brokers/dealers. Competing trading venues also provide competing execution and matching services (e.g. dark order books, crossing systems, internalisation, etc.). As long as investors can access consolidated data (through mandatory disclosure) and use technologies to split up orders (Madhavan, 1995), trading venues may be able to offer diversified services to meet multi-faceted investors' needs and to produce strong economies of scope (interaction of many users and liquidity pools and between pools). Those needs are very diverse (Harris, 2002) but can be perhaps summarised as:

- Handling big size orders (hedging, inventory, etc.),
- Investing in information (arbitrageurs, informed traders, etc.),
- Closing a position as fast as technically possible (close to real-time) and
- Minimising costs.

For all these reasons, the market will most likely not coalesce in a single pool of liquidity. The provision of new services and competitive fees may then increase volumes even further (order creation). Several empirical studies have shown so far that competition/fragmentation has produced beneficial effects on market structure by reducing spreads, fees and attracting new liquidity in some markets (Glosten, 1994; McInish & Wood, 1996; Battalio et al., 1997; Boehmer, 2005; Foucault & Menkveld, 2008; for a review, see O'Hara & Ye, 2009; Riordan et al., 2009; Angel et al., 2010; Gresse, 2010).

Cream-skimming. On the other hand, market fragmentation may have some drawbacks for liquidity as it reduces beneficial liquidity externalities (economies of scale). Orders will be diverted on other venues and not consolidated in a single order book, with implications for the likelihood of execution and potential unintended consequences on liquidity (Mendelson, 1987). Furthermore, orders will stop competing on the same order book with potential 'cream-skimming' effect. In effect, conflict between order creation and diversion may push intermediaries and trading venues to select part of the demand (typically the uninformed one, since less risky), leaving remaining order flows to deal with informed investors. The cream-skimming activities of intermediaries (outside the electronic order books) and some venues can spread orders in the market with strong adverse selection problems for markets that suffer from discrimination (in particular, if it is a quote-driven dealer market; Hagerty & McDonald, 1996; Easley et. al., 1996; Battalio, 1997; Gajewsky & Gresse, 2007). The impact of these potential distorting effects will depend on the overall size of the market, if the market is big enough the effects of cream-skimming activities will be fairly limited for liquid shares, while effects on less-liquid markets may need to be assessed case-by-case. Finally, fragmented markets have to deal with fragmented surveillance systems and rules. Authorities need to make sure that organisational and surveillance requirements are fully and uniformly applied across all trading venues. Ongoing supervision should then make sure that practices are sufficiently implemented.

Figure 19. Market fragmentation versus liquidity fragmentation

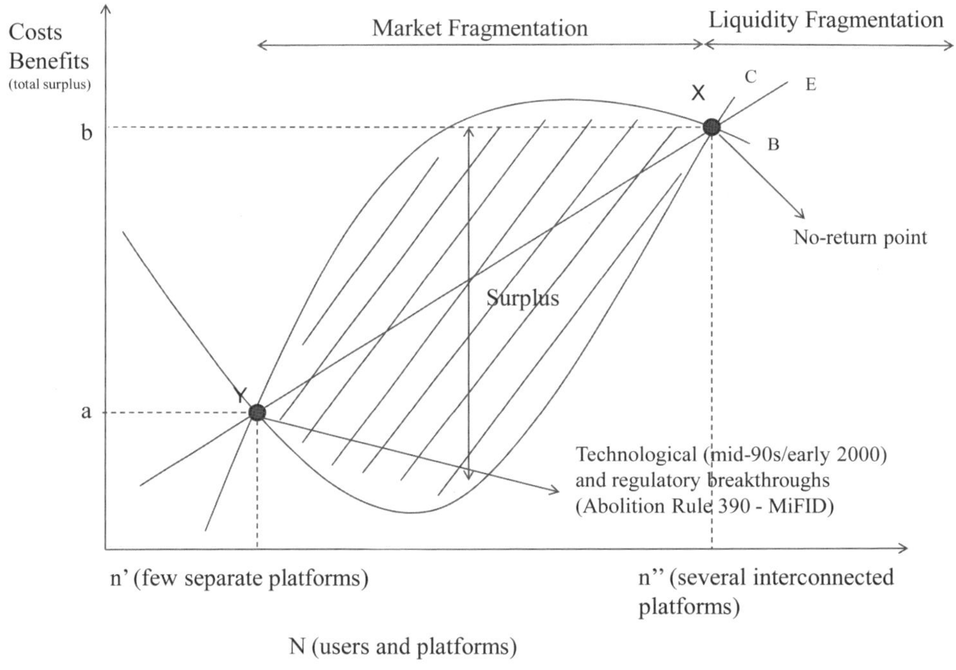

Source: Authors.

Market vs liquidity fragmentation. The graph above explores the market structure dynamics. B and C are respectively functions of benefits and costs for all market participants (e.g. investors). Their value varies as a function of the number of users and competing platforms. Two potential equilibria may be found (Y and X).

The benefit function B is a concave function that represents the evolution of benefits for all market participants associated with an increase of users and platforms. The first equilibrium Y refers to the market setting before new technologies and the abolition of concentration rules unleashed platform competition. Before reaching Y and immediately afterwards, the cost function is very steep given big economies of scale (due to a few disconnected platforms that have reached the 'critical' volumes in Y). Similarly, benefits increase fast, as – on the one side – investors can access a trading platform to match other interests and avoid expensive bilateral negotiations and – on the other side – trading platforms can gradually reach their profitability and benefit from a combination of economies of scale and scope from Y onwards.

In effect, the development of advanced technologies (e.g. automated trading and internet) have lowered sunk and access costs, thus the thesis that national exchanges were natural monopolies with limited economies of scale was gradually dismissed. This situation led regulators to abolish concentration rules, which had protected that market equilibrium (Y).

The combination of regulatory and technological breakthroughs (more recently in Europe than in the US) has promoted market fragmentation and competition between platforms. As a result, costs for setting up trading platforms (sunk costs) and trading costs for final investors have further gone down. Beneficial effects due to a greater number of users (economies of scale) and multiple platforms (economies of scope) have increased benefits for final investors – who can access better-tailored execution services – and for trading platforms – which benefit from a potentially higher range of investors and services to compete on. This situation has created a highly competitive landscape around costs of trading and offered diversified 'bundled' execution services (e.g. direct electronic access services)[131] in order to gain a bigger part of the surplus.

---

[131] Competition between replicable bundles can be fierce and somehow beneficial. Conflicting views arise when a bundle is deemed to create non-replicable 'portfolio effects',

As a result of these competitive forces among trading platforms and investors on the order flow (informed versus uninformed), market fragmentation/competition may generate costs, such as market impact for larger size orders and costs for routing orders across several trading venues. Therefore, once passed the equilibrium Y and after reducing costs, greater benefits await market participants due to the combined effects of economies of scale and scope. Costs (e.g. costs of interconnection) and lower benefits (such as reduced profits for trading platforms) for market participants will push the two functions towards another equilibrium (X). This point is at a higher level than Y, where the market absorbs the entire surplus, regardless of its distribution. The stability of this equilibrium is unknown, since it is up to the market (and regulators) to understand that a greater number of competing platforms may cause greater costs than benefits, even if the number of users would increase. Hence, the strategic behaviour of market competitors – which look for an opportunity to seize a bigger part of that surplus – may result in liquidity fragmentation and strong negative externalities. Empirical studies are not conclusive about the 'optimal market capacity' for trading platforms that financial markets can currently bear. Economides (2008) argues that perfect competition (with zero marginal costs) would provide a network that is smaller than the socially optimum. Hence, the second equilibrium (X) implies a non-perfectly contestable market.[132]

---

weakening the concept of 'efficiency defence'; see Case COMP/M.2220, General Electric/Honeywell, Commission decision of 3 July 2001 and Evans & Salinger (2002).

[132] A perfectly contestable market is a market in which barriers to entry and exit are absent (Baumol et al., 1982). The threat of potential 'hit-and-run' strategies keeps markets highly competitive. Besides other critical assumptions, an important one behind this theory is the absence of sunk costs. In the case of financial markets, those network infrastructures suffer fairly high sunk costs that are going down thanks to technologies. Accordingly, even though the market becomes more and more 'contestable' due to shrinking sunk costs (thanks to new technologies), these costs will not be zero; therefore competitors may need to benefit from a quasi-perfectly competitive and contestable market in order to have enough incentives to set up a competing network infrastructure.

Box 7. A case study of national stock exchanges: Next steps after the demutualisation

In the last two decades, national stock exchanges have undergone evolutionary changes in their governance and business models. Three major trends happened to be part of these changes:

1) Demutualisation
2) Consolidation
3) Diversification

The demutualisation of European national stock exchanges started in the early 1990s and had been ongoing for more than a decade (for a review, see Levin, 2003). Nowadays, the once nationalised and user-governed stock exchanges are for-profit entities facing fierce competition from new trading platforms, but they still keep part of their institutional role in financial markets (Lee, 1998). For instance, they still provide primary markets (listings) and 'junior' markets for small and medium enterprises (SMEs).

National stock exchanges have been leading the process of consolidation, since the process of demutualisation started, and in reaction to the prospects of abolishing the concentration rule and opening up execution services to competition. Exchanges have been working to increase their economies of scale in order to compensate the drop in trading revenues. This situation brought a period of intense talks around potential mergers and some important ones eventually took place. For instance, the merger in 2000 between Paris, Amsterdam and Brussels ('Euronext'), followed then by Lisbon (2003). The merger between the London Stock Exchange and Borsa Italiana was part of this process too. In addition, a final act (for the moment) was the merger between the NYSE and Euronext in 2007 that created the world's biggest exchange.

Currently, exchanges are important players that are redesigning their business models to keep pace with changes in market structure. In effect, consolidation is also driven by the importance of acquiring sufficient know-how and economies of scale to develop their business model in other parts of the value chain or to reinforce their original vertical (silo) models (see Figure 20.).

'Diversification' is the word that better identifies current market developments in the business of exchanges. These firms have massively invested in strategic mergers and new trading platforms, in particular by successfully acquiring new MTFs (such as Turquoise, Smartpool and NYFIX Euro-Millennium) or running their own (see Table 6) in order to build know-how on new trading mechanisms (e.g. automated dark order books or HFT). Investing in technologies to increase speed and capacity of infrastructures is key for their future. For instance, NYSE Euronext recently launched its new universal trading platform (for all markets) and LSE Group will soon launch the new Millennium platform for the main UK markets (after the start of Turquoise with this system).

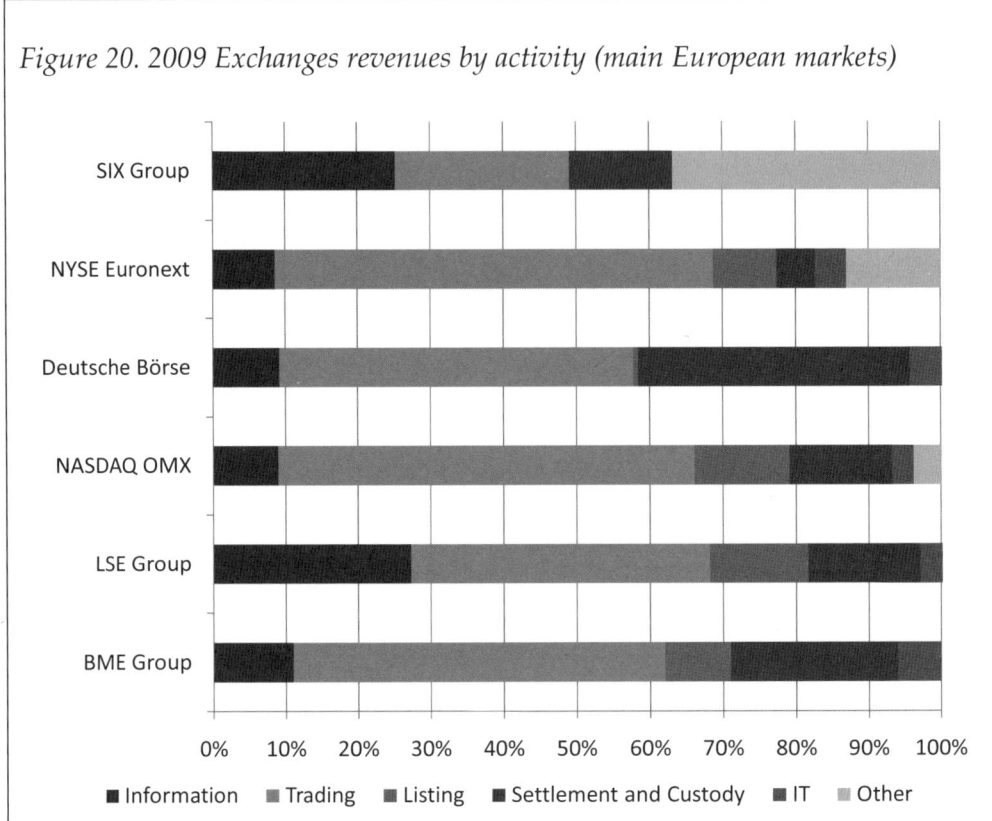

Figure 20. 2009 Exchanges revenues by activity (main European markets)

■ Information ■ Trading ■ Listing ■ Settlement and Custody ■ IT ■ Other

Source: FESE.

Table 6. MTFs run/owned by exchanges

2008	2009	2010
16	19	26

Source: CESR MiFID Database (accessed on July 1st).

Business diversification has also been pursued by developing trade execution services for assets other than equities. For instance, for Deutsche Börse (through Eurex) and NYSE Euronext (after the acquisition of LIFFE in 2001), such services are already profitable. The proposed merger between NYSE Euronext and Deutsche Börse is aimed at giving a boost to diversification[133].

---

[133] For more details about the merger proposal, see http://www.nyse.com/press/1297768048707.html.

> Furthermore, regulatory changes have effectively promoted greater use of organised trading platforms for non-equity products, together with advanced data services to keep up with competing post-trading services and market fragmentation (by consolidating data across asset classes). Exchanges will have to give more emphasis to their expertise in these areas in order to compete with incumbent dealer markets and other actors.[134]

5.4 Classification and obligations of trading venues: A 'new' role for internalisation?

Trading platforms bring together buyers' and sellers' interests in financial instruments to promote best allocation of capital in financial markets. Trading platforms can be classified as either neutral or non-neutral.

A 'neutral' trading platform allows matching and public dissemination of executable bids and offers (or asks), which are typically consolidated in an open limit order book (displaying best bid/ask offers) that may or may not be pre-trade transparent. Binding manifestations of interest are sent to the platforms by investors, typically through their intermediaries or dealers, who can also trade on their own capacity. Access to the platform is defined on a non-discretionary basis and the company running the platform does not trade on own account or act on behalf of investors either as a principal, agent or 'riskless counterparty'.[135] This is the main characteristic of so-called 'multilateral trading mechanisms'. MTFs contribute to price discovery by publishing meaningful pre-trade information (executable quotes), which allows traders to execute their orders almost in real-time. Furthermore, liquidity providers may commit capital to support continuous trading.[136] An 'undiscriminating' platform has three main characteristics (Madhavan, 1992; Glosten, 1994):

i) It will breakdown with high asymmetry of information (adverse selection and moral hazard).
ii) It lowers spreads for small quantities (cheaper and more accessible for retail and small professional investors; 'fairer' markets).

---

[134] For an interesting view on the role of exchanges, see Harris (2010).
[135] Recital (6), MiFID. By contrast, "'Dealing on own account' means trading against proprietary capital resulting in the conclusion of transactions in one or more financial instruments"; Art. 4, MiFID.
[136] For a review of potential trading mechanisms, see next section.

iii) It invites competition between trading platforms as lower execution fees will attract more investors.

Figure 21. Trading platforms and MiFID

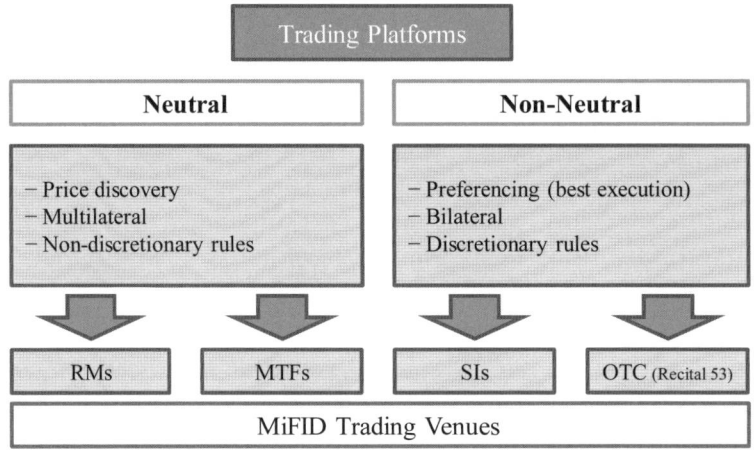

Source: Authors.

A 'non-neutral' trading platform brings together buyers' and sellers' orders that are already on its own books ('own account') or are part of dealings carried out by wholesale counterparties (e.g. asset management companies). Therefore, execution services are provided as part of activities to handle in-house orders (internalisation) or to cross them on internal crossing networks (over-the-counter, OTC). Both activities can be considered 'preferencing' activities (Lee, 2002) developed by banks and brokers/dealers in order to promote best execution outside MiFID official venues (RMs, MTFs and SIs), as well as to increase competition on pricing with main markets. These forms of trading present a trade-off between the risks of market fragmentation and 'cream skimming' on the one side, and better prices and lower dealing costs (in particular, for the institutional demand) on the other. A 'discriminating' platform (Glosten, 1994), finally, makes markets:

1) Less likely to breakdown (it selects liquidity) and
2) Unresponsive to competitive reactions (liquidity is typically 'locked-in' by switching costs and competition may not be profitable as liquidity is limited.[137]

---

[137] However, technologies have brought down switching costs and introduced new trading methodologies. This is actually increasing competitive reactions also on these platforms for

MiFID designed a set of official trading venues operating as trading systems for shares admitted to trading on RMs. On the one hand, there are two major categories of 'neutral' and non-discretionary trading venues providing order execution services under MiFID: regulated markets (RMs; Arts. 4.14 and 42), and multilateral trading facilities (MTFs; Art. 4.15). The Commission is consulting on the proposal to introduce a new category of trading venue for OTC derivatives, the so-called organised trading facility (OTF, see Box 9), which represents the evolution of current inter-dealer platforms currently classified as MTFs. The definition propounded by the Commission does not clarify yet if the platform will be a discretionary or non-discretionary trading system.

As trading venues, RMs and MTFs perform order execution services with the 'same organised trading functionality' (Recital 6, MiFID). However, RMs have more stringent requirements for admission to listing and trading, higher disclosure costs for issuers and obligations to monitor potentially abusive practices and preserve orderly trading.[138] Specifically, securities regulation has always recognised an important role of RMs for investor protection; this may have affected the way in which MTFs have been sometimes treated by national authorities.[139] CESR (2010b), in this respect, has formally proposed to level these rules, which will oblige MTFs:

i) To have the same arrangements as RMs for conflicts of interest in their operations,
ii) To be equipped with adequate mechanisms to manage the risks to which they are exposed and
iii) To set arrangements for the sound management of technical operations (e.g. risks of system disruptions).

The third requirement will need to be extended also to OTFs (European Commission, 2010b, p. 19).

Finally, in order to trade a share admitted to trading in another regulated market, regulated markets have to wait 18 months from the original admission, plus the publication of a summary note to the prospectus by the issuer, while MTFs run by investment firms are not

---

the provision of execution services.

[138] These other requirements are mainly coming from Art. 43 MiFID, the Transparency Directive (2004/109/EC) and the Prospectus Directive (2003/71/EC).

[139] See Moloney (2008, pp. 797-813).

requested to follow this procedure. As explicitly stated by MiFID (Recital 6), these players operate with the same business model and thus should be subject to the same set of rules.

Systematic internaliser. On the other hand, the Directive also established a new trading venue, the so-called 'systematic internaliser' (SI). This venue executes trades on own account on an 'organised, frequent and systematic basis' (Art. 4.1.7, MiFID), outside RMs and MTFs. It applies non-discretionary rules in handling trades and pre-trade transparency for client orders on liquid shares (for illiquid ones, only on request) below the standard market size (SMS).[140] However, besides publication issues, pre-trade transparency is not meaningful since quotes are not executable because execution happens at the discretion of the SI. The contribution to price discovery is therefore minimal.

Conclusion # 12

Competition between trading venues on prices and execution services and between investment firms on the provision of other investment services has generated some positive effects, in terms of promoting investments in trading platforms and reducing trading costs for shares. Competition needs, however, to be fair and based on a level playing field between MiFID-official trading venues and their structural characteristics.

In this respect, this report acknowledges the importance of ensuring a harmonised approach across national supervisory authorities in the application of MiFID requirements for official trading venues. This may require a further alignment of the remaining differences in the legal obligations (and supervisory practices) applied to regulated markets (RMs) and multilateral trading facilities (MTFs). This alignment of legal obligations already exists in some European countries (e.g. the UK).

Box 8. The regime for systematic internalisers

The low number of firms currently registered as systematic internalisers (only 12) has suggested that the current regime may not be a great success. Along with CESR's advice (2010b), the SI regime does contain some ambiguities in its text. In particular, Art. 21.1 (Implementing Regulation) sets the conditions to be considered where trading venues execute trades on an "organised, frequent and systematic" basis on own account (bilateral trading mechanism). These conditions – to be considered all together – are:

---

[140] Art. 27, MiFID; Arts. 21-25, Implementing Regulation. The Standard Market Size (SMS) is defined in Annex II, Table 3 of the Implementing Regulation, which changes in relation to the average value of transactions.

> 1) The application of non-discretionary rules and procedures and the activity has a material commercial role;
> 2) The development of activities through personnel or automated technical systems, with no consideration if they are also used for other purposes; and
> 3) The continuity and regularity of the activity.
>
> Condition 1, in particular, has raised doubts about the term 'non-discretionary' having the same meaning as for RMs and MTFs. CESR (2010b) suggests keeping this reference but clarifying that it was originally intended only to avoid non-systematic trading (including this clause in their commercial policies).'Dealing on own account' is by definition a discretionary activity, so the requirement cannot refer to the trading system itself. Furthermore, by assessing whether the activity is a significant source of revenue, competent authorities should be able to determine the materiality of the commercial role covered by the firm. CESR suggests setting a threshold for the activity to be considered 'significant'. By contrast, the Commission (2010b, p. 17) proposed to replace the more vague condition of 'material commercial relevance' with a quantitative threshold above which, if the firm also meets the other two conditions, it will be required to register as SI to the competent authority.
>
> Condition 3, finally, does not explicitly clarify what is the meaning of a continuous and regular activity, besides what common sense would suggest.
>
> In addition, some pre-trade information (quotes) displayed by SIs is not meaningful since it is often one-sided and in a very low size (even one share). Therefore, de facto the market does not see liquidity and activities on the venue. In order to keep the level playing field even for retail traders in RMs and MTFs, CESR suggested to fix a minimum quote size (10% of SMS of any liquid share in which the firm is SI). Quotes then need to be two-sided and periodic trading data reports should be published more regularly (e.g. monthly; CESR, 2010b). Finally, SIs are not properly flagged in the post-trade disclosure, which has prompted CESR to propose a flag for trades executed by internalisers (ISO 9362). CESR's proposal on quotes, flagging and trade reports has been also endorsed by the Commission's recent consultation report.

5.4.1 Shedding light on over-the-counter equity trading

OTC trading. Besides internalisation, another form of 'preferencing' activity has been historically offered by brokers, and known as 'internal crossing'. Part of the liquidity in the market – even for liquid equity markets – has always followed a different way of execution, generally called 'upstairs trading' (Madhavan, 2000). Those services provided on a discretionary basis have been evolving with time and are currently offered through sophisticated internal crossing engines. These engines utilise complex algorithms to achieve best execution, by either matching internally or executing on MiFID official venues (RMs and MTFs). These internal crossing systems are also more commonly defined as broker-dealer crossing systems (BCSs, or broker-dealer crossing networks BCNs if several BCSs interact in one or more pools of liquidity). In addition, 'crossing' activities are also subject to fiduciary duties and conduct of business rules (Arts. 19, 20, 21, MiFID; OTC) as well as arrangements to disclose conflicts of interests. While post-trade transparency obligations apply to them, they are not affected by pre-trade transparency or organisational requirements (CESR, 2010b).

MiFID captures internal matching activities offered by brokers/dealers through the definition of 'transactions carried out on an OTC basis'. Three conditions should be met for trades to fall under the definition of OTC equity trade (Recital 53, MiFID):

i) Transactions must be *ad hoc* and irregular;
ii) Dealings take place with a wholesale counterparty; and
iii) Dealings must be above the standard market size (SMS).

The interpretation around the implementation of these conditions is currently different across the industry. Market views consistently diverge around the business nature of BCNs, which for some perform the same business as RMs and MTFs and therefore should be classified as such.

Market views. One side of the market believes that there is part of OTC trading that should be traded on RMs/MTFs and SIs and are therefore subject to strict pre-trade transparency requirements and more effective post-trade reporting, while they acknowledge the importance of OTC trading in the MiFID text. Most will agree that all trading happening in Europe, including the one taking place under the OTC label, should be properly classified in order to preserve market quality and prevent any significant part of the market from escaping pre-trade transparency without any economic justification (see below) and other MTFs rules on access, discretion and surveillance. This part of the market argues that OTC performs the same function as RMs and MTFs, and if not properly classified, could increase liquidity fragmentation and weaken investor protection.

Moving from the assumption that the OTC trade reports used were meaningful and mostly accurate, a recent study tries to shed more light on OTC trading (Gomber & Pierron, 2010). Using current data on OTC trades, the authors show that about 39% of OTC trades are below retail size, 48% are below standard market size, 87% are below large-in-scale and 73% are too small to have a market impact according to their proprietary methodology. According to them, this should be enough to clarify that these networks deal with trades below the standard market size, even though orders are partially sent to regulated markets and MTFs. In addition, crossing systems are designed as 'multilateral' trading mechanisms that match trades, acting as 'riskless counterparties'. Hence, 87% of trades could potentially escape the size-related pre-trade transparency waiver imposed on RM and MTF trades (Gomber & Pierron, 2010). These findings imply that the MiFID conditions to be considered 'OTC trading' are not met and therefore there should be a proper classification for these trades under current MiFID-official trading venues (see below).

This first position concludes that, even if OTC trades would be considered bilateral, 52% of them seem to be escaping MiFID rules of pre-trade transparency for SIs. In any case, they see BCSs as multilateral trading systems, that are systems managed by firms not operating on own account or taking any risk in the transaction (recital 44, MiFID). As a result multilateral trading systems should be classified as RMs and MTFs.

A countering view contests the abovementioned interpretation of recital 53. In their view, broker-dealer crossing systems (BCSs) are fully compliant with MiFID, which recognised their role in financial markets. However, those platforms should be better classified in the new MiFID text.

124 | Reshaping Market Structure

Figure 22. Transparency obligations for venues under MiFID

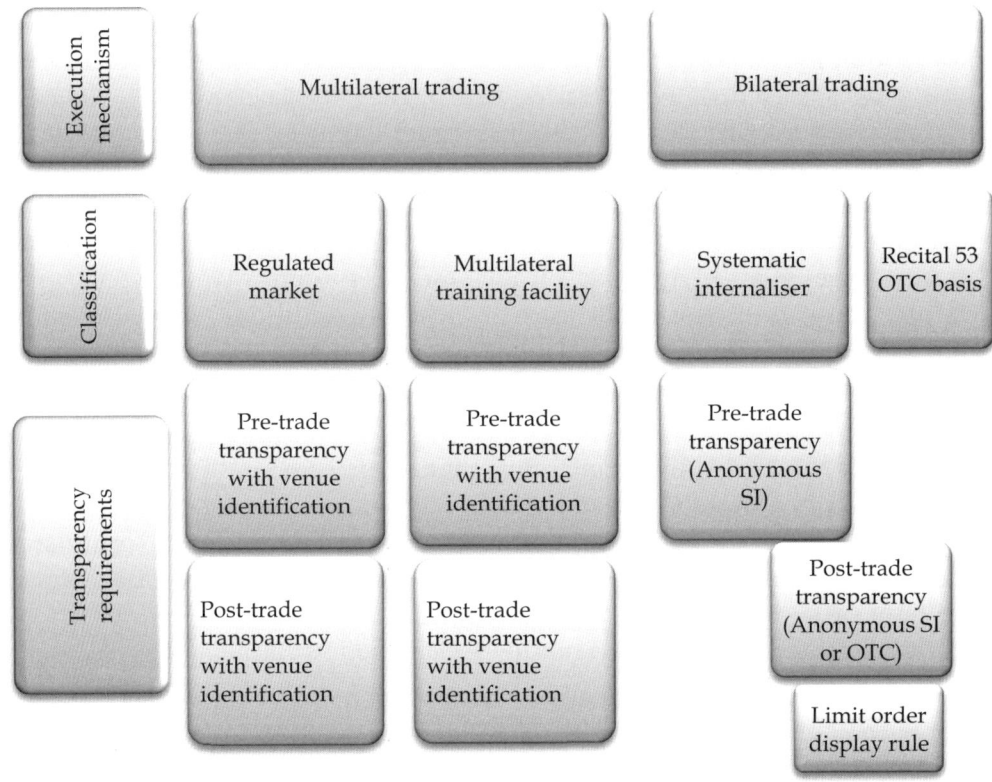

Source: Gomber & Pierron (2010, p. 11).

According to this second position (see graph below), the advanced brokerage services offered to clients (wholesale counterparties) through the use of BCNs meet the MiFID conditions for trades 'carried out on an OTC basis', since they are:
- Dealings with wholesale counterparties (e.g. asset management companies),
- Dealings ('parent' orders) above the standard market size and
- Dealings irregularly transacted with brokers/dealers.

Figure 23. Broker-dealer crossing system

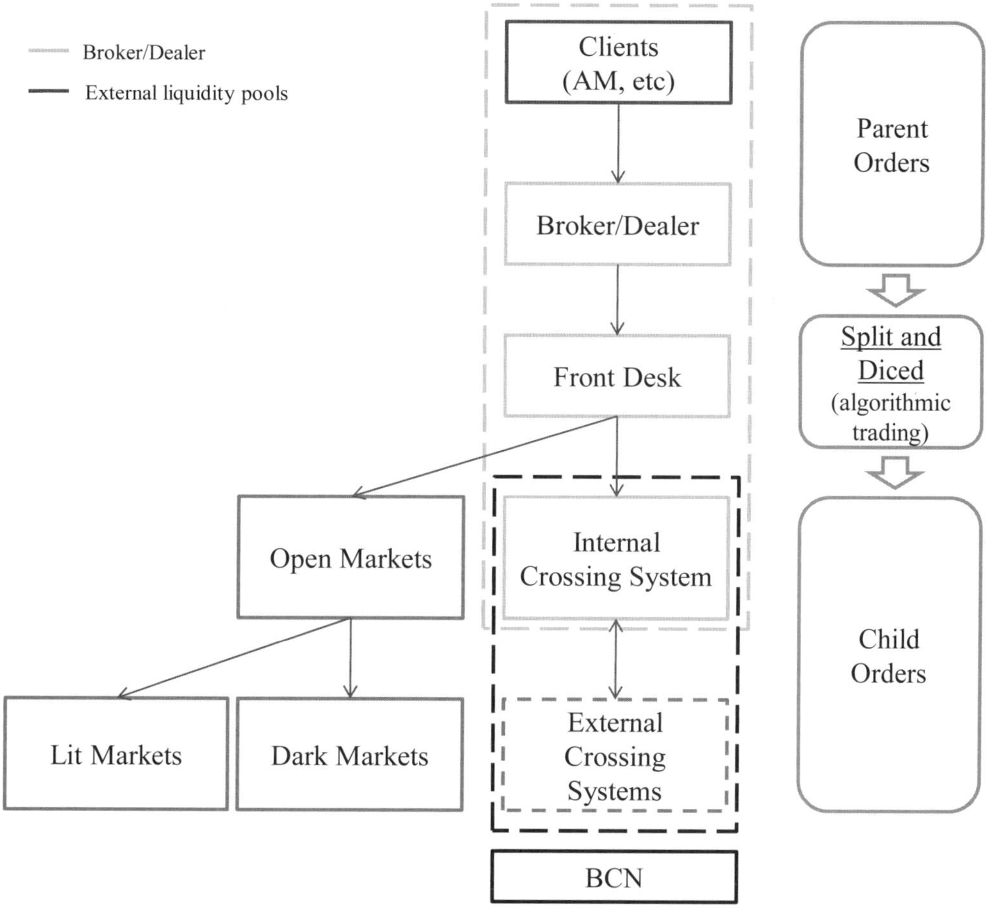

Source: Authors.

They note that trades may be below the standard market size only after the broker/dealer has accepted to execute the trade and split the 'parent' order into 'child' orders, eventually routing them to several trading venues to minimise market impact (including internal crossing systems, as BCSs or BCNs, but also RMs and MTFs). They argue that the Directive refers to 'parent' orders since fiduciary duties and business conduct rules apply to the 'parent' order as a whole and not separately to each 'child' order. Nevertheless, in their view, most trades are sent to regulated markets and MTFs for execution, while usually less than 1/3 is 'internally' crossed. They argue that advanced brokerage services need to interact with internal crossing systems, which allow a smoother handling and execution of big orders. The general rationale for trading OTC is best execution of trades outside official markets. Moreover – besides the exemption of recital 53 – this position also argues that BCSs cannot be considered 'multilateral' since they do not act as 'riskless counterparties' since the 'riskless' position is part of the execution they carry on behalf of their clients. Since MiFID obliges them to provide best execution and apply other conduct of business arrangements, they should not be considered acting as 'riskless counterparties'. In addition, recital 44 says that RMs and MTFs should be managed with non-discretionary rules, which is not the case for BCSs. Most of all, they claim that internalisation is gradually becoming an indispensable complementary execution service to those offered by official markets, rather than a competing service as originally feared.

Finally, some players claim that imposing a trading threshold may represent a threat for the provision of complex and tailored brokerage services, as it needs to be accurately and constantly updated. Clarifications of the defining criteria of 'OTC trades' under MiFID and availability of data for full assessment and enforcement of best execution, and other conduct of business rules are needed. Once these aspects are defined, the burdens of the obligations would set a 'natural' threshold to the development of these trading systems with no threat to price formation processes in the open markets, since it would become highly costly to carry them out on a broad scale.

Commission's proposal. The European Commission (2010b, p. 11) has proposed a 'new sub-regime for BCSs, which will *de facto* assign a new classification to these venues under MiFID organised trading facilities (see next box). This classification will work by setting two boundaries: i) if third parties will enter orders in the crossing system, the BCS would transform the system in an MTF; ii) if the broker/dealer executes internally against its own capital, the system would change in a SI.

This proposal tries to accommodate conflicting views and it may represent a radical change for the definition of SI and MTF. For instance, if third parties enter orders in the system, it does not necessarily mean that the system is based on non-discretionary rules (such as an MTF). Therefore, this proposal will *de facto* modify incentives to provide discretionary execution services (e.g. upstairs trading) under MiFID, with unclear broader implications.

Being a sub-category of OTF, the broker/dealer running the BCS may also need to add an identifier for post-trade transparency requirements and report the daily number, value and volume of transactions. It will also add an identifier to transaction reports, to show when the transaction is executed on the system.

Figure 24. Proposal for broker dealer crossing system (BCSs)

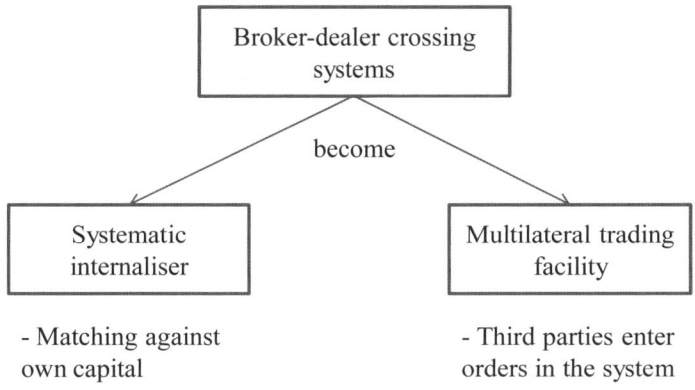

Source: European Commission (2010b).

> **Box 9. Organised trading for OTC derivatives: EU and US discussions**
>
> Following the G20 commitments,[141] the European Commission has proposed that "where appropriate, trading in standardised[142] OTC derivatives[143] [will] move to exchanges or electronic trading platforms" (EU COM, 2010b, p.12). Besides the fact that some trading on fixed income products (bonds and structured products) and OTC derivatives takes already place through platforms registered as MTFs across Europe, the Commission – taking up the positions of the European Parliament (Langen, 2010) and CESR (2010g) – has proposed a new category of venue, the so-called 'organised trading facilities' (OTFs; EU COM, 2010b, p. 13).

---

[141] In particular, G 20, "Declaration on strengthening the financial system", London Summit, 2 April 2009 (http://www.londonsummit.gov.uk/resources/en/PDF/annex-strengthening-fin-sysm) and G 20, "Leaders' Statement: The Pittsburgh Summit", Pittsburgh Summit, 24-25 September 2009.

[142] Standardisation is a multifaceted concept. It "refers to specific technical processes, economic and legal terms of a financial product that allow a straight-through processing (STP) of a derivative transaction" (Valiante, 2010, p. 11). A product is standardised when the interaction between those aspects does allow an STP of the transaction. The use of electronic means is only one aspect of standardisation. Other relevant aspects are uniform contractual agreements and the use of plain vanilla terms, where possible.

[143] For a definition, please see Section 4.4.5.

> The Commission suggests that OTFs should meet the following conditions:
> 1) Non-discriminatory[144] multilateral access;
> 2) Support pre- and post-trade transparency obligations;
> 3) Report transactions to trade repositories; and
> 4) Have a dedicated facility for execution of trades.
>
> For the consultation document, ESMA would set requirements to determine when a derivative is sufficiently liquid to be traded exclusively on OTFs or other organised venues. The decision could be based on liquidity measures such as frequency of trades and average size of transactions, as well as additional criteria such as the degree of investors' participation. Ideally, requirements may need to coordinate with rules proposed for swap execution facilities (SEFs) in the US. Since the market for OTC derivatives is global, uncoordinated responses could create regulatory arbitrages.
>
> Furthermore, rule-making should take into account that non-equity products (in particular, OTC derivatives) usually have a different market structure than equity markets (limit order books), with dealers posting executable quotes at investors' request (Request For Quotes model; RFQ) or through bilateral transactions. The RFQ model is required by the nature of the transaction that is essentially bilateral, and by the nature of the demand that is mostly institutional and require a certain degree of customisation. A greater push towards standardisation and organised trading should balance benefits of a more transparent and orderly setting with costs entailed by lower availability of customised derivatives and so greater possibility to leave in the system some risk not properly hedged (Valiante, 2010, p. 45).[145]
>
> Trading in bonds and structured products is already partially done on organised trading venues like MTFs, but transparency obligations do not necessarily apply to them, due to the exemption in MiFID (Recital 46). In effect, there is a risk that the requirements for OTFs may overlap with those for MTFs, as they provide a execution service. The border between being qualified as a MTF rather than an OTF should be clearly spelled out.
>
> In order to promote more organised and transparent trading for non-equity asset classes, the Commodity Futures Trading Commission (CFTC) has proposed[146] that those systems should have robust risk controls and should display either indicative or executable quotes from members. In order to avoid

---

[144] The Commission does not clarify if 'non-discriminatory' should have the same meaning as 'non-discretionary', as currently defined by MiFID for RMs and MTFs (recital 44).

[145] CESR (2010g) believes that trading of standardised derivative products on organised trading venues is to be encouraged by regulators, even though not mandated at this stage.

[146] Commodity Futures Trading Commission (CFTC), "Core Principles and Other Requirements for Swap Execution Facilities", (www.cftc.gov).

> unintended consequences for market structure, trading venues should be able to deploy both RFQ and electronic order book trading systems. In effect – for US regulators – this solution would allow a gradual shift from currently bilateral trading to SEFs by enhancing the opportunity for dealers to compete on executable quotes whenever possible, without necessarily undermining the management of their huge inventory positions (by publishing an indicative quote or falling under a large-in-scale waiver). The US proposal, at the moment, does not clarify whether these venues will have non-discriminatory access and pre-trade public transparency obligations, such as EU OTFs. The RFQ model under SEFs should have at least five market participants from which other participants can simultaneously request quotes. The order book model, if chosen by market participants, should develop a platform in which all of them can post bids and offers for other participants and decide with which of the displayed bids and offers transact.
>
> Finally, in Europe, some trading platforms – registered as MTFs – have already started to bring together, through organised trading on order books, executable quotes and interests of dealers and other market participants that have chosen to stream their quotes on these platforms. Public pre-trade disclosure is limited to non-executable quotes, such as the mid-price.

OTC trade disclosure. Besides specific positions on market structure and how equity trading on an OTC basis currently occurs, there is a consensus that the quality of OTC data needs to be effectively improved, reducing inconsistencies (duplicative reporting) and increasing granularity (in particular, through the use of specific flags). Post-trade transparency requirements for OTC trading have been introduced by MiFID for the first time in many countries. According to CESR (2010b), up to 38% of EEA trades occur on an OTC basis, but it also recognises serious risks of misreporting and double-counting. These data are collected by Thomson Reuters from market data sources that collect themselves data as defined by MiFID. At such levels, OTC trading may raise doubts about its beneficial role in European capital markets. Some argue that this size – despite being historically high for Europe – contradicts the MiFID concept of OTC being an exceptional type of execution. Separately, since all OTC trading is by definition 'pre-trade dark', if this figure is correct, such level of non- pre-trade transparent trade may undermine market quality and price formation mechanisms.

However, there are two important caveats to the interpretation of this data. First of all, given the poor consistency and quality of OTC data, the publicly reported OTC may not be the same as what is actually traded OTC. Secondly, and even more importantly from the perspective of either of the two positions outlined above, CESR's data only include the market share of OTC as reported through Markit BOAT or national exchanges. In effect, these data do not permit a trade-by-trade analysis or break down the overall 38% figure without assuming any double-counting or misreporting (see Box 10). These issues contribute to increasing uncertainty and opaqueness in the market. Without such an analysis, it is impossible to draw from the market share of the OTC alone any definitive conclusions about whether the OTC classification is being correct and whether, as a consequence, there is sufficient transparency and market quality in the market.

OTC breakdown. In this respect, a recent study (Nomura, 2010) reports an earlier investigation made by the UK Financial Services Authority (FSA) that estimates the share of reported OTC trades affected by double counting.

Figure 25. OTC 'printed' vs 'actual' equity trading

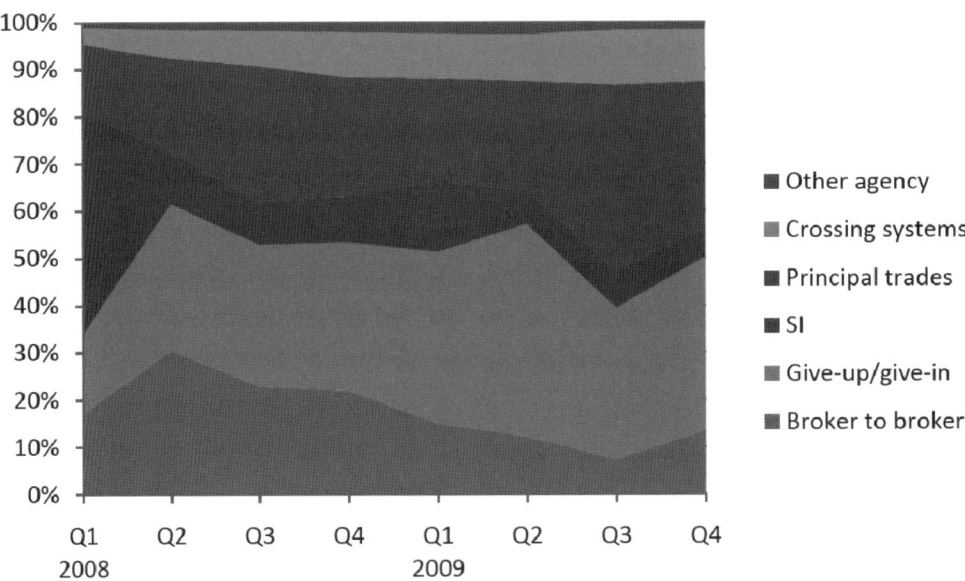

Source: FSA (from Nomura, 2010).

Since some trading venues are not officially recognised by MiFID and divergences exist between the regulatory and economic definition of trade, what the Directive considers as trade to be made transparent does not necessarily match the definition of trades that contribute to price formation. Therefore, there is a difference between what is 'printed' as defined by MiFID and what really contributes to price formation ('actual trading').

As suggested by the figure above, in the UK market, roughly 35-40% of OTC trading represents 'give-ups' from brokers,[147] plus other categories of trades that may not be considered as real liquidity, either price forming or informing. In addition, CESR (2010g) investigated other cases of double-counting or misreporting (see box below).

Box 10. OTC equity transaction type standards

In order to improve the quality of OTC trade reporting, CESR (2010g) has proposed the introduction of transaction type standards.[148] These standards should increase granularity and help at the same time to breakdown OTC trades into data that should be reconsolidated as either price forming or informing data, while avoiding double counting or misreporting.

Hence, CESR proposed a flag for each type of transaction below:
i) Benchmark trades (when price is calculated over time, as result of different variables, e.g. VWAP (volume-weighted average price);
ii) Agency cross trades;[149]
iii) Give-up/in trades;
iv) Ex/cum dividend trades; and
v) Technical trades.[150]

In order to avoid double reporting due to the complex application of Art. 27.4 (implementing regulation), CESR also clarifies that it should generally be the 'executing broker' that makes the report. If it is unclear who the 'executing broker' is, the 'selling investment firm' provides the report.

---

[147] Give-up trades are orders executed by a broker (A) on behalf of another one (B), who is officially executing it on behalf of a client. Since the order should be made by the broker B on behalf of the client, broker A should give up the trade (once executed) to broker B. In this way, the trade is printed when broker A buy shares on behalf of broker B and when the trades are given up and bought/sold by broker B in order to justify his/her execution to the client.

[148] To amend Arts. 3 and 27(1)(b), Implementing Regulation.

[149] When a broker brings together clients' orders to buy and sell, both transactions conducted as one transaction.

[150] 'Technical trades' is a generic category that includes 'non-addressable liquidity' or 'exchange of shares […] determined by factors other than the current market valuation of the share' (CESR, 2010g, p. 11). This category should include back-to-back transactions to ensure the proper functioning of the financial system.

Therefore, the Committee has highlighted three potential sources of double-counted or misreported trades:

i) Riskless principal (the investment firm buying and selling on own account simultaneously to make the report);

ii) Agency cross (the investment firm 'crossing' the two trades should make the report); and

iii) Single/Multiple OTC transaction on behalf of a client (only the 'selling' investment firm or the trading platform where the trade has been sent should make the trade report, if not agreed otherwise).

An example of double reporting is when a client orders to buy 10 million shares at a guaranteed 2 hour VWAP. The investment firm decides then to split it into child orders of 6 million shares on the main RM, 3 million on a MTF and 1 million on another MTF. The investment firm will adjust the average price to the actual VWAP for client booking. The uncertainty surrounding who should report in this case obliges the investment firm – under MiFID I – to report as OTC the client booking of 10 million (client-leg). However, the market also sees 6 million + 3 million + 1 million as traded shares (market leg). Therefore, trade reporting will show 10 million as execution on MiFID-official trading venues and 10 million as OTC, even though the real trading volume was 50% of what has been reported and none of it 'over-the-counter'.

The CESR proposal clarifies that only the market-leg should be reported either by the selling investment firm or by the RMs or MTFs (if orders are sent to the market). In the abovementioned example, all 10 million shares would be trade reported by the RM and the two MTFs. In the case of BCNs, the trades that are matched in the internal crossing system would be trade reported by the executing (crossing) investment firm, while other trades sent to the market would be reported by the trading venue where orders have been sent for execution.

Conclusion # 13

It is within the scope of this report to clarify the different views around the classification of trading venues and OTC trading (BCNs). However, this report does not challenge the role that OTC equity trading plays in financial markets, but rather acknowledges it, in particular where it comes to guaranteeing effective best execution for complex institutional orders. Therefore, the review of MiFID should not ban these trading activities but rather recognise their relevance by properly classifying them.

This report also acknowledges the importance of ensuring a harmonised approach across national supervisory authorities in the application of MiFID requirements to official trading venues. This may require a further alignment of the legal provisions and supervisory practices applied to regulated markets (RMs) and multilateral trading facilities (MTFs). This alignment already does exist in some European countries, such as the UK where the remaining differences have been levelled.

> *Data employed in the run-up to the MiFID review by the Committee of European Securities Regulators (CESR) to ascertain the size of OTC equity trading are inadequate. Analysis based on this data cannot be considered conclusive and has probably led to overestimates of the size of this market. More effort needs to be made to accurately assess market quality in Europe and clarify the actual size of OTC equity trading, its origin and its impact on price formation processes. There is a compelling need to improve the quality of market data by reducing inconsistencies and increasing granularity through the use of harmonised flags.*

Box 11. The role of issuers

Issuers play a crucial function in financial markets, as they promote innovation and a more efficient allocation of resources in our economies. Through the access to capital markets, they favour a better allocation of resources by bringing together those who need them with those who have a surplus of capital and wish to allocate it in the best way possible. Issuers represent the direct link between financial markets and the high street, in particular for small and medium enterprises (SMEs) that have limited possibilities to access alternative funding channels. After a single or multiple listing, it actually matters where financial instruments are traded in secondary markets (Amihud & Mendelson, 1996; Di Noia, 2001). On the one side, fragmentation may discourage issuers' participation if they do not keep control over the value of their shares over time. Some believe that a right for the issuer to decide to go public and where securities should be traded in secondary markets should apply. Such a proposal would entail the right of issuers to, at least, be duly informed and asked for acquiescence in relation to their issued securities in order to be traded in venues different to that/those of issuance. The proposal would not be claiming for the ban of multi-market trading, but rather the need for issuer to be informed and in agreement to such fact. On the other side, assuming interconnection between trading venues, multimarket trading may allow more efficient pricing, lower costs and greater investor protection (those who provide liquidity to issuers).

In this sense, competing flows of information may also generate prices more akin to the firms' fundamental value. It is highly controversial that once the issuer has placed financial instruments (mainly shares) and collected capitals at relatively low cost, the management of the company (or the shareholders' majority) should be able to influence the way these instruments are traded in secondary markets, even though they are not the company's property anymore. Conflicts of interests between issuer and trading venues or their members may impose additional costs. A proposal that would allow issuers to decide in which secondary markets their shares should traded, however, has been historically challenged by both market and policy-makers (e.g. the SEC[151]).

It is also relevant, in particular, to ensure that the interconnection among venues is effective and does not permit the formation of 'inferior prices' or market abuses due to potential arbitrages with main markets or proper supervision cannot occur (extreme case). Finally, the possibility to trade instruments freely across trading venues is a crucial aspect for market liquidity; it broadens both the appetite of investors and competition between trading venues, although venues may ultimately suffer from any competitive constraint set by the issuer. For SMEs, finally, the Commission (2010b, p. 20) proposed a special regime in order to facilitate a cheaper access to capital, as well as to enhance inter-linkages between markets.[152] A set of requirements would apply to firms with market capitalisation below 35% of the average market capitalisation. In this respect, the regime proposed does not seem necessarily to rely on a set of lighter requirements but rather on adapting current rules applying to trading venues and their members to SMEs' size and nature. The framework of rules will be defined in the framework Directive, which will leave space to member states to tighten or loosen the regime in line with the specific market conditions. This set of principles may boost a race among member states to increase the level of standards, as long as the market recognises these aspects as a further incentive to provide capital to SMEs. Otherwise, as it seems to be in this case, the incentive for member states would be to lower regulatory barriers in order to further reduce costs of access for SMEs and end investors, as long as appropriate protection for both parties will still be in place.

5.5 Some aspects of market microstructure for organised trading

The microstructure of financial markets has been deeply researched in the last decades. However, technological developments bring rapid and sweeping changes to the structure of markets, which may need further investigation. This section will look at the following topics:

i) Market settings (e.g. auction versus dealer markets);
ii) Trading tools (high-frequency trading, algorithmic trading, direct

---

[151] The Unlisted Trading Privileges Act of 1994 made official that no approval from the SEC was needed to trade securities (not only shares) in other markets than the market where they were issued. See, Pub. L. No. 103-389, 108 Stat. 4081 (1994) (codified as amended at 15 U.S.C. 78l (f) (1994)). The US Congress has always expressed its favour towards multimarket trading and that "an issuer does not have the right to veto exchange trading of its securities"; Release Discussing Exchanges' and NASD's Proposed Rule Changes, Exchange Act Release No. 34-22,026, 50 Fed. Reg. 20,310, 23,313-14 (1985).

[152] For a more accurate proposal, see Demarigny (2010).

electronic access); and
iii) Other micro-structural issues (e.g. decreasing average size of orders).

As mentioned above (see footnote 48), liquidity in financial instruments depends on depth, resiliency and breadth of the market. To allow an efficient interaction between these variables, the market microstructure needs to be designed according to several factors, such as financial stability, the role of financial regulation, efficiency, market integrity and investor protection.

5.5.1 *Market setting: The role of trading mechanisms*

The market structure of capital markets defines the set of rules and mechanisms that lead the interaction among different trading interests and platforms and the incorporation of information into prices, by minimising frictional costs (implicit and explicit trading costs). These rules may involve price and quantity discovery (Francioni et al., 2008). Market microstructure is generally influenced by two factors: i) the nature of liquidity suppliers and demanders (traders' motives); and ii) external factors, such as technological developments. In particular, the automation of trading has produced radical changes in order routing, information dissemination and trade execution (Domowitz, 1996), which use complex mathematical algorithms. As explained below, technological change is a two-way process; technology has influenced market structure, which in turn has stimulated investments in technology. Similarly, the level of market transparency comes as a result of the design of market microstructure, but can also ultimately stimulate changes in the structure itself.

The key aspect of a trading mechanism is "transforming the latent demands of investors into realized transactions. This transformation is based on price discovery, the process of finding market-clearing prices" (Madhavan, 1992, p. 608), which is to a great extent influenced by the level of market transparency. In general, two types of trading mechanisms let markets decide transactions' clearing prices:
i) Auction markets
ii) Dealer markets

The former puts investors in competition (e.g. limit orders; see Boehmer et al., 2005) to find the best market-clearing price ('downstream' competition). The latter stimulates 'upstream' competition between dealers to offer the best bid/ask quotes (e.g. RFQ models). Both trading mechanisms can be continuous or periodic. A continuous trading mechanism entails the uninterrupted submission and matching of bids and offers, which can be submitted by investors (auction markets) or dealers/market-makers (dealer markets). A periodic trading mechanism brings together those binding interests (typically collected over time) at some point in time.

Auction markets are widespread in financial markets. There are two types of auction markets:

i) Batch (call) auctions
ii) Continuous auctions

Batch auctions collect over time bids/offers from investors and execute these orders at a particular point in time at a single price (to maximise volumes, call auction) or at slightly different simultaneous price. Call auction are frequently used in financial markets, especially in the opening of markets when liquidity is low and the market needs to find a market-clearing price to start its session.

Continuous auction markets are the most diffused form of trading, which allows amassing many transactions in one place and generating economies of scale that abate (implicit) transaction costs (Economides & Schwartz, 1995). The use of continuous auction markets and their transparent setting has been increasing in the last decades, as the flows of cross-border financial transactions have soared. The global interconnection of financial markets has been made possible thanks to the development of automated forms of trading and to new communication technologies (e.g. the internet), which have brought together liquidity demand and supply across markets, especially for liquid financial instruments.

According to this background, open limit-order book (OLOB) – so-called 'order-driven market' – have become a widespread form of auction market, since it permits continuous trading in which investors' public reservation prices are submitted simultaneously and consolidated in a single order book, which shows the best bids and offers at different price levels. This market design has some relevant characteristics:

i) The need for high volumes to allow continuous trading (efficient system for small trades; Baruch, 2005);
ii) A meaningful competition between orders (information reward[153] as

---

[153] Investors must receive proper reward from their investment in information (which can assume different forms; on fundamentals, rumours, etc.). The order flow, therefore, should contain private and public information. Traders who act on the belief that they own private

a result of information asymmetry) and a greater flow of information into prices; and

iii) A sufficient level of transparency (allowing investors to see the order flow and make their investment decisions accordingly).

Auction markets are inherently more transparent than other market settings, since the price formation mechanism needs transparency to foster competition between investors. The resulting outcome is more information-efficient prices, which may ultimately reduce volatility (Baruch, 2005). Efficient prices also support the evaluation of assets and hence better risk management processes.

Furthermore, alternative ways can promote competition between investors and raise the incentives to submit bids/offers, keeping volumes high. In particular, the flexibility of the execution system and thus the possibility to enter different limit order types allow investors to compete with each other on the basis of their information (see next box). In effect, traders will submit orders on the basis of the information they consider private and will behave strategically[154] when it comes to i) liquidity and ii) asset value. They submit orders on the basis of information such as potential arbitrages, information on the fundamental value of the asset or the need to divest own liquidity.

Box 12. Order types

Limit order books make possible the interaction between several types of orders. Besides the modality and conditions for the execution, orders always include a binding interest to buy or sell a financial instrument when certain conditions are met. The set of conditions applicable to orders that a trading platform can adopt on its system is potentially unlimited.

Therefore, below are summarized the most-used types of orders:
- Unconditional limit[155] (when a trader enters an order to trade a number of shares at a certain price that is not yet verified);
- Market (when a trader enters an order to trade a number of shares at the currently displayed price or at the closest value);

---

information – which in the end is already public and embedded into prices – are called 'noise traders'.

[154] They will base the decision on their beliefs about other traders' future choices.

[155] The report generally uses 'limit orders' and 'unconditional limit orders' interchangeably.

- Marketable (an order at the limit or better price);
- Tick sensitive (an order to sell or buy at an uptick or a downtick);
- Stop/Take profit (market or limit-sell or buy order for an open position, respectively long and short position, triggered when the price moves through the stop price in order to contain losses or take profits from the position held);
- Market-not-held (an order to leave the decision of execution to the broker);
- At-auction (orders only allowed for the call auction at the end or beginning of the day; if not executed, these orders are typically cancelled);
- Immediate-or-cancel, IOC (a market order that requests the immediate execution of the order; if part of the order is not executed at that market price, it should be cancelled);
- Fill-or-kill, FOK (a slightly different IOC order since in this case the order should be cancelled in full if it cannot be filled at that immediate price);
- Market to limit (another variation of IOC and FOK; if the order is not executed in full at the current immediate price, the rest of it will be cancelled and re-entered as limit order with price equal to the price of the executed part of the initial order);
- Trailing stop (a sell order that sets a stop price at a fixed number of ticks below the market price, which will follow the market price where above the executed price; if the price is below the execution price the stop price will be the floor that will be triggered if the price reaches this value);
- Market-if-touched (a buy or sell market order triggered when the price reaches a certain level; a combination of a market and limit order);
- Box Top (a market order that is automatically changed in a limit if the order is not executed at market price).

These orders are all market or limit orders that may or may not apply detailed conditions, in relation to the strategy that the trader wants to achieve (limit risk, speed of execution, price improvements, etc). Further, these orders can be pre-trade displayed or hidden when waivers apply and combined together to pursue trading strategies. Finally, all orders can be seen as orders with a limit price subject to certain conditions. For instance, a market order is a limit order in which the limit price is the market price at that specific instant.

Sources: Harris, 2002; Comerton-Forde & Rydge, 2004 (www.interactivebrokers.com).

Order flow competition. To meet investors' needs, several types of orders interact on the order book and get executed in a sequential order. The order flow competition between traders through orders has been partially investigated. Many types of limit and market orders may create several equilibria between orders that have not been researched enough. For instance, Foucault (1999) suggests that the volatility of the asset is the main determinant of the equilibrium between market and limit orders. In effect, when the volatility of the asset increases there is more possibility for limit orders to be picked-off by new information and suffer adverse selection (winner's curse). Market orders will be more costly in terms of price impact and spread because there will be more competition between investors in their use. This situation also explains why trading at the end of the day is dominated by market orders, as the probability of execution of limit orders decreases.

As suggested by Parlour (2010), in a world in which information moves faster across assets classes due to technological developments and financial interconnection, the order flow is intrinsically more informative and the costs of adverse selection due to fast-moving information encourages the use of market orders, which may be seen as limit orders with price set at the market value in the instant of the observation of the order flow. In addition, the increasing need to look at shorter time horizons to fill the gap in returns caused by the dismal growth of developed economies has further increased volatility of asset values, which are affecting the microstructure of financial markets. Financial institutions are massively investing in routing technologies and speed of execution, since investors need to observe the order flow in real-time to use market orders. In effect, since volatility has created a strong disequilibrium between market and limit orders, the only way to win competition between market orders and improve the liquidity of the order book is to increase speed and volumes. More speed and higher volume ultimately reduce the portion of the price on which non-retail investors can compete on and create potential risks in terms of capacity for trading platforms. In the past, immediacy of execution was possible through specialists acting on the trading floor. Today, the only way to see the order flow and reduce market impact by investing accordingly is through investments in technologies such as smart order routers and direct access with high-frequency trading tools. Retail investors were and will always be slower than professional investors. However, the typically small size of their limit orders protects them from market impact and the reduction of tick sizes (see also next section). Finally, order-driven auction markets are designed to handle small trades at the lowest transaction costs but only as long as the market for that financial instrument is sufficiently liquid.

Table 7. Auction versus dealer markets

Auction Markets	Dealer Markets
PROs - High transparency - Price information efficiency - Order flow competition - Low transaction costs (especially for small trades)	PROs - Handling of illiquid products and block sizes - Resilience (to information asymmetries) - Execution certainty
CONs - Market impact - Market breakdown (information asymmetries) - Operational risks (capacity)	CONs - Costs - Opacity (price formation) - Accessibility (if OTC) - Low competitive pressures

Source: Authors.

Dealer markets. Another form of trading, often complementary to auction markets (dealer markets can be designed as multilateral auction systems), is the dealer market. In this market setting, trades are typically dealt with quote-driven dealer markets or bilateral negotiations with the support of an intermediary that submits executable bid/ask quotes. The submission of quotes can be: i) bilateral or ii) multilateral.

Bilateral models are usual in bilateral OTC transactions, which are in general used in illiquid markets where financial instruments may need further customisation. The RFQ model (see Box 9) also represents a bilateral dealer market since executable quotes are only available on request by that specific counterparty through the use of an inter-dealer platform. RFQ markets have been developed for less-liquid products such as corporate bonds or structured products, while OTC bilateral contracts are still the main negotiation mechanism for many types of derivatives.

Dealer markets can be designed as (multilateral) auction model, through a 'quote-driven' market or a facilitator. In the former, dealers submit executable quotes on a continuous basis or periodically (batch auction system). A dealer competes with other dealers/market-makers on the size of the offered bid/ask spread. A quote-driven market is a market model used for liquid markets such as stocks or futures (e.g. NASDAQ). Given free entry into market-making business, quote-driven systems are equivalent to continuous auction mechanisms (Madhavan, 1992). In the latter model, a facilitator (e.g., inter-dealer platform) brings together different buying and selling interests as riskless counterparty (multilateral trading system) but it does not interpose itself to counterparties and the transaction between the buyers and the seller is based on a bilateral RFQ model. Therefore, quotes are only indicative and may vary in a pre-defined range. The trading platform remains a neutral (and 'multilateral', as Recital 6, MiFID) trading system if non-discretionary rules to submit quotes by dealers (inter-dealer platform) and orders by clients and dealers (dealer to client) apply.

Figure 26. Dealer markets (trading models)

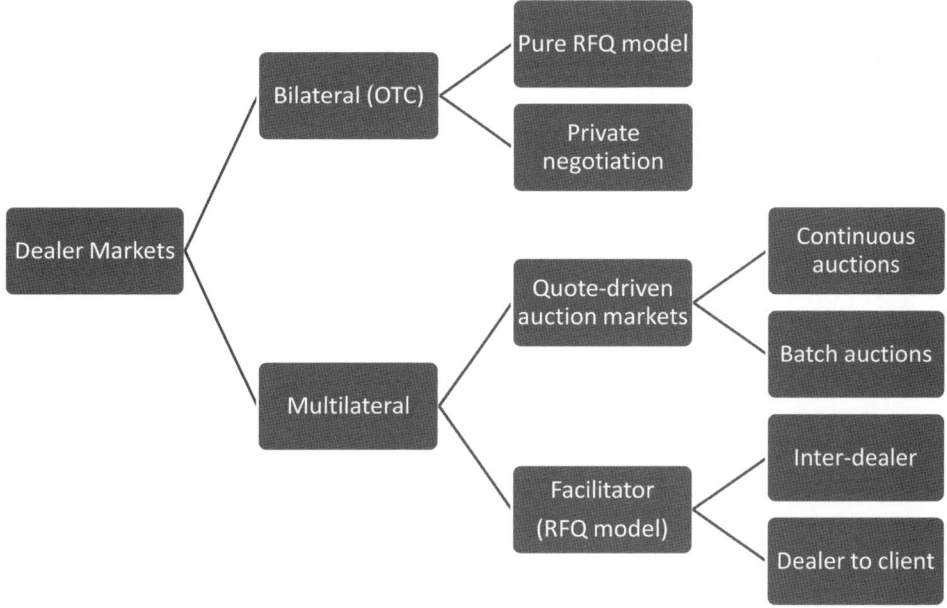

Source: Authors.

Benefits and costs. On the one hand, dealer markets may be beneficial for some asset classes. In particular, these markets can ensure order execution with minimal exposure risk (market impact; Pagano & Röell, 1993). This effect is achieved through a system of competing dealers that exploit their informational advantage; namely, the possibility to see the order size and price before it is executed, which does not necessarily happen in order-driven markets (Malinova and Park, 2008). This informational advantage comes as a reward for their investments into capital commitments and advanced technologies. The use of capital on own account also ensures that investors can trade highly-customised and illiquid financial instruments to better meet their risk profiles, by minimising information leakage. Some investors may also get better terms if they can exploit a contractual power (institutional investors) or bring a kind of liquidity that maximises the possibility of dealers to benefit from their market knowledge. The informational advantage of market-makers (due to their investments in market knowledge) and their intensive capital commitment in the development of bilateral or multilateral platforms, make dealer markets potentially more resilient to information risks than order-driven markets. Dealers also provide markets with innovative ventures and financing, as well as tools to manage particular risks that would be prohibitively costly in other market settings.

On the other hand, the extreme flexibility of these market settings is usually offset by fairly high costs to deal with financial products. For instance, corporate bonds should be financial instruments with lower trading costs than the related stock of the company as they are less risky (Biais & Green, 2007). However, this is usually not the case because the market for corporate bonds is often very illiquid (as explained above) and a market with dealers that commit capital seems so far to be the only structure able to deal with this constant illiquidity. In addition, the pricing mechanism is not as transparent as in OLOBs since it is not based on the reservation price of investors, but on the proprietary valuation models of dealers. Bid/ask spreads in dealer markets are the outcome of these models and can only be influenced by the potential threat of competing market-makers/dealers, which may offer more aggressive bid/ask spreads in order to erode rivals' market shares and increase volumes. In effect, another potential drawback of dealer markets is the structurally high concentration levels of the dealer industry (capital is limited!), which may ultimately determine monopolistic or oligopolistic settings. A model with 'monopolistic/oligopolistic dealers' may be undesirable not only in terms of output and prices –which are typically fixed above marginal costs– but also because the assignment of stocks between dealers may be arbitrary and lead to a sub-optimal distribution (Stoll, 1978).

Finally, accessibility for retail investors to some bilateral dealer markets may be difficult without the support of intermediaries, who typically pass the higher costs on end investors. It may even impossible (as for OTC derivatives instruments) because dealers may decide to deal only with some specific counterparties due to counterparty risk and product complexity.

The ability to price discriminate – thanks to their information advantage – makes this market setting more suitable for discriminating platforms (see section 5.3). Accordingly, market-makers move first and propose price schedules. Hence, if the market is less-liquid and the information asymmetry fairly large, some authors suggest that dealer markets (with one specialist or competing market-makers) may be both more resilient and efficient, thereby making it easier to reach equilibrium (Glosten, 1989; O'Hara, 1995). Dealer markets are therefore designed to deal with less-liquid markets, as long as this 'low-liquidity condition' is always verified.

Hybrid markets. Capital markets have developed different market microstructures, dominated by OLOBs or dealers. In particular, equity markets regularly combine auction markets (OLOBs) with the presence of liquidity providers (market-makers/dealers) that offer liquidity to the market to ensure the continuity of trading. In this way, markets try to combine the benefits of both market designs, ensuring a high degree of transparency (with due exemptions and delays), market integrity, and investor protection (for uninformed traders). This market setting combines the efficient pricing mechanisms of auction markets, and greater protection for retail investors, with stronger resilience to market shocks (information asymmetry). Stronger resilience comes from the capital committed by liquidity providers in order to ensure continuity of trading and to always maintain available executable quotes.

5.5.2 The evolution of trading: Market efficiency and financial stability

Automation and the internet. The automation of trading and the introduction of the internet have fostered quick developments in capital markets in the last two decades, in particular for equity markets, pushing volumes up and making markets in general more accessible. The possibility for investors to more easily compete amongst each other on a global basis and across asset classes has led them to invest even more in advanced technologies for trading with a rapid increase of volumes. In particular, current markets are experiencing faster and greater flows of information into prices. This situation has made the order flow more informative than ever before, but private information embeds many complex variables (such as risk exposures, gross positions, macroeconomic outlook, and regulatory boundaries) that have increased the complexity of trading strategies and ultimately asset volatility (as rationale behind the financial system's bias towards 'boom and bust' cycles; Group of Thirty, 2010).

Easier and cheaper market accessibility has brought a new wave of investors and raised volumes, which remains at higher levels than at the beginning of the 21st century, despite the recent financial crisis. This situation has inevitably promoted a shift in the structure of financial markets. Equity markets, in particular, have gradually moved from more opaque quote-driven dealer markets to OLOBs run by advanced trading platforms able to process millions of trades in the blink of an eye.

Algorithmic trading. As a consequence, complex flows of information (e.g. multimarket trading, risk exposure, etc) need trading software that can collect and process a wide range of variables in order to reach an investment and trading decision, as well as route orders across multiple venues (Biais, 2010). The introduction of algorithmic trading technologies aims at replacing the human trader with machines that overcome cognitive limits of human beings and process complex information quicker and completely. Further, algorithmic trading reduces search costs and market impact by splitting big size orders and automatically executing them on several venues (split & dice strategy; see figures below).

Figure 27. Average trade size on SETS

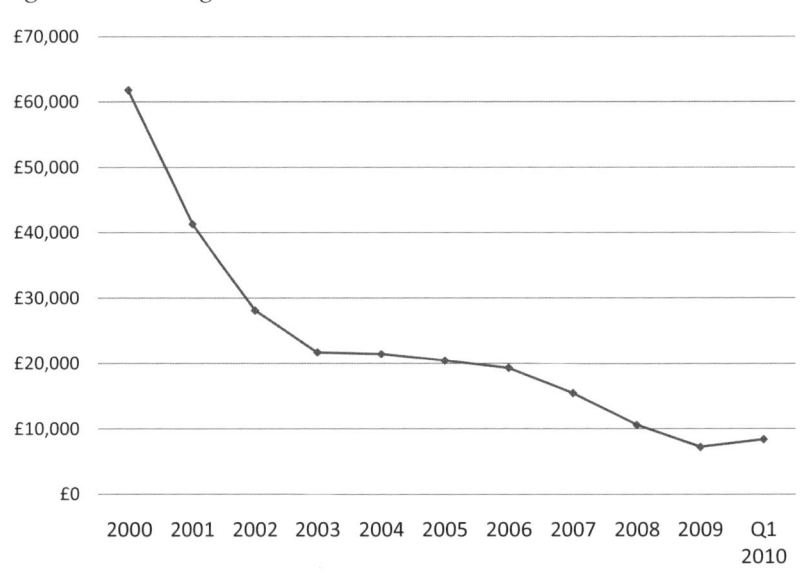

Source: LSE Group (2010).

Figure 28. Average value of orders executed for most liquid European shares

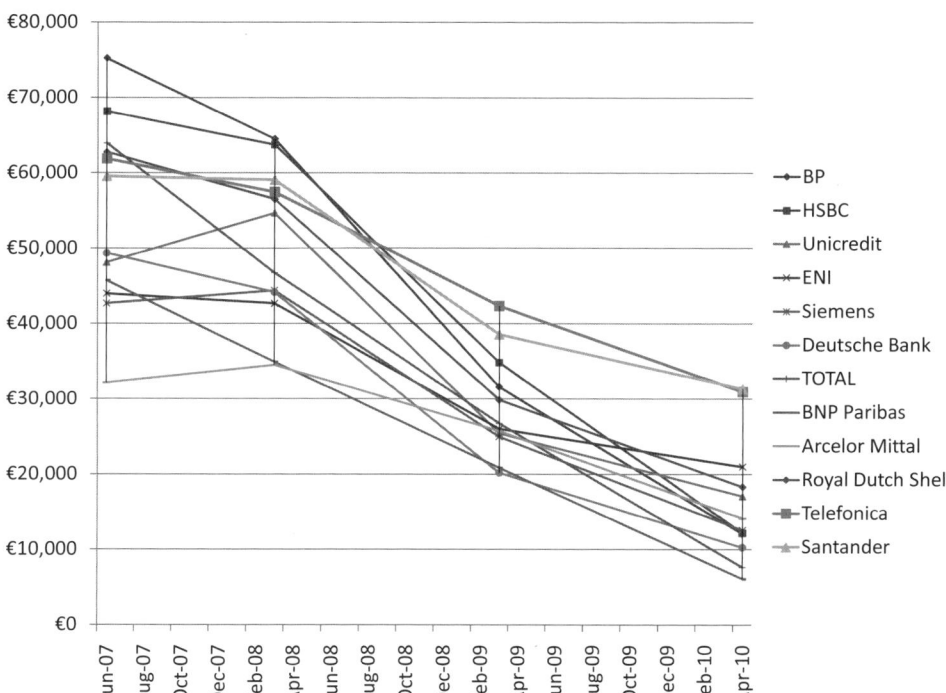

Source: CESR MiFID Database.

The figures above show the trend in the average size of orders respectively for the London Stock Exchange SETS and for some of the most liquid EU shares. The decline should reflect a substantial increase in the use of 'split and dice' strategies, which are based on trading algorithms that route orders across markets after the big 'parent order' has been split into small 'child orders'. The average size of retail orders has not followed the same pattern. Nevertheless, the figure above suggests that MiFID has also contributed to this decline by perhaps increasing competition in execution services, thereby pushing investment firms to invest in new technologies and diffuse them at a faster pace. In effect, besides the decline in the average value of executed orders from 2007, the second figure also shows that the difference between average values of orders among liquid shares is drastically reducing to a tiny range (except for Telefonica and Santander). This may be the result of a wider use of new trading technologies, which typically treat orders and split them in a similar way. On average the market seems to deal only with retail orders. Hence, this situation should create more liquidity for small retail trades and less liquidity for institutional orders that do not use 'split and dice' strategies (explaining in part the growth of dark pools of liquidity; see Section 4.2.1).

Algorithmic trading (AT) gives more speed and strategic thinking to the investment decision. This trading activity, however, may also generate costs. Firstly, it raises the asymmetric information between fast and slow traders, which may discourage slow traders from investing and create disequilibrium, thus volatility. No evidence that AT raises volatility has been found so far (Hendershott & Riordan, 2009). Secondly, the increased number of messages and potential human errors in defining the most appropriate algorithm during the trading day may generate operational risks and ultimately cause market crashes (see next Box), with potential spiral effects due to the interconnection between orders on the order flow. This situation would irremediably harm the investor confidence that keeps global financial markets together (in particular OLOBs).

AT can be:

1) Directional (market trend) or market neutral (HFT),
2) Short or long,
3) Fully or partially hedged and
4) Short-term or overnight.

Algorithmic trading solutions are typically embedded in proprietary software made in-house or outsourced to external IT companies.

Finally, investing in algorithmic trading presents high fixed costs, mitigated by relevant economies of scale. Network effects and the risk for slow traders to be easily picked off bring market participants to run to get the best algorithmic trading technologies. However, on the one hand, overinvestment may not be socially useful but, on the other, trading platforms may need to have harmonised monitoring practices to avoid downside spiral effects (Biais, 2010).

Box 13. The US 'flash crash': What can be learned?

On 6 May 2010 – between 2.40pm and 3.00pm – US stock markets experienced a previously unseen phenomenon. Within a few minutes, the S&P 500 index plummeted by almost 100 points (-8.2%) and the Dow Jones Industrial Average by over 1,000 points (-9.2%). Indexes then recovered their previous levels almost 20 minutes later, at the end of the so-called 'flash crash'. Some stocks, such as Procter & Gamble, dropped nearly 40% before rebounding. The whole market swung within a 10% range down in 10 minutes due to a series of events.

The SEC report (2010b) split the crash into two major events: i) a liquidity crisis in the E-Mini (and SPY) future contracts[156] market; and ii) a liquidity crisis in the main stock index market (S&P 500). The general market trend on that day was already affected by downward pressures from the morning due to the European debt crisis, with high volatility (S&P volatility index was above 22%) and an overall sentiment of uncertainty concerning the global economic outlook. The e-Mini future contract market was very thin (the traded value was around $2.65 billion, 55% less than the early morning).

The market crash propagated from a liquidity crisis in the e-Mini future contracts. In effect, against this background of low liquidity, an investment fund trader submitted an aggressive selling algorithmic programme for a big position in e-Mini contracts (75,000, for a value of $4.1 billion [157]), which was a hedge for an existing position in equity. Only two other sell programs of that size were executed in the previous 12 months in that market. In addition, those other sell programs took 5 hours to complete the execution, while in this case the same number of contracts was executed in 20 minutes. The strong sell pressure, according to SEC findings, was initially absorbed by high-frequency traders ('HFTs'), which support previous evidence on the supply of liquidity offered by algo-HFT when the market is volatile and fairly thin (Hendershott & Riordan, 2009; Chaboud et al., 2009), together with fundamental buyers and cross-market arbitrages, which transferred the selling pressure to equity markets. However, HFTs do not hold big positions for a long time so they started to sell aggressively in e-Minis, causing an increase of HFT trading, increasing volumes (HFT generally trade high volumes but do not hold more than 4,000-5,000 contracts). The artificially high volumes made the initial 'sell algorithm' feed the market with more sell orders. The trader had set this algorithm at 9% of total volumes in the previous minute, without considering price and time, which ended up generating 75,000 contracts that could not be absorbed at once. The human error of the trader was the assumption that higher volumes meant higher liquidity. HFTs began to sell and buy contracts among each other, while the market was going down and the buy-side demand dropped to less than 1% of the morning's levels. In short, the market actually dried up because of the uninformed use of advanced trading technologies (see graph below).

---

[156] The 'E-Mini' is a stock index instrument traded in electronic future and equity markets. It is a derivative product designed to replicate the S&P 500 Index. The number of outstanding contracts is not fixed at any given time. This type of product was introduced by CME in the 1997 and trades exclusively on the CME Globex electronic trading platform 24h a day (SEC, 2010b). The first liquidity crisis also concerns the S&P 500 SPDR exchange-traded fund (SPY), which replicates the S&P 500 index as well. For simplicity, the report only mentions the e-Mini market since both markets were affected by the same kind of events.

[157] The value of contracts traded was down from the morning to $2.65 billion.

Cross-market arbitrageurs transferred the downward pressure to equity markets, which fell of 3% like the e-Mini market in 3 minutes. Demand collapsed and the buy-side only held 1,050 e-Mini contracts and equity markets lost another 2%, bringing the total to 5%. At that moment only 35,000 contracts of the sell algorithm were executed and the market was stopped for a few seconds by CME, due to the awkward trading activities and in an attempt to reduce selling pressures. When the market resumed, in effect, it started to recover but the net imbalance between buyers and sellers was of over 30,000 contracts (for sellers). The sell algorithm then completed its sell programme at 2.51pm due to the restored liquidity attracted by the quick recovery, with high losses overall for the investment fund since no price and time conditions were added to the algorithm.

Figure 29. Aggregated S&P 500 market depth

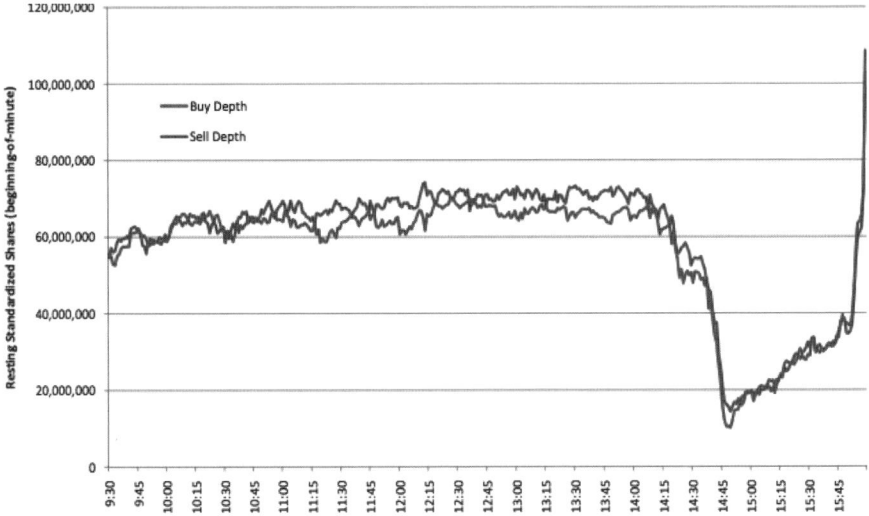

Source: SEC (2010b).

In the equity market, besides the initial fall of the index, the fall and pause of the e-Mini market sparked fears that there was a more fundamental reason than just human error behind the price decline. Therefore, some market-makers and liquidity providers widened spreads or withdrew from the market, causing selling pressures to continue their action and buying interests to go even lower. As a result, prices started to behave irrationally since markets started to match stop-market orders with stub quotes originally set by market-makers at levels away from current market prices in order to fulfil continuity of two-sided quotes obligations, even when a market-maker had withdrawn. As soon as the market participants verified the integrity of their data and trading systems, sell-side and buy-side interests returned and the market quickly recovered its previous value, but with big losses for some market participants. As the SEC reports, after the crash, the exchanges and the Financial Industry Regulatory Authority (FINRA) agreed to cancel orders that were clearly a result of 'errors' in the trading rules.

> To sum up, the crash was the combination of human error with the use of stop-market orders by main US exchanges, which pushed prices to behave irrationally, so generating heavy losses not only for the traders that run the algorithm but also for markets. The SEC also concluded that pausing trading systems was beneficial and that there should be clear and sound procedures to break erroneous trades to ensure certainty and strengthen investors' confidence. In the aftermath of the flash crash, the authority introduced 'circuit breakers', which are procedures to halt trading across markets when prices swing in the previous 5 minutes of a value higher than 10%. According to these rules, systems should be paused for 5 minutes. Finally, it is thought unlikely that the same phenomenon would occur in Europe, given that, on this side of the Atlantic, there is a more limited use of stop-market orders and much less-liquid ETFs markets (low interconnection). However, it would be beneficial for Europe to also adopt a set of rules to interrupt price volatility in extreme circumstances, taking the solution in the US as a benchmark.

High-frequency trading. As mentioned above, the general increase of asset volatility has changed the equilibrium of order flow competition (for OLOBs), beyond any classification by asset class. Greater competition for market orders between investors has led market participants to invest hugely in IT services and high-frequency trading (HFT) technologies, which allow investors to 'see' the order flow and execute orders in almost real time, i.e. in microseconds (and soon 'nanoseconds'). HFT is gradually becoming indispensable for algorithmic trading strategies but it has also supported the emergence of other strategies. In particular, as anticipated in Section 3.3, HFT may pursue the following three major strategies (AFM, 2010; Chi-X, 2010):

1) Market-making
2) Arbitrage
3) Informed trading (or speculation)

Firstly, HFT may supply liquidity to markets through systems able to analyse the order flow at the fastest speed technically possible, reducing risk-sharing on inventory positions. As suggested in the box above, HFT may absorb temporary imbalances between buy and sell orders. HFT has the important function of temporarily absorbing market shocks. However, HFT positions are usually market-neutral (non-directional), hedged and continuously updated (high cancellation rate), and closed-out by the end of the day (AFM, 2010). Market-making means that the role of HFT is temporary, so in the event of extreme imbalances, markets would need to restore fundamental demand to avoid market collapse (for instance, by halting trading across markets for a short timeframe).

Secondly, HFT allows cross-markets and arbitrage across asset classes to benefit from price anomalies. Moreover, it also permits so-called 'statistical arbitrage', which uses historical datasets to find repeating patterns in the price trends that can be profitably exploited.

Thirdly, HFT may use low-latency execution to pursue strategies based on investments in information. Three examples are: trading according to indicators that try to predict future performance; placing and cancelling orders to find hidden liquidity; or screening algorithms to find failures and profit from them.

Both algorithmic and HFT are widely diffused and more often used as complementary tools to achieve specific trading strategies. These technologies are essential for institutional investors and brokers/dealers, and, as a result, new trading strategies are becoming widespread (see Section 3.3). These new strategies are often deemed to increase volatility but no empirical evidence has been found so far that supports this view (Hendershott & Riordan, 2009; Chaboud et al., 2009; Broogard, 2010).

The implementation of trading strategies through algorithms and HFT needs trading tools that can operate with the lowest technically possible latency (proprietary and roundtrip).[158] To reach the highest speed, and therefore the lowest latency, several factors need to be considered. Among the most important ones are the following (AFM, 2010):

1) Complexity of the trading algorithm (e.g. smart order routing),
2) IT infrastructures (computing power),
3) Efficient connection (network latency in terms of capacity, speed and stability of data),
4) Physical distance from the data source (trading platform) and
5) Access services to the platform.

Investment firms and trading platforms are investing in IT infrastructures and special services to reduce latency (respectively,

---

[158] Latency is the time/delay that occurs for a package of data to be sent/received from one point to another. It is the technical delay caused by the inability of the physical network/infrastructure to act/react in real time. Latency can be split in round trip and proprietary (AFM, 2010). Roundtrip latency is the technical delay caused by the structure of the trading platform, which may take a minimum amount of time to accept, execute and confirm orders, besides time taken by the security check done by the firewall. Proprietary latency is the technical delay caused by the hardware, software, IT infrastructure, and access arrangements of brokers/dealers, or investment firms or investors (direct access) that transmit orders to the platform for execution.

proprietary and roundtrip latency), such as co-location services,[159] connection services (e.g. optical fibres, connection capacity) and direct electronic access (DEA) services. Several European equity markets (e.g. NYSE Euronext, Oslo Börs) are moving their trading systems close to the major European financial centre (London) to offer similar advanced execution services and higher speed of execution (by reducing physical distance) through proprietary trading systems, often provided by third parties. Some investment firms are physically relocating in a mid-position among several platforms with the support of latest high-speed connections. This solution or multiple co-locations can ultimately reduce the risks of liquidity fragmentation and improve arbitrages across trading venues.

Direct electronic access. Amongst advanced trading services, direct electronic access (DEA) arrangements can potentially reduce latency, costs, and trade errors (Celent, 2008); but they may have multi-faceted implications. These services, in particular, may have beneficial effects for clients (low entry costs and administrative hurdles of membership), sponsoring firms (attracting HFT volumes, coupled with volume discounts of trading venues), and trading platforms (attraction of new liquidity). DEA arrangements allow firms that are not registered intermediaries (or investment firms under MiFID rules[160]) to have direct access to the trading venue through: i) using an intermediary's member status/contract; or ii) becoming direct member or direct access (IOSCO, 2010b).

In the first case, a non-member will be able to directly access the trading venue to execute orders by using:

1) The intermediary's infrastructure (Direct Market Access, DMA) or
2) Its own infrastructure, but under intermediary's control and rules (Sponsored Access or SA).

Sponsored access, in particular, lowers the economic barriers to enter a platform. It allows direct access to markets for more participants, with

---

[159] Co-location services have de facto substituted the role played by the 'floor' trading in the past. Instead of bringing together specialists and investment companies' traders on the floor to get information and execute orders faster, today's main equity markets put together – in the same room, close to the central data server – the servers of trading specialists, brokers, dealers, market-makers, and investment firms.

[160] To which apply also rules on regulatory capital, Capital Requirements Directive, Directive 2006/49/EC (Art. 12, MiFID).

their own technology, without intermediaries. In both DMA and SA, the intermediary is responsible for the customer's conduct[161] and transactions are flagged with the ID code of the intermediary. Moreover, the intermediary monitors customers' activities (and eventually reports anomalies to authorities; FSA, 2008) and typically applies specific requirements to get DEA to the trading platform. In addition, trading venues may unilaterally decide to restrict access only to certain type of customer. DMA permits the intermediary to apply pre-trade filters and post-trade controls, since orders are directed to markets through intermediaries' infrastructure. The proportion of trading value done through Direct Market Access is expected to grow up to 15% by 2011 (Celent, 2008).

For SA services, intermediaries typically receive a 'drop copy' of the order at the same time when it is sent to the market (AFM, 2010). This situation makes it difficult to apply pre-trade controls, even though it allows faster execution because only pre-trade filters set by the trading venue are actually applied. Pre-trade filters are particularly important to detect erroneous trades or human errors ('fat fingers'), rather than for detecting market abuses. Ex ante and ex post controls are applied to SA services by the trading venue or by third parties on behalf of the intermediary as well. SA is a typical service for a small number of highly sophisticated intermediaries and their clients. IOSCO (2010b) suggests applying:

1) Specific requirements to DEA customers, such as limits to transactions' notional value,
2) Pre-trade controls and
3) Post-trade controls.

In the case of Direct Access (DA), firms that are not investment firms under MiFID may be granted membership to the trading platform. In such cases, they would apply both their own internal controls and the controls of the platform by executing orders directly on the trading venue, using their own ID code. As a consequence, in order to avoid credit risk, members should apply sound financial requirements and become clearing members of the CCP for the purpose of balancing their trading activities with

---

[161] Even though IOSCO (2009a and 2010b) recognises that it may be difficult in certain jurisdictions to act against a non-member for violation of market rules or it may be difficult to show an intermediary's lack of supervision.

potentially high notional values (IOSCO, 2010b). The European Parliament (Swinburne, 2010) has recommended a clamp-down – with an explicit ban – on DEA 'naked' arrangements, which grant market access without filters to intermediaries and trading venues ('unfiltered' market access). This Report does not find evidence that such agreements have been put in place by any European trading venue.

Overall, DEA arrangements create specific challenges:

1) Risks of market manipulation and insider dealing if only traditional controls apply, for instance, by offering much smaller and not harmonised tick sizes that can make supervision more complicated, especially if HFT is involved;
2) Risks of creating an unlevel playing field (unfairness) by allocating limited physical space on a discriminatory basis, as for co-location services, or because of the geographical position;
3) Risks that the limited capacity of trading venues to receive/send messages can restrict access in a discriminatory way; in this regard, the adoption of incremental fees for messaging may be a less invasive way to keep control of the platform's capacity constraints;
4) Risks that human errors or erroneous trades may happen more frequently, with devastating effects on investors' confidence; and
5) Risks that members may not be sufficiently capitalised in case they would be held responsible for their actions (credit risk; in particular with DA).

In order to face these challenges, the Commission (2010b) is consulting market participants on the possibility to amend MiFID as follows:

1) Require HFT over a specific threshold to be authorised as investment firms,
2) Impose new general organisational requirements and non-discriminatory clauses,
3) Set a minimum tick size,
4) Impose an obligation on HTFs trading a significant number of shares to keep providing liquidity on an ongoing basis (as for market-makers) and
5) Require to keep (limit) orders on the order book for a limited amount of time before cancellation or, alternatively, requiring firms to keep their cancellation over execution ratio over a specified level.

On points 1 and 4, in particular, it should be noted that HFT is difficult to define (CESR, 2010b, p. 40)[162] and if defined it would not be easily identifiable on the order book. It seems that the Commission refers to HFT where it pursues market-making strategies, since large positions may boost the credit risk of HFT firms. Notwithstanding that credit risk is a potential issue for all traders accessing financial markets with insufficient financial resources, it is rather the way in which traders access financial markets (in which HFT can be more easily identified) that needs to be further scrutinised. IOSCO (2010b) suggested setting minimum standards for DEA customers, which include 'appropriate financial resources' and 'appropriate procedures' to assess customers' knowledge and technical proficiency, or setting position limit filters that avoid exceeding credit limits and gaining exposure to 'unacceptable risks' (p. 22). Hence, since HFT uses DEA arrangements (trading or not on own account), by regulating the three ways how traders access markets directly – with no direct intermediaries' involvement (but partial responsibility) – would be an easier-to-handle and more functional approach (for instance, by requiring of the DA that their members are investment firms and/or clearing members).

Moreover, point 4 may raise problems of incentives for HFTs to provide liquidity, if they are obliged to do so on an ongoing basis. As illustrated above, HFT supplies and consumes liquidity in different circumstances, and since they are not allowed to offer spreads, it would reduce their incentives to trade high volumes if market-making obligations are imposed upon them.

On point 5, as mentioned, incremental fees based on sent/received messages may be a less invasive way and allow trading venues to fine-tune fees with the actual capacity of their trading platform. An organisational requirement to deal with capacity constraints may stimulate these changes.

Disorderly markets. The abovementioned risks (in particular, operational and credit risks) may cause disorderly markets and create financial instability if no appropriate regulation and supervision has been put in place. The Commission (2010b) suggests requiring trading venues to set appropriate harmonised procedures to halt trading 'to mitigate the risk

---

[162] It is worth noting how the regulatory approach is changing in comparison to the current MiFID text, in which regulation imposes obligations on market participants as a result of being the provider of a specific service rather than being identified with a specific status (such as, 'high-frequency trader').

of errors' (e.g. circuit breakers; Swinburne, 2010). Harmonised regulatory obligations to ensure fair and orderly trading and to monitor members' compliance with rules (e.g. 'adequate risk management systems'; FSA, 2008) may need to be applied across markets, since otherwise it would create great instability (order imbalances). Some market participants also argue that those measures should be reserved for critical situations, while solutions that allow trading continuity should be by far preferred. CESR has been requested by the level 1 mandate of the new MiFID to define binding technical standards to ensure fair and orderly markets, including DEA arrangements (CESR, 2010b).

In case markets experience outages/crashes, the FSA (2010b) has suggested fairly sound requirements, as follows:

1) Maintaining fair and orderly markets (by suspending trading activities if the orderly functioning is under threat and requiring sound arrangements to deal with technical operations);
2) Informing members/participants of trading conditions (e.g. by disseminating non-misleading information) and setting order management procedures (e.g. by cancelling orders already in the system in case of outages or cancelling transactions that come as result of erroneous matching due to price anomalies in market crashes);
3) Restarting trading with transparent and non-discretionary rules and procedures to avoid affecting fair and orderly trading on related markets (members should be clearly informed about the status of their outstanding orders, sound and transparent rules should apply);
4) Setting contingency arrangements for trading venues using the reference price of the market where trading has been suspended (also for asset classes other than equity markets). Extending these arrangements to investment firms in order to ensure continuity in meeting best execution obligations in the absence of a reference price (it may be desirable for them to have connectivity to multiple venues).

When the failure does not only pertain to a specific problem of a venue, under such market circumstances, any eventual decision by the competent authority or corresponding body to halt trading in any given security would need to be enforced among all trading venues. In addition, trading venues may need to periodically assess their trading capacity and test their systems accordingly (stress tests). Other important controls should be falling on trading venues: approval of participants; sufficient capacity and resilience to cope with high volumes; real-time market supervision; market volatility controls (trading suspensions, etc.); erroneous order cancellation (trade bust policies); and market abuse monitoring/surveillance.

Box 14. Regulatory shift: the 'growing' role of macro regulators[163]

The link between the international regulatory activities around issues of financial stability has brought significant implications for the revision of the MiFID and the work of securities regulators. Regulatory activities face three major challenges:

i) Global economic vulnerability affects sovereign tolerance for volatility in financial markets;
ii) Disagreement on economic policies will increase the need for regulation that delivers financial stability (macro-prudential regulation); and
iii) A possible trade-off between new trading technologies and market stability.

Securities regulators are not directly represented at G20 level and are more frequently compelled to comply with decisions made somewhere else. In effect, the centre of regulation has shifted from national technical issues to G20 level (with IMF playing a major role; see graph below). In terms of enforcement, however, the centre of gravity is still at national level, even though Europe is trying to increase the enforcement powers of the new European authorities. These different approaches may create some clashes between new financial regulation (which represents the current priority at global and national level) and its concrete application at national level. Benefits and costs of macro-prudential financial regulation may need to be further investigated.

For instance, exogenous factors brought about by the global regulatory framework are influencing the discussion around the functions performed by some market operators (such as HFTs and market-makers), i.e. the impact of HFT on volatility and liquidity, or the role of market-makers in concentrating risks and interconnections. New regulatory tools – coming from the top – are actually at centre of the discussion. For instance, concerning HFT, the introduction of circuit breakers or stricter financial requirements. For market-makers and financial institutions, exposed to certain macro risks in general, the introduction of trade repositories, margin/capital requirements and liquidity requirements are proposed.

---

[163] This section builds upon Barbara Matthews's presentation at the Task Force meeting on 15 October 2010 (Matthews, 2010).

Figure 30. Shifting the regulatory centre of gravity.

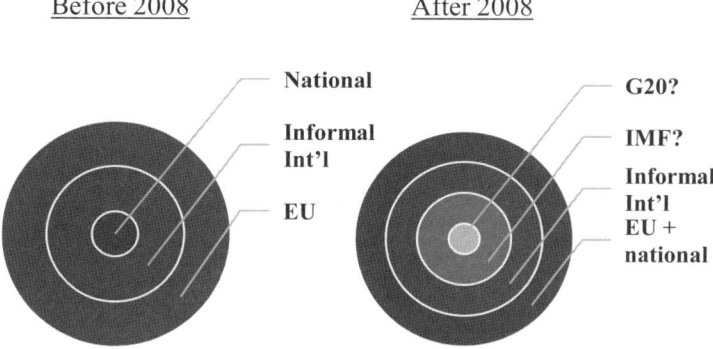

Source: Matthews (2010).

Moreover, several aspects may be deemed to impact volatility and so push regulators to rein in new areas of financial markets, with a potential impact on MiFID. These variables are:

1) Exchange rates (and FX);
2) Anaemic growth;
3) Persistent unemployment;
4) Latent or lurking inflation;
5) Deflation;
6) Budget deficits; and
7) Unsustainable sovereign debt burdens.

If new technologies are perceived as a determinant of volatility, they will be subject to stricter regulation. Regulators' attention is gradually turning towards trading networks and the implications of regulatory actions on such network infrastructures as financial markets.

In conclusion, another important aspect is data access, in terms of best execution and regulatory/supervisory actions (price, cost, speed, counterparty exposures, etc). Regulation may need to define proper mechanisms to launch early warnings and to identify systemic risks. Indirect effects of actions in parallel segments of financial markets due to their interconnectedness can increase the level of uncertainty in the market and bring tough regulatory responses.

Conclusion # 14

The systemic importance of modern capital markets highlights the inner tensions among financial stability, market efficiency and technological innovation. A well-functioning market must balance efficiency and safety, since inefficiencies will sooner rather than later raise problems of safety and vice versa. Technology plays a central role in the configuration of market infrastructure. In short, speed and volumes will likely continue to grow but trading venues may have to deal with more frequent crises and outages.

> *Overall, technological innovation, combined with new trading techniques, has brought revolutionary changes to trading platforms. Among these changes, there are major benefits, such as better order management and control of market impact; or more efficient and faster feed of information into prices, which generate diffused gains in terms of lower spreads and better price discovery.*
>
> *However, modern trading also presents a number of challenges, such as an increase in fundamental market volatility, which in turn has brought speed and volumes to critical levels. Advanced execution services like direct-market or sponsored access have radically increased speed and volumes for transactions, in an attempt to cope with increasing volatility. Yet, limits to infrastructure capacity mean that higher speed and volumes risk generating market disorder and financial instability. To overcome these challenges, intermediaries and trading venues need to strengthen their own monitoring. A coherent set of emergency procedures in case of market disruptions should be designed in consultation with market participants (e.g. circuit breakers). There are a several efficient monitoring systems already in place, which could serve as model systems. Finally, trading rules should be harmonised across markets to avoid instability arising from arbitrage.*

5.6 Access to market infrastructures for equities: What's next?

Market access. Competition among network infrastructures needs a certain degree of market contestability in order to bring costs down for final users and avoid oligopolistic settings. Current development of competition has led to a dramatic cost reduction in trading and post-trading costs, even without interoperability. Greater and cheaper market accessibility is a key objective of MiFID, to be achieved through competition and greater contestability. MiFID grants to investors/intermediaries non-discretionary market access to trading venues (recital 6), to investment firms freedom of access to regulated markets in other than their country of origin (Art. 33), and most notably it gives freedom to investment firms to decide the infrastructure for clearing and settlement (Art. 34). In addition, member states need to ensure incumbent infrastructures grant access to newcomers unless a 'legitimate commercial ground' makes the link unavailable. In this regard, the definition of 'legitimate' seems to leave some space for ambiguity. Incumbents typically allege one of the following three reasons to refuse access:

i) Efficiency and cost reduction,
ii) Not meeting specific requirements or standards set by the infrastructure itself or
iii) Technical difficulties.

'Efficiency and costs reduction' has been frequently dismissed by the Commission, which wishes to avoid high market concentrations, even if it comes at cost (see GE/Honeywell)[164]. As to 'technical reasons', these are usually assessed case-by-case by looking at available technologies and standards. With regard to the 'accessibility requirements' set by the infrastructure, these should be clearly defined and applied on a non-discriminatory basis (see Code of Conduct, 2006, §25-33)[165].

Market architecture. The opening up of competition in the upstream market (trading) has also generated some beneficial effects in terms of market accessibility for end investors. However, in the post-trading segment accessibility remains somehow limited, also affecting the overall costs of trading. Looking only at costs however, does not reflect the redistributive effects that a different market structure can generate. As a result, it is unclear how current markets can balance efficiency and competition with market integrity and stability. Excluding any ideal world of 'perfect competition', there are three possible scenarios:

1) Open architecture
2) Closed architecture and
3) Semi-open (or semi-closed) architecture.

The first scenario would require unleashing competition at every stage of the post-trading architecture, imposing painful unbundling obligations (disregarding potential economies of scope) and interoperability arrangements. The second scenario entails the creation of a 'closed' architecture, whereby market players and regulators work for further integration disregarding potential economies of scope. This market design tends to maximise economies of scale only and ignores beneficial portfolio effects and interoperability in favour of quasi-monopolies or monopolies at various stages of the post-trading value chain. Finally, there is an intermediate formula that does not seek to impose a specific market design but rather to interpret market trends and reap the benefits of scale and scope economies. For instance, this approach does not judge bundling

---

[164] See Case No. COMP/M2220 – *General Electric/Honeywell*, Regulation (EEC) No. 4064/89 – Merger Procedure, Article 8(3), (http://ec.europa.eu/comm/competition/mergers/cases/decisions/m2220_en.pdf).

[165] See Code of Conduct for Clearing and Settlement, (http://ec.europa.eu/internal_market/financial-markets/docs/code/code_en.pdf).

or mergers as harmful as long as they generate important economies of scope ('efficiency defence'), are replicable (together with the infrastructure), and do not create a big concentration in the market. In effect, according to this approach, the post-trading infrastructure should be evaluated under the 'essential facility doctrine',[166] i.e. the infrastructure should not be forced to open the access to its infrastructure as long as it does not meet all the following requirements:

1) The facility controlled by one market player is the only way to access the relevant market.
2) The facility is not replicable at a reasonable cost.
3) The monopolist refuses access to the facility or offers it at unbearable costs or under unfair conditions.
4) The absence of a valid economic justification.

On the other hand, this third approach would minimise barriers to entry and exit by promoting interoperability agreements between incumbent infrastructures and newcomers (in line with Art. 34, MiFID and forthcoming European Market Infrastructure Regulation), and minimising the presence of monopolies at any stage of the post-trading architecture, if no 'natural monopoly' conditions are verified.

Code of Conduct. To favour a more open post-trading architecture and to promote a full application of the principle originally set in MiFID (Art. 34), in November 2006, the European Commission endorsed the Code of Conduct for Clearing and Settlement, which was signed by the Federation of European Securities Exchanges (FESE), the European Association of Clearing Houses (EACH), and the European Central Securities Depositories Association (ECSDA). The Code represents the last self-regulatory effort by the industry to meet high-level objectives, before the financial crisis promoted a more interventionist approach through regulation. In effect, the Code was a valuable explorative work to achieve three goals:

1) Transparency of prices and services,

---

[166] The 'essential facility doctrine' is a theory that was originally elaborated in the US antitrust case law; see, *U.S. v. Terminal Railroad Association*, 244 U.S. 383, 1912. An extension of this doctrine was elaborated in Europe too in several cases, in particular, European Commission, *Magill TV guide/ITP, BBC and RTE*, in GUCE 1989, L 78/43; Court of Justice, *Oscar Bronner GmbH & Co. KG vs Mediaprint Zeitungs- und Zeitschriftenverlag GmbH & Co. KG, Mediaprint Zeitungsvertriebsgesellschaft mbH & Co. KG and Mediaprint Anzeigengesellschaft mbH & Co. KG*, C-7/97, p. I-7791. Amongst the most important literature, see in general Areeda (1990).

2) Access and interoperability and
3) Unbundling of services and accounting separation.

After three years, the Commission (EU COM, 2009b) made an assessment of the progress achieved so far, which highlighted how the Code of Conduct had positively contributed to price transparency. However, conflicting evidence was found with regard to 'access and interoperability' and 'unbundling of services and accounting separation' (Lannoo and Valiante, 2009). In effect, despite the Code promoting basic principles (such as 'right of standard access' and 'reciprocity') and some additional competition between infrastructures, commercial and technical barriers to cross-border access to infrastructures remain fairly high (EU COM, 2009b), in addition to other legal, economic, fiscal and social barriers that still impede the full development of a European post-trading architecture in particular for settlement services (Giovannini Group, 2001, 2003; CESAME, 2008). More competitive clearing services, however, have been effectively delivered in some markets, including silo market models (e.g. Swiss equity market), even though the situation seems to have stalled for interoperability agreements in other markets (see figure below).

Figure 31. Equity landscape before and after MiFID and the Code of Conduct

Before...

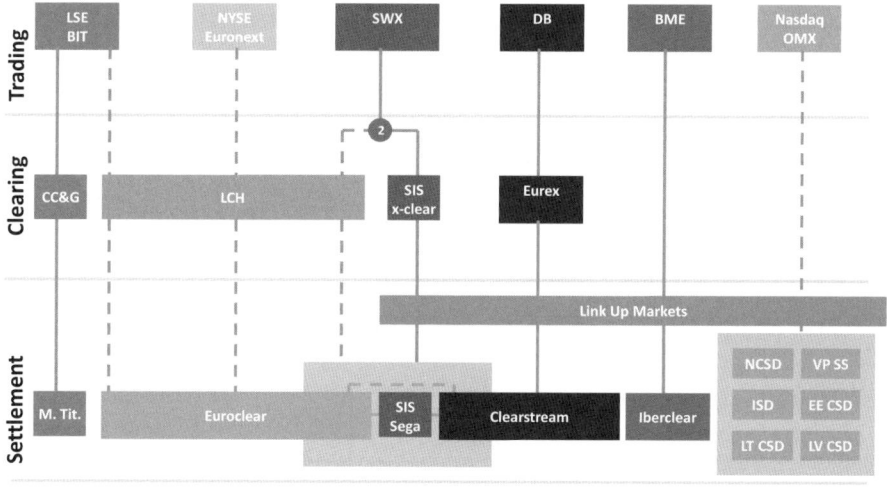

...and after the Code

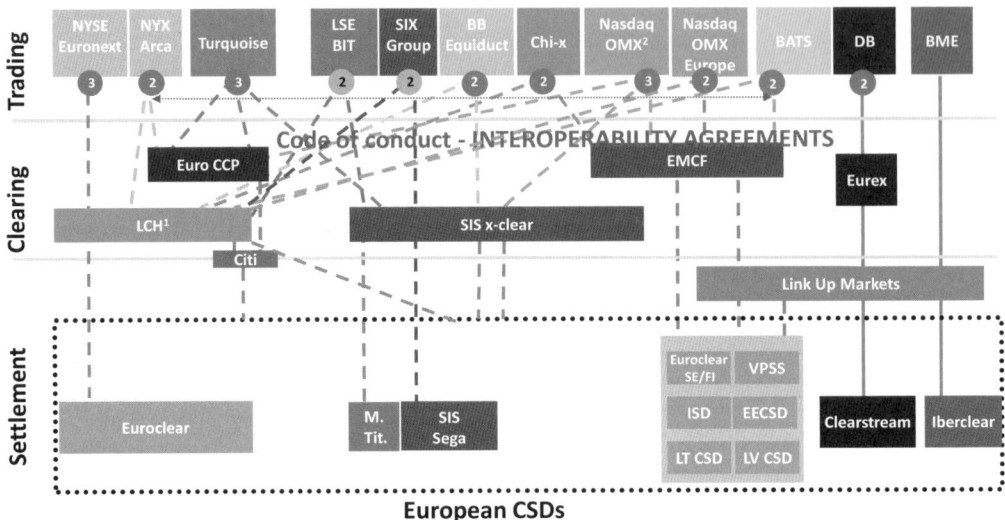

Source: FESE.

Note (from the presentation): In green the interoperability agreements in place and in yellow those on hold due to review by the regulators or to discussions between the parties. For a complete overview of the status of the requested links between post-trading infrastructures,

As shown above, after the Code came into force, many requests for interoperability and access were sent to incumbent infrastructures but only two were actually put in place. In addition, MiFID also stimulated the entry of new competing infrastructures in the clearing space.

Despite conflicting findings, costs of trading and clearing services went down by 60% between 2007 and 2009, while costs of settlement services seem to have gone down only in some markets, also due to the competitive pressures coming from the upstream trading market thanks to the introduction of MiFID (Oxera, 2009; EU COM, 2009b, p. 3). The fragmentation of European financial markets infrastructure, in particular for equities, is still led by geographical aspects (i.e. national markets; see figures above).

In the aftermath of to the financial crisis, risk reduction seems to prevail over cost reduction, which was a main objective of the Code. As a result, interoperability agreements are being more deeply scrutinised for potential threats to infrastructure integrity, while important guidelines are still in the implementation phase (Sections 3.5.3 and 3.8.3, FESE et al., 2007). In particular, the crisis drew attention to potential risks, such as competitive pressures that could lead to a race-to-the-bottom in terms of risk management practices. Moreover, asymmetry in collateralisation agreements should be the object of further examination and sound internationally-agreed standards.

The whole post-trading sector will be eventually reshuffled by an array of new European regulations. It is essential that EU co-legislators ensure strong coherence among these legal texts by giving to each piece of legislation a specific role, minimising conflicts and promoting legal certainty.

> *Conclusion # 15*
>
> *Academic literature has consistently suggested that market infrastructures, particularly for equity markets, are network structures that should operate in a competitive environment. MiFID should therefore take action to keep barriers of entry and exit low, but with due attention to economies of scope and potential efficiencies. The Code of Conduct succeeded in improving price transparency and stimulated interoperability. More remains to be done, however, to solve existent commercial and technical challenges in terms of access, interoperability and unbundling. Ultimately, MiFID will favour freedom of access by investment firms to competing market infrastructures. In effect, while the original MiFID Directive (Article 34) envisaged a level playing field in terms of non-discriminatory access to competing infrastructures, the transposition of this provision into national law and its enforcement has been inconsistent across EU member states. As such, greater efforts need to be made to ensure consistency in the enforcement of the regulatory framework. For this purpose, not only the revision of MiFID will play a role, but also concurrent legislations such as European Market Infrastructure Regulation (EMIR), Securities Law Directive (SLD) and Central Securities Depository Regulation (CSDR).*

6. Provision of Investment Services

MiFID represents an important attempt to design a harmonised framework of rules for the provision of investment service in the European Economic Area (EEA). It adopts a 'functional approach' by regulating market participants according to the actual investment service[167] they provide. Within its scope, the Directive therefore applies to all market participants, with some important exemptions.[168]

In parallel with a more competitive environment for trading venues, MiFID sought to harmonise and strengthen the level of investor protection and market integrity through two sets of rules:
1) Organisational requirements (ORs) and
2) 'Conduct of Business' (CoB) rules.

The former aims at strengthening market integrity (i.e., fighting market abuses and attempts to manipulate markets) and improve resilience. The latter targets greater investor protection and market efficiency. These rules consist of fairly detailed provisions, which should be read in conjunction with the general obligation for investment firms to "act honestly, fairly and professionally" in the best interest of clients (Art. 19.1, MiFID), and the rules on trade and transaction reporting (see Section 1).

---

[167] The definition of investment services and ancillary services can be found in Annex I, Sec. A and B, MiFID. The latter are typically provided in combination with the former. However, no authorisation to operate as MiFID investment firm should be granted if only ancillary services are provided (Art. 6.1, MiFID). Ancillary services can only be provided in combination with investment services to benefit from the European passport. The definition of investment service under MiFID should be read in combination with the exemptions set by Art. 2.1.

[168] See, in particular Art. 2.1, MiFID. Amongst others, MiFID most notably set exemptions for insurance companies, energy firms, and UCITS and pension funds (Art. 2.1(a)(h)(i)(k)).

The overarching objectives of investor protection, market integrity, and market resilience also operate as high-level principles (informing the legislation and serving as guidelines for its interpretation). For instance, in order to increase investor protection, 'investment advice', (an ancillary service under the ISD), became a core investment service under MiFID, subject to the authorisation of the competent financial authority. This means that even market players providing only this service[169] can compete at European level and need to comply with MiFID.

6.1 The nature of investment services and investors

Nature of investment services. The exchange of financial instruments – and more generally the search for the best allocation of resources – involves a wide array of (financial) services, which typically fall under MiFID, either as 'core investment' or 'ancillary' services. The nature of services sometimes raises economic and regulatory issues, particularly whenever the quality of the service is observable only after its use or is not verifiable at all. The former situation is an example of 'experience' goods, and the latter is a case of 'credence' goods.[170] Investment services, besides those activities that are not offered to third parties (e.g. 'dealing on own account'), are made up of aspects from both experience and credence goods.[171] Most notably, investment services may be affected by:

1) Strong information asymmetries between providers and customers (including limited financial education),
2) High switching costs due to 'sunk' investments (lock-in effects),

---

[169] 'Generic advices' are not included in the definition, see Recital 81, Implementing Directive.

[170] Products and services can be classified in three categories: search goods; experience goods; and credence goods. A search good consists of a product or service for which it is possible to assess the quality before the purchase. Search elements include those attributes of the relationship that are easily detected and understood by customers. An experience good, however, is a product or service for which the buyer can evaluate the quality only after the purchase and its use. Finally, a credence good is a product or service whose value and quality cannot be assessed even after its use, as features cannot be easily compared with other products or services. See Nelson (1970).

[171] For a general discussion of investor protection and competition policy issues in financial services, see Renda & Valiante (2010).

3) Cognitive biases in decision-making and judgment that affect investors and
4) Difficulties for the customer to 'shop around'.

Asymmetric information. Firstly, two particular aspects generate asymmetric information between investment firms and their clients: i) limited financial education and rationality; and ii) private information. The former is related to the type investor. In effect, retail investors have typically less knowledge of investment products and financial markets than professional and institutional ones, who usually own the necessary resources to reduce any informational gap vis-à-vis investment firms and can leverage their contractual power. However, all investors can behave 'irrationally' and increase their informational gap (see below). The latter cause of asymmetric information comes from the investment firm that finally owns private information as a result of its investments for the provision of investment services. For instance, a dealer knows better than its clients how order execution works, precisely because order execution is a core part of its business.

Switching costs. Asymmetric information between providers and customers may spark other market effects, which may include transaction-specific investments (or sunk costs).[172] For instance, for a retail investor, the relationship between the provider and the customer is often based on trust given the overwhelming difference in knowledge and access to information. This situation generates 'sunk' and switching costs, since when a customer changes provider it loses the transaction-specific cost/investment, and faces an additional, equally 'sunk' cost to familiarise with the new provider. This effect is particularly strong for investment products, where the fiduciary relationship with the service provider may be a fundamental transaction-specific asset, in particular for retail investors (see Llewellyn, 1995; next sections). Transaction-specific costs/investments may amount to switching costs, which lock in consumers and ultimately give the investment firm the opportunity to unilaterally increase its prices over its rivals since customers would de facto be locked in. Under these circumstances, competing investment firms would have to offer discounts that offset switching costs in order to attract rivals' customers. For retail

---

[172] Sunk costs are irreversible costs paid once to produce or to consume a specific service or product. They represent a barrier to entry for producers and a barrier to switch for consumers. Sunk costs linked to investment services are usually higher for retail investors, who cannot benefit from scale economies.

investors, in particular, the following costs impede switching providers (Klemperer, 1995; OFT, 2008; Renda & Valiante, 2010):

- *Transaction costs*, e.g. documentation, time, fees, search costs, other information costs, learning costs, etc.;
- *'Exit' costs*, due to, e.g. loyalty programmes, etc.;
- *Uncertainty costs*, since the quality or suitability of a product can only be observable after purchase (experience attributes), or can never be fully observed by the customer (credence attributes) and
- *Psychological costs*, mainly in the case of goods with a high significant credence attributes ('mutual trust'), such as investment advice.

In particular, experience and credence attributes represent a transaction-specific investment for customers that make switching very difficult (so-called *status quo bias*). Retail investors may potentially suffer all the above costs, while wholesale investors typically encounter only transaction costs and an opportunity costs when they switch provider. An example of opportunity cost may be the risk of suffering market impact in order execution, which can ultimately restrain institutional investors from changing provider.

Another aspect that may influence the provision of investment services, for retail investors in particular, are so-called 'cognitive biases'. These are investor behaviours that violate the assumption of 'rationality' and standard economic principles. In particular, investors (Posner, 1998; Jolls et al., 2000):

- Do not necessarily maximise their utility in every circumstance,
- Do not often have stable preferences (e.g. sunk costs and initial allocation of entitlements may dominate in their decisions) and
- Do not have the ability to process or accumulate an optimal amount of the information available in the market.

The violation of rational assumptions lies on three cognitive limits (Jolls et al., 2000): i) bounded rationality, ii) bounded willpower and iii) bounded self-interest.[173]

---

[173] For an overall analysis of potential cognitive biases resulting from these cognitive limits, see Renda & Valiante (2010), pp. 51-55. For instance, the 'overconfidence bias' means that "people tend to overestimate (to be overconfident about) the probability of an outcome if an example of the event has recently occurred (linked to the prospect theory and the precedent behaviour). Therefore, consumers are generally overconfident in their abilities and in their

Bounded rationality (Simon, 1957) refers to limits faced by human beings in terms of accessible information, mental capacity and available time. It should be distinguished from rational ignorance.[174] In addition, individuals are often 'path-dependent' in their choices, especially when they cannot fully appraise the value of something they already possess (Korobkin & Ulen, 2000; Sunstein, 2000; Jolls, 2007). As to bounded willpower, it leads people to act in conflict with their long-term interests, even though they anticipate pervasive effects in so doing (e.g. smokers). Finally, bounded self-interest may push people to care about treating others fairly because they want to be treated in the same way. Agents will act 'nicer' or 'nastier' depending on how the other party treats them. All these cognitive limits also occur with the provision of services not related to investment. However, the experience and credence attributes present in investment services can magnify the effects of cognitive limits on judgment and decision-making processes. As result, MiFID has laid out a regulatory scheme that offers greater protection to final investors with particular attention to retail investors, who suffer more from experience and credence attributes.

Moreover, due to the abovementioned costs, only an insufficient number of 'marginal' consumers is actually able to 'shop around', thereby limiting the flow of information that helps to correct market failures. In effect, by 'shopping around', informed consumers generate a positive externality on uninformed ones (as long as they are able to see them) that may have too little incentive to acquire information (Hynes & Posner 2001).

MiFID Requirements. MiFID brought together all these concerns and introduced a more paternalistic approach to consumer protection. For instance, MiFID intervenes on firm-client relationships by setting obligations such as the good faith clause (Art. 19.1) or 'best execution' duties (Art. 19 and 21, MiFID). In effect, these duties try to palliate two phenomena present in firm-client relationships:

1) A lack of effective monitoring (moral hazard) and
2) A lack of ability to assess the quality of the service (adverse selection).

---

future fortunes. For example, many people invest, believing that they can beat the stock market, or they underestimate the risk that illness or unemployment may cause difficulty in repaying a loan" (p. 54).

[174] It represents the situation in which the investor is not able to or finds it inconvenient to put effort in understanding a clear set of information in a specific amount of time.

The former has broad implications for how services are offered and disclosed to clients. MiFID organisational requirements play a primary role in containing adverse effects by promoting a more effective monitoring and discouraging moral hazard. Adverse selection, in particular, may drive good quality services out of business with consequences for the stability of the market. In this regard, MiFID business conduct rules ensure that investors are aware and able to understand the risks they take and, ideally, evaluate prices against actual product quality.

The introduction of stricter pre-trade and post-trade transparency has also increased the flow of pre-contractual and post-contractual information, which contributes to reduce adverse selection and moral hazard for end investors (besides any test of suitability and appropriateness foreseen by MiFID). It follows that MiFID organisational, conduct of business and transparency rules have been more consistently applied, with positive effects also on market structure and its long-term efficiency.

6.2 Fiduciary duties

Contract incompleteness. A contract between two parties for the provision of a product or service entails a complex web of aspects, which cannot be fully anticipated. Contracts are therefore 'incomplete' by their very own nature, no matter the sophistication or evenness of parties' contractual power.

The degree of completeness of a contract depends mainly on four factors (Hermalin et al., 2007, p. 11):

i) Specification costs
ii) Monitoring costs
iii) Enforcement costs
iv) Need for pre-contractual commitment

Firstly, high specification costs make the drawing up of the 'perfect' contract impossible for several reasons. Most notably, a contract cannot usually cover all potential contingencies in the provision of a good or service, especially when deferred in time, as it is impossible to predict all future events. This universal cost affects every contractual provision of services or goods.

Secondly, costs of monitoring that the transaction has been executed may be comparably prohibitive (or even be not observable or verifiable at all).[175] This situation hinders the possibility of devising contracts effectively.

Thirdly, contracts may not be enforced because costs can be too high in absolute or relative terms (in comparison to the potential benefits). Enforcement is strictly related to monitoring costs. If a party cannot verify the execution of a contract, a competent authority or judge may not be capable of doing so either. In this case, in addition to default rules,[176] the provision of 'experience and credence' goods or services is combined with strong remedies (e.g. punitive damages) and fiduciary duties (general clauses). In particular, when verifiability is low, strong remedies may reduce the agent's pre-contractual commitment to act in its own interest.

Last but not least, in order to enter into a contract, parties need to trust the other party's commitment; otherwise, they may not take on the risk of going into the agreement. This is particularly true in transactions where reputational aspects are crucial to the success of the deal, such as investment advice.

Investment services, as mentioned above, involve an agency relationship with high specification and monitoring costs, due to their experience and credence attributes. Moreover, even though investment services are frequently observable, the scarce ability to verify their execution (low verifiability) often makes enforcement too costly.

This complexity can have differing degrees of intensity, in relation to the type of transaction cost or information asymmetry. For instance, retail investors may feel an investment service is too complex for their level of knowledge and wholesale investors may fear the economic implications of complexity on other aspects of their business. For all these reasons, in addition to greater competition, regulators have pushed for the recognition of fiduciary duties in the provision of investment services. The concept of fiduciary duty originates from the Common Law duty of the agent (e.g.

---

[175] Observability and verifiability are indispensable to define a contractual contingency. However, they may come at high cost, since they include tasks such as investigation, measurement, documentation and monitoring (Hermalin et al., 2007).

[176] Default rules are those rules that apply to a legally binding agreement if not decided by parties otherwise. They are effective in reducing transaction costs – setting the ground for a contractual agreement – and they may encourage parties that enjoy an informational advantage to reveal their type. Default rules have the role to balance the contractual power between structurally strong and weak counterparties in terms of private information. However, default rules need to be carefully drafted as they may increase transaction costs if parties need too often to contract around them because they are or ineffective or too costly.

broker) to be loyal to the principal (e.g. investor). Fiduciary duties are typically coupled with disgorgement, that is, the restitution of any gain obtained by the agent as a result of its actions against the principal's interests (Easterbrook & Fischel, 1993). In this way, legislation has gradually overcome its formalistic approach to the law of contract (the 'sanctity of the contract') based on the fiction of 'arms-length' transactions and equally powerful counterparties. By recognising that parties do not frequently have the same bargaining power, legislation has gradually afforded more protection to the 'weaker' party of the contract. In effect, the party with in theory more contractual power can hardly impose its own contractual conditions today.

Financial regulation has followed the same trend and increased protection for final investors, moving from an original 'duty to read' to a 'duty to disclose', and now to a 'duty to behave'. In Civil Law countries,[177] a preference to deal with fiduciary relationships through bilateral negotiations (contracts) has often given a crucial role to national legislation in dealing with these issues. Therefore, by applying Common Law-based principles such as fiduciary duties, the European legislator has decided to introduce, in a pre-existing legal system mainly based on Civil Law principles, concepts that need the underpinning of strong national and supra-national enforcement mechanisms, which have been conspicuously absent at European level (Pistor & Xu, 2002, pp. 32-33).

More generally, fiduciary duties apply to situations in which there are:
1) Information asymmetries (moral hazard and adverse selection)
2) Transaction costs
3) Cognitive biases and
4) Market frictions (limited competition).

Also the literature on marketing portrays trust, satisfaction and average perceived cost (including switching costs) as key determinants of

---

[177] Civil Law countries are those countries in which law is primarily codified or designed with other written regulations, while the role of the judges is to verify their application with low space for interpretation. By contrast, Common Law countries are those where law is developed through court decisions. However, since the last century these two systems have been getting closer. For instance, a typically common law country such as the US has recently approved an enormous package of financial reforms (Dodd-Frank bill) that will need to be implemented primarily through detailed regulation.

customer loyalty (amongst others, Graf et al., 2008).

Additional cognitive biases may affect retail investors' behaviours and make the provision of investment services even less observable and verifiable, and so de facto even more akin to fiduciary duties. Wholesale investors, however, typically have the contractual power to modify contract terms if they are not devised properly, while for retail investors costs are typically too high. Hence, many fiduciary duties have been formulated differently for retail and professional investors.

The breadth of these duties is very important, though. On the one hand, strict fiduciary duties may have two unintended consequences. They may preclude investors' ability to contract around specific terms; or make pre-contractual commitment too high, generating clients' overreliance in the positive outcome of the transaction. As a consequence, a protective approach would end up damaging precisely those investors the regulation seeks to protect. On the other hand, a loose definition can make enforcement too costly and expose the beneficiary/principal to two types of agents' wrongdoing (Cooter & Freedman, 1991):

i) The fiduciary/agent may misappropriate the principal's asset or some of its value (moral hazard); and
ii) The fiduciary/agent may neglect the management of the asset (negligence or violation of the duty of care).

In the US, the fiduciary duty is recognised in two kinds of situations: when the contract explicitly recognises a fiduciary relationship (e.g. principal-agent); and when specific circumstances surrounding the transaction and the relationship occur. 'Trust', 'confidence' and 'influence' are typically those circumstances that denote the existence of a fiduciary duty (Frankel, 1983, p. 829). In effect, a fiduciary duty should not be considered as a moral belief, but legal ground should be found in the potential sources of failure for the contractual relationship (Easterbrook & Fischel, 1993). A fiduciary relation is a contractual one, characterised by unusually high costs of specification and monitoring.

Due to high specification and monitoring costs, MiFID and more generally EU regulation have gradually recognised fiduciary aspects to the agency relationship between the provider of financial services and its customers (in particular, for retail investors). The use of general clauses in the legal text, such as 'good faith' or 'fairness', has afforded judges much needed flexibility, especially in Civil Law countries,[178] to formally recognise fiduciary duties and to devise them in line with the nature of the counterparty and the relationship. MiFID, in particular, has introduced a general clause that explains the fiduciary duty between providers and clients by asking the provider to act in client's interest (Art. 19.1). However, general clauses should not be seen as vague statements, but have a clear contractual meaning. For instance, the concept of 'fairness' can be seen as a deviation from a benchmark transaction that shifts the balance in favour of the more entitled party (Jolls et al., 2000). There are two general clauses upon which organisational requirements and conduct-of-business rules are designed (see figure below):

1) The general requirement to "act honestly, fairly and professionally in accordance with the best interests of its clients" (Art. 19.1, MiFID); and
2) The general requirement to make sure that "all information, including marketing communications, addressed by the investment firm to clients or potential clients shall be fair, clear and not misleading" (Art. 19.2, MiFID).

The enforcement of fiduciary duties has been typically left to competent authorities through information coming mostly in via trade and transaction reporting, plus other substantial supervisory powers (Art. 50, MiFID) and the possibility to file civil litigations. However, no harmonised system of sanctions is in place so far in Europe. The Commission (2010b) is looking into the possibility of granting further powers of investigation to competent authorities. It is also examining the feasibility of harmonising the regime for remedies, such as sanctions based on the losses generated by the infringement, and not on the disgorgement (restitution of profits).

---

[178] Civil Law countries are those countries were law is primarily codified or designed with written regulation, while the role of the judges is to verify their application with low space for interpretation. By contrast, Common Law countries are those where law takes shape through court decisions. However, since the last century these two systems are getting closer. For instance, a typically common law country as the US has recently approved an enormous package of financial reforms (Dodd-Frank bill) that will need to be implemented primarily through detailed regulation.

Figure 32. General clauses

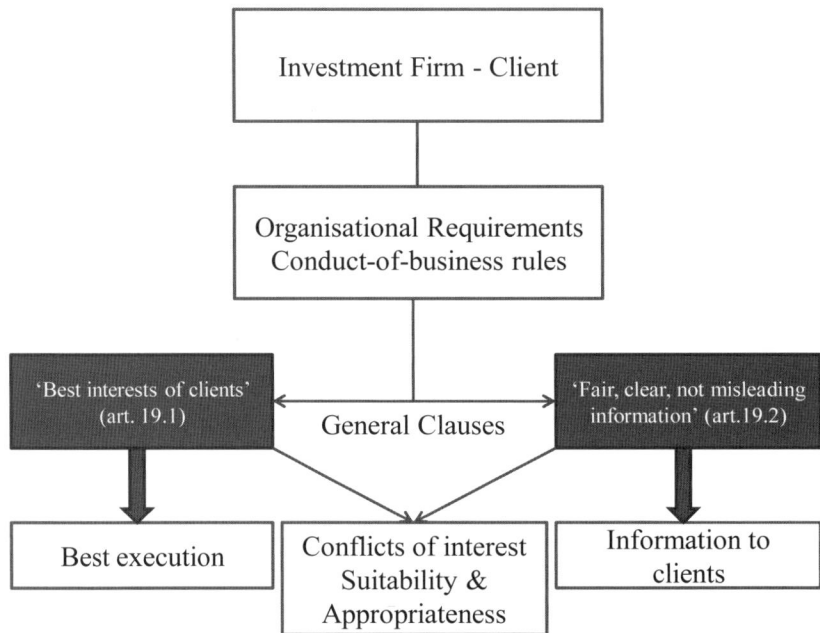

Source: Authors.

Finally, competition between investment firms may improve the quality of the provision of investment services without making it necessary to tighten legislation or monitoring. Competition may generate pre-contractual incentives to behave in the best interest of investors, but with unclear effects on the implementation of rules already in place. On the one hand, in particular, if firms do not act cooperatively, competition may reduce monitoring costs and promote greater compliance with fiduciary duties. On the other hand, however, if firms do cooperate, competition may result in a collusive equilibrium based on a shared 'soft' interpretation of fiduciary duties across firms, if they are not soundly defined.

6.3 Organisational rules

MiFID organisational requirements (ORs) aim at promoting integrity and orderly functioning of financial markets (Recital 5), as well as "integrity, competence and soundness among investment firms and entities that operate regulated markets or MTFs" (Recital 2, Implementing Directive). For instance, ORs improve monitoring and compliance with conflicts of interest rules and prevention of misselling practices by requiring disclosure, recordkeeping and other material obligations. The Directive (Art. 13)[179] sets a wide array of organisational requirements, which are needed in order to gain authorisation but can be slightly aligned with the logic of the firm's relevant markets. This list of requirements has had a major impact on the internal controls of investment firms and must be applied also by UCITS management companies if they perform portfolio management and advisory services.[180] Moreover, ORs apply not only to investment firms but also to official MiFID trading venues (RMs and MTFs, Art. 14, 26, 39 and 43). However, diverse interpretations by member states of the 'proportionate approach' set by MiFID (Art. 13.4) have promoted a fragmented implementation of these requirements across trading venues, de facto setting the scene for different rules being applied to similar activities. The review of MiFID should look at the possibility to finally align material obligations.

Besides a general clause to comply with MiFID rules and procedures (Art. 13.2, MiFID), the Directive set strict requirements to improve internal mechanisms of:

1) Compliance
2) Risk management
3) Order handling
4) Transparency to clients

Compliance. Firstly, the Directive set organisational requirements to ensure the creation of 'adequate policies' and compliance with MiFID rules through:

- A general duty to 'establish adequate policy and procedures' and comply with MiFID rules (Art. 13.2 MiFID),[181]
- The appointment of a compliance officer (objective and independent),[182]
- Obligations for tied agents (Art. 23, MiFID) and
- Recordkeeping (13.6, 25.2, MiFID).[183]

---

[179] Plus Art. 5-25, Implementing Directive and Art. 7-8, Implementing Regulation.
[180] See Casey & Lannoo (2009), pp. 141-143, footnote 3.
[181] Art. 6, Implementing Directive.
[182] Art. 6, Implementing Directive.
[183] Art. 13.6, MiFID; Art. 16, 17, 51, Implementing Directive; and Art. 7-8, Implementing

Most notably, the investment firm is required to appoint a compliance officer that should be able to independently ensure compliance, with enough powers and resources to solicit the firm to correct any policies or procedures that do not comply with MiFID obligations. The Directive also requires firms to keep records of all services and transactions (including transaction reports) taking into account proportionality with regard to the type of business and the range of investment services and activities performed. Investment firms then must retain all required records for a period of 5 years or longer if requested. Records that refer to obligations and rights for the investment firm and its clients shall be retained for a period that is at least equal to the duration of the relationship with the client (Art. 51.1, Impl. Dir.). Records shall be finally stored in data management systems and be easily accessible for future reference by competent authorities (Art. 51.2, Impl. Dir.). CESR (2010c, p.10) has remarked the importance of record keeping obligations in four areas:

i) Reception and transmission of orders
ii) Execution of orders on behalf of the client
iii) Dealing on own account
iv) Portfolio management

For some group of consumers, the investment firm should keep records of the investment advice as well. However, CESR noted that, since investment advice services are usually offered face-to-face, setting recordkeeping obligations would be costly and very difficult to implement. Other ways to improve quality of investment advice should be taken into consideration (see Section 6.3.1).

Risk management. Secondly, ORs define rules concerning the firm's risk management system. In particular, the Directive sets:

- A system of internal controls (e.g. independent internal audit, IT, etc. (Art. 13.4-13.5,),[184]
- The possibility to outsource non-core operational services (Art. 13.5),[185]
- A client order handling system (Art. 22.1 and 22.2)[186] and

---

Regulation.

[184] Art. 5, 7, and 8 Implementing Directive.
[185] Art. 13-14, Implementing Directive.
[186] Art. 47, 48 and 49, Implementing Directive. Art. 31-32, Implementing Regulation.

- The safeguard and administration of clients' financial assets (Art. 13.7, 13.8).[187]

This framework of rules aims at improving internal risk management and ensuring continuity in the provision of investment services. Furthermore, MiFID attempts to improve the control of counterparty risk, as well as economic, financial and operational risks. In particular, the Directive forbids excessive risk-taking actions by using clients' assets to deal on own account if the client has not explicitly expressed his/her consent. These rules have not prevented the recent financial crisis, but they presumably played a crucial role in limiting the negative effects of cases in which the broker/dealer also offered custodian services and made use of clients' assets to deal on own account or did not segregate assets with third parties, putting additional credit risk on assets that should have been protected from bankruptcy procedures (e.g. the Lehman Brothers case). However, asset segregation with third parties is currently foreseen by MiFID only for clients that are not credit institutions. Clients can eventually oppose the decision to segregate the assets but only with regard to a specific entity, however.

In addition, MiFID (Recital 27) exempts investment firms from applying client asset protection rules when full ownership of funds and financial instruments has been transferred to cover any client obligation. The Commission is looking into this matter and may decide to remove this possibility (at least for retail clients' assets), which was a main issue in a recent bankruptcy procedure (Lehman Brothers; EU COM, 2010b, p. 70).[188] Investment firms would also be required to improve disclosure on asset segregation and diversify the placement of client funds using different third parties.

Transparency to clients. Finally, MiFID has set organisational requirements, which amounts to a new discipline for information disclosure to clients, with the particular role of containing conflicts of interest.

More specifically, the Directive defines:

---

[187] Art. 19, 20, 42, 43, 48, and 49, Implementing Directive.

[188] The Commission proposes to give an option to member states to exclude title transfer collateral arrangements in case of professional clients and eligible counterparties.

- Rules on personal transactions,[189]
- Conflict of interests rules and inducements disclosure (Art. 13.3, 18.1, and 18.2)[190] and
- Information to clients rules (Art. 19.2, 19.3 and 19.8).[191]

Disclosure to clients should protect clients' interests and information should be "fair, clear and not misleading" (Art. 19.2). Most notably, MiFID organisational requirements introduced new rules to prevent investment firms from acting in conflict with their clients' interests by identifying, managing and, if they cannot be eliminated, disclosing these conflicts to prospective clients before approaching investors to offer a transaction. In order to comply with the general clause on "acting honestly, fairly and professionally in accordance with the best interest of a client" (Art. 19.1), the investment firm should disclose fees, commissions and non-monetary benefits (inducements) that are neither directly generated by the investment service provided to clients nor do they help to increase the quality of the service (Recital 39, Impl. Dir.). This rule aims at limiting undue influence by interest groups on the provision of services to clients. Furthermore, the legal text should be consistent with the forthcoming legislative proposal on Packaged Retail Investment Products (PRIPs),[192] which will define the terms of pre-contractual information. The Commission also proposed to increase the level of information to be disclosed to clients when dealing with complex financial instruments (EU COM 2010b, p. 58). Information about risks/gains ex ante and ongoing quarterly reports on the instruments and their underlying should be disclosed to clients.

New proposals. The European Commission (2010b) is reviewing some of the organisational requirements discussed above. In particular, concerning inducements, it is currently foreseen that if the amount of inducements cannot be clearly determined, the method of calculation should be disclosed (Art. 26 (b)(i), Impl. Dir.; CESR, 2010i). As MiFID does not define the requirements to be disclosed in the form of a 'methodology', in line with the Commission's view, this has created difficulties to quantify or provide a tool to quantify the level of inducements. In this respect, the

---

[189] Art. 11-12, Implementing Directive.
[190] Art. 13.3 and Art. 18, MiFID; and Art. 12, 21, 22, 23, and 26 Implementing Directive.
[191] Art. 24 and 27, Implementing Directive.
[192] European Commission Communication, *COM(2009) 204 final.*

Commission has proposed to introduce:
1) *Ex-post* reporting obligations,
2) More details and templates for disclosure to clients,
3) Other requirements to be assessed by supervisors to define if inducements enhance the quality of the service,
4) A ban on inducements provided by a third party in case of portfolio management services and
5) A ban on inducements provided by a third party for intermediary providing independent advice.

Inducements may not only distort incentives to provide an investment service in the best interest of clients, but they may also be used to give compensation to brokers that may potentially distort incentives.

The Commission (2010b, p. 65) also proposes to clarify and modify rules on activities concerning "dealing on own account".[193] Most importantly, orders executed using matched principal (so-called 'back to back' transactions[194]) would be considered as 'dealing on own account', but they would not fall under the Capital Adequacy Directive (Dir. 2006/49/EC). They would not fall either under MiFID, unless the transaction was tagged as 'market-making' or was executed outside organised MiFID venues "on an organised, frequent and systematic basis" (Art. 2.1(d)).

Moreover, the Commission (2010b, pp. 66-72) proposes to strengthen authorisation and organisational requirements in general. In particular, members of the board of directors would pass a 'fit and proper' test, which would evaluate their time commitment and other aspects relevant for the exercise of their functions. The Commission also proposes to promote the inclusion in the board of non-executive directors with supervisory functions.

---

[193] "'Dealing on own account' means trading against proprietary capital resulting in the conclusion of transactions in one or more financial instruments", Art. 4.1(6), MiFID.

[194] Back-to-back transactions consist of a chain of securities transactions among multiple counterparties (typically investment firms) involving the purchase and sale of a security, for settlement on a single date. It may refer, for instance, to the case in which the investment firm C buys a security from investment firm A and, at the same time, it sells the same security to investor B during the same day. These are transactions perfectly matched with very limited risk for the investment firm C.

Sales policies. Additional requirements would need to be taken into consideration for the launch of products, operations and services. The legal text would be modified (EU COM, 2010b, p. 68) to include these requirements, which would need to be applied before the financial instrument is offered to clients (sale policy). In particular, investment firms should:

i) Run a 'compatibility test' with clients' needs.
ii) Strengthen duties of compliance with MiFID rules and risk management of the product.
iii) Subject products to stress test as 'appropriate' (Art. 5, Impl. Dir.) and periodically review distribution and performance of products and services.
iv) Ensure that staff receive appropriate training for new products.
v) Ensure that the board has more effective control on these aspects.

In this way, MiFID introduced a further layer of organisational requirements to be applied before approaching the client. Sales policies are generally designed to increase the guarantee and the protection of investors, rather than to improve pre-sale services or increase the possibility of investors to 'shop around'. In this sense, increasing the protection of investors does not necessarily mean improving their awareness of the risk they take.

Telephone recording. In addition, the proposal entails the removal of member states' discretion upon the use of recording for communications between the investment firm and the client. Recording would become mandatory while still preserving individuals' privacy and respecting the rules on data protection. Member states may extend the obligation to services other than "the receipt and transmission of orders and execution of orders and transactions concluded when dealing on own account in all financial instruments" (e.g. portfolio management; EU COM, p. 75). Records would be stored for at least 3 years. This type of organisational requirement would be a strong deterrent against market abuses and promote greater compliance with MiFID rules, but it would come at a cost for market participants and competent authorities. (CESR, 2010c). However, it would promote greater enforcement across Europe, in particular if supervisory arrangements between authorities on their use are effectively harmonised.

> **Conclusion # 16**
>
> *Organisational requirements play a crucial role in ensuring business continuity, market integrity and investor protection. A proper implementation of the Directive should be ensured by harmonising ORs and supervisory practices across Europe and removing ambiguities in the legal text. Moreover, strengthening consistency with other upcoming regulations would avoid inefficiencies and promote a uniform regime of investor protection and market integrity within Europe, which would increase legal certainty and the attractiveness of investment services.*

6.3.1 Investment advice: Striking the right balance

The 'advice'. Investment advice is topic subject to heated debate in Europe, in particular after the scandals that shook financial markets a few years ago (e.g. Parmalat) and more recently as a result of the financial crisis, both of which have dramatically impaired investors' confidence. The nature of the investment advice service lies on a trust-based and usually long-term relationship, which emerges from a situation of strong informational asymmetry between the provider and the client (mostly retail investors). This relationship has wider implications and it usually qualifies as a transaction-specific investment (TSI), as illustrated in the seminal contribution by Williamson (1975). In effect, customers face 'sunk' investments/costs that typically deter them from switching providers (changing provider frequently means losing the previous TSI and facing an additional one in order to become familiar with the new provider).

The information and behavioural biases involved can lead to rather high 'perceived' switching costs, difficulties in evaluating alternatives, and consequently low price transparency and customer mobility.[195] This leads customers to rely on proxies to establish the value of a given investment option – the proxy, in this case, being the advice received by their service provider. For this reason, so-called 'relationship banking' is brought into the sphere of consumer protection. In more detail, the provider-customer

---

[195] In this respect, the retail financial services sector can be said to differ noticeably from other economic sectors. For example, in the telecommunications or energy sectors consumers are less likely to suffer from an information asymmetry, provided that they have visibility of the quality of service and relative price of the offer. At the same time, the elements of "trust", "transaction specific investments" and "bounded rationality" are much less important in these fields. Finally, especially in the telecommunications sector, consumers are more likely to shop around for better offers.

relationship can be described by two dimensions: i) the 'depth' of the relationship, stemming from the 'off-contract' relationship (typical in some brokerage services), and ii) its thickness, defined as the information conveyed to the bank through the multiple financial contracts and services. In particular, the thickness of the provider-customer relationship offers customers a range of potential advantages, but may also give the informed provider the opportunity to capture rents by engaging in hold-up behaviour and false representation of both market and contractual conditions. In many cases, this relationship is strengthened by personal feelings with the person who represents the provider.[196]

Independence. Investment advice is usually provided by investment firms that also offer other investment services. This situation, next to the abovementioned aspects, highlight the importance of proper 'advice' for the efficient allocation of capitals, which needs to overcome the risk of conflicts of interest. The investors' quest for 'independent advice' has drawn attention to improving the quality of this service. Divergent views emerge around the specific way investment advice could be boosted to help restore investors' confidence. On the one hand, those who believe that greater disclosure and stricter organisational requirements can enhance the quality and attractiveness of investment advice. In particular, in a report sponsored by EFAMA (2010), asset managers suggested implementing, amongst the others, four actions at point of sale:

1) Disclosure of the nature of the distributors' services,
2) Full and detailed disclosure of all cost items and the principles of remuneration arrangements,
3) Introduction of a standardised advisor certificate and
4) Granting investors a right of withdrawal.

Disclosure should include the origin of the income of the adviser, whether it comes only from the fees charged for the advice or depends on the products sold and in which way. This side of the market challenges the idea that imposing an independent charging structure, with no alternatives, will increase the costs of advice and ultimately discourage investors from using, with strong direct and indirect repercussions on the efficient allocation of resources in the market. All information should be disclosed to investors before signing the contract, in order to allow them to 'shop

---

[196] For a more comprehensive analysis of the interaction between switching costs and cognitive biases, see Renda & Valiante (2010).

around'. Disclosure would increase investors' confidence in the advice service, thereby promoting its use. Moreover, the advice service needs to meet the suitability test in MIFID (see next section), which helps to improve its quality and design the service in the clients' best interest.

In the area of pre-contractual information changes in MiFID will need to be reconciled with other regulatory initiatives at European level (such as PRIPs, IMD review, and Prospectus Directive).

On the other hand, some market participants (in particular, retail investors) claim that – besides the importance of improving disclosure and the role of the suitability test – there should be a thorough review of the incentives which impede advice to be 'independent'. In particular, they argue that, in order to be considered 'independent', the investment advice should be based on an 'independent' system of remuneration, by receiving only fees for the provision of the service. No commission should be set by product providers (see box below). The strict independence of advisers could be achieved by severing the links between fees and products. However, this severance should be handled with care by allowing alternative forms of advice to be ultimately offered to clients.

Box 15. A new regime for investment advice: the FSA's proposal

The UK Financial Services Authority (FSA, 2010a) proposed the introduction of a new system of 'adviser charging' for retail investment products. If investment advice is to be disclosed as 'independent', it would need to have its own charges either upfront or taken from the investment returns. Furthermore, charges should not be supplemented with other commissions given by product providers, even in form of non-monetary benefits (inducements). The purpose is to ensure the independence of advice for retail clients and avoid the rules being circumvented through the use of 'soft' commissions. Fees should be contracted and fully disclosed upfront (even potentially 'ongoing charges')[197]. In addition, only advisers who provide a fair and independent analysis on a wide range of retail investment products would be considered 'independent' under the FSA proposal. The adviser would have to demonstrate that he/she conducted a fair and independent analysis of the 'relevant market' for investment products. The 'relevant market' would include all retail investment products that are capable of meeting investors' needs. Since the range of products is potentially very wide, it would be preferable to elaborate this definition in order to fully implement it. Investment advice that does

---

[197] For instance, the periodic review of the performance (FSA, 2010a, p. 27).

> not meet these requirements would be named 'restricted', or 'non-independent'. This service will anyway need to meet the suitability test under MiFID.
>
> This new compensation scheme will impact consumer access to advice, possibly by both reducing the number of advisers and increasing its cost. The proposal, however, aims at enhancing "the market's reputation and build consumer confidence, improving sustainability of the sector in the longer term" (FSA, 2010a, p. 18). Anyway, the proposal would not prohibit the provision of 'restricted' investment advice but only force its disclosure. The authority also commissioned an impact study, which concluded that the introduction of this charging system could result in "an 11% reduction in the number of advisers; a 9% reduction in total revenues across all advisers, and an 11% reduction in the number of clients advised, assuming that other firms did not expand and there were no new entrants" (Oxera, 2010). New entrants would require high initial investments to build sufficient reputational capital. This situation may create high barriers to entry the market of advice services. However, it carries high potential benefits in terms of more efficient allocation of resources and reduced opportunity costs by avoiding investors being redirected towards more expensive investment products against their interest. However, both costs and benefits are difficult to quantify, so the overall effect is unclear.

New proposals. The Commission (2010b, p. 56) has also proposed a number of measures to improve investment advice:

1) Enhancing disclosure to clients by stating whether the service is based on an 'independent and fair' analysis;

2) Defining 'independent and fair' analysis as one that considers a wide range of investment products and is carried by a firm that does not accept any payments or benefits from product providers;

3) Increasing reporting to clients about performance and market value of the financial instruments recommended, and to keep updated information about the client; and

4) Clarifying, when applicable, if the investment advice is also provided online.

This proposal does not clarify whether investment advice that does not comply with the definition of 'independent and fair' advice would remain available to investors. The UK proposal from the FSA does allow so-called 'restricted' advice, that is, advice under conflicts of interest, to be offered as an alternative to independent advice. The proposal from the Commission does not clarify whether the fee can be embedded in the costs of the investment product and if both remuneration systems can coexist. In addition, no proposals have been formulated where the adviser is a company owned by a group that also offers the sale of other investment products. In this case, the conflict of interest may also be high, since – even though the investment firm does not receive any monetary or non-monetary benefit for the advice – the whole group benefits from the activity of the adviser.

> **Conclusion # 17**
>
> *Some market participants claim that – besides the importance of improving disclosure and the role of the suitability test – there should be a thorough review of the mechanisms of incentives, which prevent advice from being 'independent'. In particular, they argue that to be considered 'independent', investment advice should be based on an 'independent' system of remuneration, by receiving only fees from the clients. No commission should be set by product providers. Other market participants argue that obliging investors to pay for the advice would increase the access costs to these services and dramatically reduce the use of advisory services, with potential long-term costs for end investors. They suggest keeping the possibility to remunerate distribution through commissions, but with the requirement to improve disclosure on the nature of the services, in particular disclosing if the advisor is solely remunerated by the client or whether he is remunerated by a product provider. Full disclosure of all costs items and remuneration arrangements should be made before signing the contract. This would improve the ability of investors to choose the service that best suits their own interest. In the area of pre-contractual information, changes in MiFID will need to be reconciled with other regulatory initiatives at European level (such as PRIPs, IMD review, and Prospectus Directive).*

6.4 Conduct of business rules

The final piece of the investor protection puzzle under MiFID is a set of rules to regulate the conduct-of-business (CoB). CoB rules provide some contractual definitions for the set of fiduciary duties that apply in a transaction in investment services.

Accordingly, the Directive recognises a fiduciary obligation between clients and service providers through its general clauses and specific CoB rules, such as:

i) Best execution (Art. 19.1 and 21);[198]
ii) Conflicts of interest rules (Art. 13.3 and 18);[199]

---

[198] Art. 44-46, Impl. Dir.
[199] Art. 21-25, Impl. Dir.

iii) Suitability and appropriateness tests (so-called 'know-your-customer rules'; Art. 19.4 and 19.5)[200] and
iv) Other relevant requirements (in particular, information to clients,[201] client agreements,[202] orders handling,[203] and marketing rules).[204]

In addition, MiFID rules specify exemptions for eligible counterparties (Art. 24) and define client classification (see Section 6.4.2).[205] The constant growth in the last decades of asset under management and the widespread provision of investment services and products have brought regulators to set the rules of the game on how investment services are actually provided to end users. In effect, as portfolios become more tailored to the needs of investors and to more volatile market trends, the exposure to complex financial products may increase. Against this background, CoB rules are becoming more and more important. In addition, by regulating CoB, MiFID has managed to harmonise an important part of investor protection in Europe. The Commission is also looking at the extension of CoB rules to firms exempted by MiFID ex Art. 3 (EU COM, 2010b, p. 52).

6.4.1 Conflicts of interests under MiFID

Definition. Conflicts of interest (CoIs) arise where the interests of a market intermediary are "inconsistent with, or diverge from, those of its clients, investors, or others" (IOSCO, 2007, p. 6). In this respect, it is in the nature of the business of an intermediary to face CoIs since it needs to exercise discretion in the provision of investment services and has to deal with numerous kinds of clients. These aspects make CoIs ubiquitous in financial services.

In effect, CoIs need to be seen as 'part of the deal', inherent to the provision of investment services, since they cannot be suppressed completely, but regulators can work to minimise both the conflicts themselves and their negative effects. This regulatory task is performed by analysing whether CoIs are exploited and are imposing further agency

---

[200] Art. 35-37, Impl. Dir.
[201] Art. 19.8, MiFID, and Art. 40-43 Impl. Dir.
[202] Art. 19.7, MiFID, art 14.3 and 39 Impl. Dir.
[203] Art. 22, MiFID and Art. 47-49 Impl. Dir.
[204] Art. 19.2, MiFID, Art. 24 and 27, Impl. Dir.
[205] See also Art. 28 and 50 Impl. Dir.

costs (Walter, 2006). Divergence of interests in an agency relationship may be driven by two factors: i) information asymmetry and ii) transaction costs. In addition, these two elements depend heavily on market frictions, and in particular on the level of competition between market players and their reputational capital. Notably, reputational risk in financial services plays an important role, since its uncertainty and unpredictability may drastically reduce expected revenues and put pressure on the management to commit to the service provided. However, reputational capital is difficult to measure and may not represent an asset for those managers who do not commit to a long-term relationship with the investment firm.

There are three types of conflict (IOSCO, 2010d):
1) Firm/client
2) Client/client and
3) Infra-group conflicts.

The first concerns a direct conflict between the provider and the client. For instance, the broker may favour its own proprietary desk at the client's expense. The 'client/client' conflict refers, for example, to an intermediary that favours a group of institutional investors over its retail clients. The third is the activity of an international dealer group that favours one of the group's investment firms in one member state to the detriment of a firm of the group in another member state. These conflicts are more difficult to detect since there are exogenous variables, such as legal and fiscal cross-border implications, which can severely raise the costs of monitoring and detecting the potential wrongdoing. At retail level, these conflicts are even stronger since information asymmetry and transaction costs are much higher. Controls should therefore be devised according to the nature of the counterparty.

MiFID has designed a system of internal controls to prevent, identify, manage and eventually disclose CoIs (Art. 18), in line with the general clause to act in clients' best interests (Art. 19.1). With this sound statement, the Directive attempts to secure two important objectives: consumer protection and market integrity. In particular, the Directive designed a system of organisational (disclosure) and CoB requirements, which aim to prevent, manage, identify and disclose CoIs in sensitive areas, such as brokerage and/or proprietary trading, securities offerings, advice, and asset management services (Recital 26, Impl. Dir.).

Controls over CoIs can be essentially either internal or external. Internal controls may consist of (IOSCO, 2007; 2010d):

- An internal committee to check conflicts and the functioning of internal controls,
- CoIs policies (to design control tools and compliance mechanisms, even infra-group, Art. 22, Impl. Dir.),
- Clear guidance to refrain from acting in case of conflict,
- Information barriers and restrictions (e.g. Chinese walls; Art. 22.3(a), Impl. Dir.) and
- Disclosure to clients (*caveat emptor*; Arts. 18-19).

Besides disclosure requirements, internal measures are designed to work primarily ex ante as active and passive organisational arrangements. Moreover, once the conflict has been identified but cannot be eliminated, it should be disclosed in line with the principle of *caveat emptor*, which foresees that the client must be informed about the CoI but still bears the ultimate responsibility. In this regard, disclosure is effective if it represents a sufficient warning, which prevents the client from pursuing the transaction in some cases. Ineffective disclosure can be counterproductive and can induce self-interested agents to behave more aggressively (protected by the disclosure requirements). In addition, if disclosure is not clear enough (e.g. examples), investors may experience a cognitive bias and ultimately increase their trust in the intermediary (Enriques, 2006).

MiFID leaves some flexibility to member states to design their own rules to control CoIs at organisational level (Art. 22.3, Impl. Dir.). This provision aims to ensure that rules and procedures are designed in line with the specificities of the country where CoIs emerge. However, this flexibility has boundaries set by MiFID Level 1 (Art. 31), which do not allow member states to draw up requirements additional to those defined by the Directive. On the one hand, too much flexibility could unleash a race-to-the-bottom among member states to attract more business and capital. On the other hand, a rigid set of rules would not allow member states to design the factual rules and procedures to fight conflicts of interest in line with the social, cultural, legal and economic context of the country. It is unquestionable that there are countries in which CoIs are met with a higher level of tolerance, which calls for stronger controls and sanctions. Under sound and effective organisational arrangements, supervisors would be able to bring legal suits on behalf of clients, especially where the clients are retail investors who are deterred by the costs of litigation. Currently, however, the system of sanctions across member states is highly fragmented. This situation may create space for supervisory arbitrages in favour of countries applying low administrative fines.

Finally, external controls may also help to limit the side effects of CoIs. In particular, regulation in related areas, civil litigations, supervisory powers and a highly competitive environment can increase the level of prevention, identification, and management of CoIs. In effect, the way CoIs manifest themselves may differ depending on the selling practices involved. For instance, 'steering' practices are frequently used in services that offer advice on investment products, whenever the portfolio of options presented to the client includes the advisers' own products. 'Steering' consists of stressing to the investor the advantage of subscribing to a more costly product because of the re-edit this generates for the advisor, which is not clearly disclosed to the client. Sometimes this amounts to an intentional misjudgement of the individual's risk by the financial intermediary to extract a rent in a specific period, by imposing specific requirements or additional fees. Other examples of CoIs arise with the provision of corporate finance services, such as pricing the value of a company that is also a borrower from the same intermediary. This situation may induce the intermediary to overprice the value of the company to be able to raise enough money in a future security offering (e.g. IPO).

New proposals. As mentioned above, the Commission (2010b) is looking at the possibility of harmonising and strengthening the current regime of sanction, if there is a violation of MiFID rules, as well as introducing the principle of civil liability for investment services providers in order to level investor protection across the EU. Managing conflicts and structuring incentives for the distribution of financial products are major concerns for the definition of new implementing measures for CoIs.

Conclusion # 18

MiFID rules on conflicts of interest represent a first step in the introduction of a common approach across Europe for the prevention, identification, management, and disclosure of such conflicts. Further initiatives to strengthen the current regime and align supervisory practices would enhance the treatment of these conflicts and benefit financial markets. A harmonised set of sanctions, however, should be combined with flexibility for member states to adapt rules and procedures in line with their national contexts, in order to ultimately guarantee the goal of a sound and safe environment of protection for investors.

6.4.2 Client categorisation

To complement the recognition of fiduciary duties, MiFID introduced a regime of client and product classification through which it assigns different levels of protection to clients. According to MiFID, the level of protection offered by CoB requirements should be related to the clients' classification. The Directive, therefore, defines two main categories of clients:

i) Retail (Art. 4.1 (12)) and
ii) Professional (annex II, Sec. 1, MiFID).

Retail. All investors that are not classified as 'professional' fall under the 'retail' category (definition by exclusion) and enjoy the highest level of protection afforded by MiFID, typically through the application of all ORs and CoB rules. However, they may ask to be treated as 'professional', if they pass two tests: a basic test (which assesses the expertise, experience and knowledge of the client); and a specific test (which requires the investor to meet two out of three 'wealth-related' thresholds, as defined by Annex II, Section 1, MiFID).

Professional investors are those who have the expertise and are able to make their own investment decisions. To them, a 'softer' regime applies that takes into account their more sophisticated nature, e.g.: they only receive client information on request. MiFID 'rules' are the same overall for both retail and professional investors, but are tailored to the nature and needs of each group of investors. Professional investors are, amongst those listed in Annex II, Section 1.1 MiFID, investment firms, credit institutions or insurance companies. They can ask to be treated as retail clients but the other party has to agree. They may also request to become an eligible counterparty.

Eligible counterparties. The Directive, in effect, introduced a third 'special' category, called 'eligible counterparties' (ECP; Art. 24).[206] This group of entities includes the most sophisticated clients, such as investment funds – either alternative investment funds (AIFs) or UCITS. Only few CoB rules and ORs apply to them, such as client agreement rules (Art. 18) and order handling rules (if acting as broker; Art. 19.8). Professional investors may request to be treated as ECPs if their member state has decided to implement this possibility. These investors need to meet a different test

---

[206] ECPs are "investment firms, credit institutions, insurance companies, UCITS and their management companies, pension funds and their management companies, other financial institutions authorised or regulated under Community legislation or the national law of a member state, undertakings exempted from the application of this Directive under Article 2.1(k) and (l), national governments and their corresponding offices including public bodies that deal with public debt, central banks and supranational organisations.", Art. 24, MiFID.

from the one adopted for retail investors to be considered professional. Professional investors must meet two out of these three criteria (Annex II, Section 1.2):

1) Balance sheet of more than €20 million,
2) Net turnover of more than €40 million and
3) Own funds of more than €2 million.

The 'light touch' regime applies to ECPs when they offer services such as execution of orders; dealing on own account; reception and transmission of orders; or any related ancillary service.

Client classification should be defined before providing the service and should be included in the contract or anyway stated in writing. Retail investors cannot be classified as 'ECPs', while financial institutions (including ECPs) can be classified on request as 'non-professional' (retail; Art. 24.2, MiFID). All other combined classifications are possible. For instance, the management company of an investment fund may ask a dealer, executing an order on its behalf, to provide best execution following 'retail' instead of the 'professional' standards, since the fund mainly collects investments from retail investors. The firm/dealer also needs to agree to this request and if it so does, it would have to apply the relevant retail or professional tests when offering services to such eligible counterparties. Some segments of the market suggest that portfolio managers should be entitled to require reclassification as 'retail' clients, since there is a mismatch in their rights and obligations. Portfolio managers are eligible counterparties under MiFID but they manage money on behalf of professional and retail clients, and they have the obligation to act in the best interest of their clients when placing orders for execution. Others, however, consider this request to be inappropriate because it may also be used for activities unrelated to retail clients, and most notably because this would no longer justify that portfolio managers gain directly (through commission on profits) from rules that should go directly to serving retail clients. In effect, their role goes beyond the execution on behalf of investors.

New proposals. It is a commonly held view that the client categorisation regime should not be radically changed (CESR, 2010c; EU COM, 2010b). Current proposals, however, concern (EU COM, 2010b): the possibility to extend the general clause of Art. 19.1 to ECPs; the limitation of the ECP regime only to non-complex products and the exclusion of non-financial institutions from the ECP regime; the abolishment of the presumption that professional investors have the necessary expertise and knowledge; and the exclusion of municipalities[207] from being classified as ECP or professional per se. In particular, abolishing the presumption of expertise and knowledge for professional investors would require investment firms to treat them as retail clients. This situation, on the one hand, increases the general level of protection in the market, but it boosts overall costs of dealing with clients, on the other. To reduce the imbalance of this trade-off towards costs, an opportunity to opt out of the protection for retail clients should be left available to be unilaterally exercised at any time for those who consider themselves to be 'professional' investors. However, there is also a bias that comes into play. A homogeneous application of retail investors' protection rules may need the implementation of sophisticated and burdensome protection tests, which may be perceived as high sunk costs for investors to comply with standard procedures (such as complex and long questionnaires). They may ultimately decide to opt out to avoid those time-consuming obligations. Abolishing such distinctions may therefore generate unclear effects on the provision of investment services.

> **Conclusion # 19**
>
> *Although the crisis showed that some of the eligible counterparties (ECPs) were not able to understand risk 'properly', the client categorisation regime should not be subject to a major overhaul. Since portfolio managers are eligible counterparties under MiFID but manage money on behalf of professional and retail clients and have the obligation to act in the best interest, some market participants suggest that portfolio managers should be entitled to unilaterally require the reclassification as 'retail' clients. Others, however, advocate the inappropriateness of this request since their role is more than execution on behalf of investors, but they would directly gain (commissions on profits) from rules that should theoretically only benefit retail investors.*

6.4.3 Suitability and appropriateness tests

"The duty of suitability rejects the prevailing paradigm of *caveat emptor* and forces providers to internalise the harm that they cause when they exploit information asymmetries to the detriment of customers." (Engel & McCoy, 2002, p. 1334).

The fiduciary relationship between the provider of investment services and the client implies an obligation to act in the best interests of the latter (Art. 19.1). In accordance with this general clause, MiFID CoB rules

---

[207] CESR (2010c) referred instead to 'local authorities'.

include a duty to make an adequate investigation of investors' suitability[208] through a specific suitability test ('know your customer' obligation)[209] and an appropriateness test ('know the security'),[210] to ensure that the investor has a professional knowledge of the risk involved in the service provided (Hazen, 2006).

The suitability and appropriateness tests are respectively articulated in Articles 19.4 and 19.5. Investment firms must acquire three types of information about their clients (or potential clients), to be able to decide if the service is 'suitable' for them:

1) Knowledge and expertise
2) Financial situation and
3) Investment objectives.

The 'suitability test' applies to discretionary portfolio management and advisory services. In other words, the 'suitability test' applies when the service offered includes an element of recommendation or discretion. Since the concept of suitability is fairly abstract, in practice there is a need to translate it into a meaningful service for clients. For professionals, these requirements apply less stringently since the provider can presume that the investor has enough knowledge and expertise and, particularly for advice, that the investor is able to sustain any financial risk (Art. 35.2, 36, Impl. Dir.). Implementing legislation may need to further specify several aspects of the suitability test, which is already described more extensively than the 'appropriateness test' in the Implementing Directive. Simple risk profiles may not be enough, so firms may need to look at the cultural and behavioural attitudes of their clients, as well as at other risk diversification measures (e.g. geographical aspects). There is a lot of subjectivity/hindsight in every transactions involving investment services

---

[208] The suitability rule was originally defined in USA as an antifraud device (violation of the Rule 10b-5 under section 10(b) SEC Act 1934, 17 C.F.R. § 240.10b-5, 2001). See *Clark v. John Lamula Investors, Inc.*, 583 F.2d 594 (2d Cir. 1978). In the EU, instead, the suitability rule was created as a rule to protect investors' confidence and to foster market integrity; see Art. 19.4, MiFID and Art. 35-37, Impl. Dir.; Moloney (2008).

[209] US Courts consider "unsuitable" an investment that is incompatible with the investor's objectives and if the broker recommended it, even though she knew or reasonably believed that the investment was inappropriate. See *Kreenan v. D.H. Blair & Co.*, 838 F. Supp. 82, 87 (S.D.N.Y. 1993).

[210] See *Alton Box Bd. Co. v. Goldman, Sachs & Co.*, 560 F.2d 916, 922 (8th Cir. 1977).

that may push people to give less consideration to aspects related to the performance (through risk profile assessment) than it was originally thought. Hitherto, assessing other aspects than risk profiles would improve the reliability of the suitability test. It is also worth noting that the implementation of suitability requirements among member states may have raised barriers to market products in some countries. It would be worthwhile to explore the consequences of a fragmented implementation.

Benefits and costs. The introduction into the regulation of very specific requirements to assess risk profile and suitability may become a 'mythical search' for a risk-free solution for consumers. The last pioneers who left for this search never returned. Rather than focusing only on the appropriate level of risk for investors, trying to mimic investors' choice, a more workable alternative would be to make sure investors are fairly 'informed' about the risks they decide to incur, which is one of the original objectives of MiFID. Responsibility should ultimately fall on investors. However, a loose definition of suitability that shifts the whole burden onto investors is not desirable either. Above all, service providers need to assist investors in their decisional process. Notably, an array of aspects (behavioural and financial) should be considered in a suitability test. Most of all, firms should look at the risk attitude and the decision style of consumers when they create a personalised investment portfolio. Only the combination of these aspects will allow a meaningful rating process of products and clients, thereby leading firms to provide a more suitable service. Finally, supervisors should make sure that the implementation of suitability requirements is uniform since differences in national implementation can create costly barriers to the cross-border provision of services, as well as important fractures in the level of protection for end investors. The suitability and appropriateness tests are among the main pillars of the CoB rules introduced by MiFID, and are meant to strengthen the protection of investors and the quality of the services provided to them. This protection is particularly relevant where firms are providing cross-border services through an EU passport. However, the roll-out of the infrastructure to perform these two tests has required uniform implementation and has come at a significant cost. One-off costs to upgrade systems and update clients' information are among the most important, next to the costs of assessing the compliance of services and products with the MiFID framework (FSA, 2006b, p. 18).

> **Conclusion # 20**
>
> *The suitability test is a crucial aspect of the provision of investment advice and portfolio management services. Views diverge slightly on how to assess the knowledge, financial situation and objectives of investors, and in particular, on how deeply the suitability test should look into investors' habits and their willingness to undertake risk. Some members regret the lack of harmonisation in the implementation of suitability requirements for discretionary portfolio management. These members would welcome action by ESMA to improve legal certainty and reduce barriers to market investment products across the EU. However, other members do not think any intervention is needed in this regard and are satisfied with the current level of harmonisation.*

The 'appropriateness test' applies for non-advised services, such as reception and transmission of orders.[211] Whenever the firms realise that according to the information provided the product or service offered is not appropriate for the client, the firm shall warn the client. Such warnings could be provided in a standard format. The 'appropriateness test' applies when the client does not rely on the firms' recommendation or advice.[212] The amount of information the investment firm needs from the client concerns the client's knowledge and experience in the investment field relevant to the service offered (Art. 19.5) and this information depends on the complexity and risk of the product. As mentioned above, the investment firm can assume that professional clients have enough knowledge and experience to understand risks. Besides, the information about clients that needs to be collected refers to (Art. 37, Impl. Dir.):

1) The types of service, transaction and financial instrument;
2) The nature, volume, and frequency of the client's transactions and
3) The profession and level of education.

For non-complex financial instruments, clients can opt out of these safeguards (appropriateness test), asking for an 'execution-only' service. 'Non-complex instruments' (Art. 38, Impl. Dir.), currently under MiFID, are:

1) Shares admitted to trading on RMs,
2) Money market instruments,
3) Bonds and other securitised debt (with no embedded derivative),
4) UCITS and

---

[211] See Casey & Lannoo (2009, pp. 46-53).
[212] Giraud & D'Hondt (2006, p. 52).

5) Other non-complex financial instruments (Art. 38, Impl. Dir.).

Remaining instruments are classified as 'complex', so investors using those them cannot opt out of the appropriateness test. In case of non-complex instruments, for execution-only services provided without an appropriateness test, retail clients should be adequately warned, the service should be provided at the initiative of the client, and the firm has to comply with CoIs rules (Casey & Lannoo, 2009).

New proposals. The definition of 'complex' vs 'non-complex' financial instruments is under discussion (CESR, 2010c and EU COM, 2010b, p. 55). Two options have been proposed (EU COM 2010b, p. 55):

1) Excluding all financial instruments that embed a derivative and all UCITS that adopt complex strategies (to be defined) from the non-complex category;
2) Removing the distinction between complex and non-complex financial instruments, and applying the appropriateness test to all financial instruments.

The first proposal requires a revision of the UCITS Directive in order to define which UCITS follow complex strategies. In this regard, it is hard to split the complexity factor from the risk factor and, for UCITS in particular, units are typically sold to investors under the latter's presumption that the product is non-complex and moderately risky given the 'security' image of the brand. If more complex and perhaps riskier strategies are pursued through UCITS, it should be left to the UCITS Directive (2006/65/EC) to differentiate complex and non-complex UCITS.

The second proposal may create higher costs for those market participants whose offer concentrates on non-complex products. Moreover, the impact of competition among investment firms on investor protection rules is uncertain, since typically those protection rules prescribed by MiFID are not actually priced by the investors, who do not tend to require these services if not unilaterally offered. With strong competitive pressures and insufficient supervision, incentives to apply these requirements might consistently be insufficient.

Conclusion # 21

MiFID foresees a different regime for 'execution-only' services based on the product classification between complex and non-complex financial instruments. Any change should take into account that complexity does not necessarily mean more risk. The objective should be to verify if the product is in line with investors' understanding of the ultimate risk that they are going to bear. Regulation should not decide the level of risk investors want to take.

> *Some market participants believe that certain UCITS might have become too complex to be easily understood by investors and so to skip the appropriateness test, at least for retail clients. Others, instead, argue that classification, in particular for UCITS, should remain as such, since a change in classification could damage the UCITS brand outside the EU.*

Box 16. MiFID and asset management at a crossroads

MiFID has had widespread implications for several areas of financial markets, in particular for the asset management business. Besides the application of MiFID to portfolio management services, it is the interaction between MiFID and UCITS that raises concerns. In particular, MiFID sets a formal exemption (Art. 2.1 (h)) that has not been *de facto* applied. In effect, UCITS are currently exempted from the appropriateness test as non-complex financial instruments, which means that they are part of the Directive. UCITS management companies are then classified as ECPs under MiFID, therefore best execution or suitability tests are not applied, unless agreed otherwise. Besides these formal exemptions, there are several aspects that put UCITS under the MiFID spotlight. UCITS typically apply and get the status of professional investor, but they also ask to be treated as retail investors, since the investment product is mainly designed for retail investors. The UCITS Directive also provides for similar organisational requirements as those in MiFID (Recital 1, UCITS Implementing Directive 2010/43/EU) to create a level playing field between UCITS managers and MiFID investment firms undertaking portfolio management services.

Overall, there are other aspects that emerge with the revision of MiFID as points of discussion that may affect the debate on UCITS. Among others, the following aspects would have an impact on the asset management industry:

- Unilaterally granting retail best execution to managers of retail funds (without the need for the agreement of dealers);
- Modifying current definitions of complex versus non-complex financial instruments;
- Investigating the status of the implementation of suitability requirements for investment advice and discretionary portfolio services; and
- Changing the charging structure for investment advice and its basic requirements, and promoting greater inducement disclosure.

The interaction between these areas may have important implications for the future of the industry, in particular for the convergence between alternative and traditional investments (if no differential status would be granted to traditional investments) and on the traditional distribution channels (by changing the role and nature of investment advice).

6.4.4 Grasping the definition and economics of 'best execution' obligations

Setting the scene. MiFID (Art. 19.1) requires that an investment firm act "in accordance with the best interests of its clients" to ensure a high level of investor protection. Besides the general clause, which de facto sets an important fiduciary duty, the article sets a dynamic obligation of 'results' (Giraud & D'Hondt, 2006), which calls for investment firms to ensure best execution when they offer:

- Execution of orders on behalf of the clients (Art. 21, MiFID),
- Reception and transmission of orders in relation to one or more financial instruments (Art. 45.4, Impl. Dir.) and
- Portfolio management (Art. 45.4, Impl. Dir.).

These duties apply to all financial instruments, except spot foreign exchange instruments. Best execution obligations, should therefore be achieved by:

1) Taking "all reasonable steps" to obtain the best net result for the client, "taking into account price, costs, speed, likelihood of execution and settlement, size, nature or any other consideration relevant to the execution of the order." (Art. 21.1, MiFID);

2) Drafting an effective and detailed order execution policy that includes the execution venues and the parameters of choice, and then getting the client's agreement (Art. 21.2, 21.3, MiFID); and

3) Demonstrating, at the request of the client, that execution has been carried out in accordance with the existing execution policy, which allows the achievement the best possible result (Art. 21.3, 21.4, MiFID).

From these detailed requirements, some argue that the Directive aims at imposing an obligation of 'means'. So far, however, regulators have not clarified yet whether MiFID's original spirit was towards 'results' (dynamic approach) or 'means' (static approach).

Definition. Firstly, MiFID draws up a comprehensive definition of best execution, which takes into account all potential factors that can affect a financial transaction (as there is not a universal definition of best execution). Such factors can have different meanings that should be then considered.[213] For instance, costs can be seen as 'implicit' or 'explicit' and

---

[213] Please, see in general, FSA (2006), p. 15-18.

they can assume different forms according to multiple factors, such as the nature of the client.

In this regard, the criteria to be considered by investment firms when performing best execution of an order are the following (Art. 44.1, Impl. Dir.):

i) Specific instructions given by the client,
ii) Nature of the client (retail or professional),
iii) Nature of the financial instruments and
iv) Nature of the execution venues.

What should be considered as best execution for retail clients (typically price and costs) may not be the same for professionals (Art. 44.3, Impl. Dir.). The difficulty of drawing up a precise definition of what is best execution is obvious in today's financial markets. Accordingly, the Directive does not give an easy-to-enforce definition of best execution either. The legal text tries to grasp all factors influencing a financial transaction, but does so in a general manner. However, this situation is not necessarily a detriment to final investors for two reasons, which should always be verified. On the one hand, general clauses are typically set to define a fiduciary duty, which should by definition fill gaps in incomplete contracts, i.e. when it is too costly and difficult for the contracting parties to specify all relevant terms. This situation does not call for detailed provisions in the law, but rather requires stronger enforcement tools and judicial review and the flexible application of best execution requirements (Macey & O'Hara, 1997 & 2005). On the other hand, when transaction costs are sufficiently low, a broad definition allows counterparties to bargain and 'contract around' the duty of best execution or customise it (even 'opt out') . In addition, technological developments (Smart Order Routers, SORs) support the customisation of best execution policies, even in a context of great market fragmentation where best execution cannot be easily verified.

Nevertheless, a strict regulatory definition can increase verifiability but the quality of the execution (investment) service would be potentially lower, with ultimately potential negative effects on demand. A too precise definition of best execution may exacerbate *ex ante* commitment and so inefficient investments. Current legal text sets the boundaries in which competing investment firms tailor execution policies in line with clients' interests. More should be done to increase verifiability by improving the content of execution policies and the quality and depth of market data.

Execution policies. Secondly, as said, a loose contract may provide enough flexibility to contract around (or opt out) at the risk of distorting ex ante commitments. Pre-contractual investments, however, are primarily based on execution policies. By improving the quality of execution policies, the contract therefore becomes less vague. In particular, by promoting:

- Quality of execution policies and
- Observability and verifiability of best execution (through better and more data).

On the quality of execution policies, MiFID obliges investment firms to make a list of execution venues where the intermediary is going to execute the orders, and a list of the factors affecting the choice of a specific trading venue (19.3 and 21.3, MiFID).[214] Best execution policies should receive the client's consent, and firms must review their policies once a year or whenever a 'material change' occurs, for instance when "a significant new execution venue emerges" (FSA, 2006a, p. 34), and assess them on a regular basis (Art. 45.6 and 46, Implementing Directive). In addition, member states should require investment firms to monitor the effectiveness of execution arrangements (Art. 21.4, MiFID) and national authorities may expressly ask investment firms to be able to demonstrate to clients that the transaction is compliant with their execution policy and so with best execution requirements (Art. 21.5, MiFID). To facilitate disclosure to clients about the execution policy, the Commission (2010b) has therefore proposed to introduce a template for policies.

MiFID also allows for different types of best execution policies, especially in relation to the selection of the venue for diverse asset classes and clients. Execution policies do not need to be defined on an order-by-order basis (dynamic approach) but in general (static approach).[215]

---

[214] This list must be reviewed periodically, taking into account "execution venue fees, clearing and settlement fees and any other fees paid to third parties involved in the execution of the order" (Art. 44.3, Impl. Dir.). Effective barriers to add new venues can be (among others, CESR, 2010h, p.5): (1) The lack of interoperability between clearing houses, so the inability to choose a 'clearer of choice'; (2) Local rules which prevent remote membership of exchanges or complex re-registration processes; (3) Different regulatory regimes and clearing and settlement requirements in several countries, creating obstacles to competition between venues; (4) Absence of a central counterparty continues to be a clearing problem for some venues; (5) Distance – speed (or latency), mitigated by new facilities, e.g. hosting facilities, IT developments etc.; and (6) System costs, integration to back office and settlement systems.

[215] See, in particular, FSA (2006), p.12.

However, the regular review of best execution policies currently provides some space for introducing dynamicity in the way investment firms provide best execution. The interpretation of what 'dynamic' means is perceived differently by the market. Some argue that dynamism refers to the obligation to modify execution policies on an order-by-order basis (led by a general obligation of 'results'). In this sense, dynamic order execution may be more efficient and convenient for clients than static approaches, which only meet the minimum legal requirement (Ende et al., 2008). Some others believe that 'dynamic' generally means reviewing the execution policy if major events occur and assessing the effectiveness of execution arrangements periodically as required by MiFID. In this respect, in their view, there are no pending issues with regard to execution policies, besides a need for a proper implementation of current MiFID requirements and the lack of high quality data to verify best execution.

Observability and verifiability. Thirdly, broad legal definitions call for greater enforcement of execution policies by national financial authorities. However, current legislation leaves gaps that make enforcement difficult, such as the difficulty to assess factors other than price and speed, and the current design of best execution duties, which allows exemptions and do not make directly accountable specific trading practices.[216] Moreover, the lack of quality data on execution for financial instruments makes comparability of post-trade information complicated.[217] MiFID requires firms to act in their clients' best interest (Art. 19.1), which constitutes a good-faith clause that should allow judges the necessary discretion to decide whether best execution has effectively taken place. However, since MiFID also defines what constitutes the client's 'best interests', it impairs judiciary discretion and rather favours the principle of caveat emptor. This principle is not satisfactory either, due to the lack of verifiability, which means investors have to choose among execution policies that may not

---

[216] For instance, the US case law recognises as 'industry practice' - therefore not considered violation of the best execution duty - accepting a rebate for directing order flow to a particular broker or trading venue; see Macey & O'Hara (1997), pp.195-196.

[217] CESR is also looking to define an appropriate execution metric in order to measure execution (on a quarterly basis) in shares (for other financial instruments it has been postponed to a future discussion) and it may ask execution venues to produce reports on execution quality using metrics set by CESR. CESR (2010), "Investor Protection and Intermediaries", *op. cit.*, pp. 18-26.

always be implemented properly. Observability and verifiability are considered minimal informational requirements for an event to define a contractual contingency (Hermalin et al., 2007). Best execution is characterised as a contractual term but it is not verifiable, even though observable (monitoring costs that are too high). It is therefore fundamental to improve the available quantity and quality of execution data (CESR, 2010b), which can also reduce the transaction costs of contracting 'around' the best execution requirements, as set by the Directive. Bargaining something that is not verifiable does not make any sense 'contractually'. The Commission (2010b) also believes that better and more data should be combined with an effective civil liability for the investment firm.

Market structure. Best execution duties influence two different areas: market structure and investor protection (Macey & O'Hara, 1997). Best execution de facto is only the one that the market is willing to provide, thus order flow markets must be competitive. Best execution is synonymous with low transaction costs. It is achieved when the least number of resources are lost in intermediation, for the execution services industry (Harris, 1996). Best execution policies must ensure that, when the abovementioned conditions are met, the investment firm screens the whole market, in particular those execution venues that can offer best execution to clients. On the one hand, the duty of best execution may sustain a competitive environment between trading venues, as incumbents are indirectly forced to deliver better quality of execution (in terms of lower implicit and explicit trading costs), due to the investment firms' commitment to deliver best execution. This pressure reduces the incentives to define an oligopolistic setting with newcomers to the market, and among investment firms (as they ought to compete around quality and dynamicity of execution policies). On the other hand, this duty comes from a more important recognition of a fiduciary relationship between client and investment firm and aims at protecting end investors. Strong information asymmetries between client and investment firm may impede the definition of what precise factors should be taken into account to achieve best execution for a specific client (McCleskey, 2004).

The lack of an immediately applicable definition of best execution and the fear of undermining the structure of the US national market system led the SEC to impose a strict definition of best execution (around the best available price, i.e. National Best Bid and Offer, NBBO) and require brokers to report execution performance statistics (SEC, 1962). In this regard, the US regulators decided to fix an enforceable requirement (price) under securities regulation and to leave to markets, under competition, the provision of related services that help to achieve best execution (such as speed, multi-market trading, etc).

Non-equity markets. For non-equity financial instruments, traded OTC or on inter-dealer platforms, best execution may rely on other relevant aspects such as national legal rules, counterparty risk, products and market feasibility. In particular, it may be relevant to consider the volumes traded on a specific platform, as well as the type of organised venue or the details of the dealer that represents the counterparty in an OTC transaction. In line with the type of venue where the transaction is executed, execution policies should consider the most appropriate approach.

Nevertheless, it may be difficult to find comparable data for some complex derivative or credit product, or to see pre-trade information on prices. The kind of transparency obligations adopted for equities may not be as beneficial as for other types of markets and products (see Section 1). For instance, buying a bond that is only traded OTC for a retail client may not be compliant with the price factor of best execution since the counterparty would only agree to sell at a specific price set unilaterally (due to the low size). There is no space for negotiation and it is not verifiable if the trade could have occurred with a different dealer (the information is simply not available). In a RFQ trading model there is more chance that the investment firm can choose between few competing bid/offer prices and therefore to apply best execution obligations.

Conclusion # 22

Best execution duties lie at the foundation of the fiduciary relationship between service providers and clients. Execution policies and data are essential aspects of the effectiveness of these legal requirements. MiFID tries to grasp all factors influencing the best execution of a financial transaction, and does so in a very general manner. A strict legal definition (price-only) would assume that other services needed to achieve best execution (such as speed, transaction cost analysis, etc) would be efficiently provided by the market itself under competition, with no need of a formal legal protection. A broad definition, however, is not necessarily detrimental for final investors as long as execution policies are properly implemented and data allows sufficient verifiability of execution. Conflicting views emerge between those who argue that execution policies should be designed around a 'dynamic' obligation of 'result', i.e. complying with the minimum legal requirements is not enough in their view to achieve best execution. Other participants however challenge the view that issues with best execution come from execution policies, which are MiFID-compliant. Investors themselves receive full information about their execution policies. Both recognise that those issues emerge from a consistent lack of data on execution quality from trading platforms, which are under discussion within the debate on the new transparency regime.

Overall, MiFID requires firms to act in their clients' best interest (Art. 19.1), which constitutes a good-faith clause that should allow judges the necessary discretion to decide whether best execution has effectively taken place. However, since MiFID also defines what constitutes the client's 'best interests', it impairs judiciary discretion and rather favours the principle of caveat emptor. This principle is not satisfactory either, due to the lack of verifiability, which means investors have to choose among execution policies that may not always be implemented properly. Observability and verifiability are considered minimal informational requirements for an event to define a contractual contingency.

Best execution also impacts on market structure. Best execution de facto is synonymous of low transaction costs and is achieved when the fewest resources are lost in intermediation. Best execution policies must ensure that, when the abovementioned conditions are met, the investment firm screens the whole market, in particular those execution venues that can offer best execution to clients. Hitherto, the duty of best execution sustains a competitive environment between trading venues, as incumbents are indirectly forced to deliver better quality of execution, due to the investment firms' commitment to deliver it.

7. A NEW REGIME FOR COMMODITY DERIVATIVES

Commodities markets play a fundamental role for our economies. They ensure that demand and offer of commodities find their best market clearing price. MiFID acknowledged the different context into which firms may need to enter in a financial transaction in commodity derivatives by giving full exemption to those firms providing investment services in those instruments, if their main business or the core activity of the group is not the provision of investment services or the transaction is done for hedging purposes (when dealing on own account; Art. 2.1 (d) (i) (k) (l), MiFID). The Directive de facto grants a broad exemption to groups such as energy companies, which frequently use derivatives to cover exposures (see figure below). For instance, energy companies providing electricity need to cover their exposures since electricity cannot be stored and its availability is subject to many endogenous (e.g. infrastructure, alternative renewable energies) and exogenous variables (e.g. weather). The need to hedge those risks requires energy companies to be heavily involved in trading activities on-exchange and over-the-counter.

In order to minimise regulatory burdens on such hedges, the text of the Directive currently grants full exemption for the provision of investment services related to commodities, except if this is part of a group whose main business is the provision of investment services (e.g. dealers). The exemption is not by instrument (commodity derivatives are included in the definitions of Annex I, Section C, MiFID) but by use (hedging) or main business/activity of the firm. No sound definition of how 'hedging' activities can actually be classified is currently available.

206 | A NEW REGIME FOR COMMODITY DERIVATIVES

Figure 33. Exemptions for commodity instruments and firms

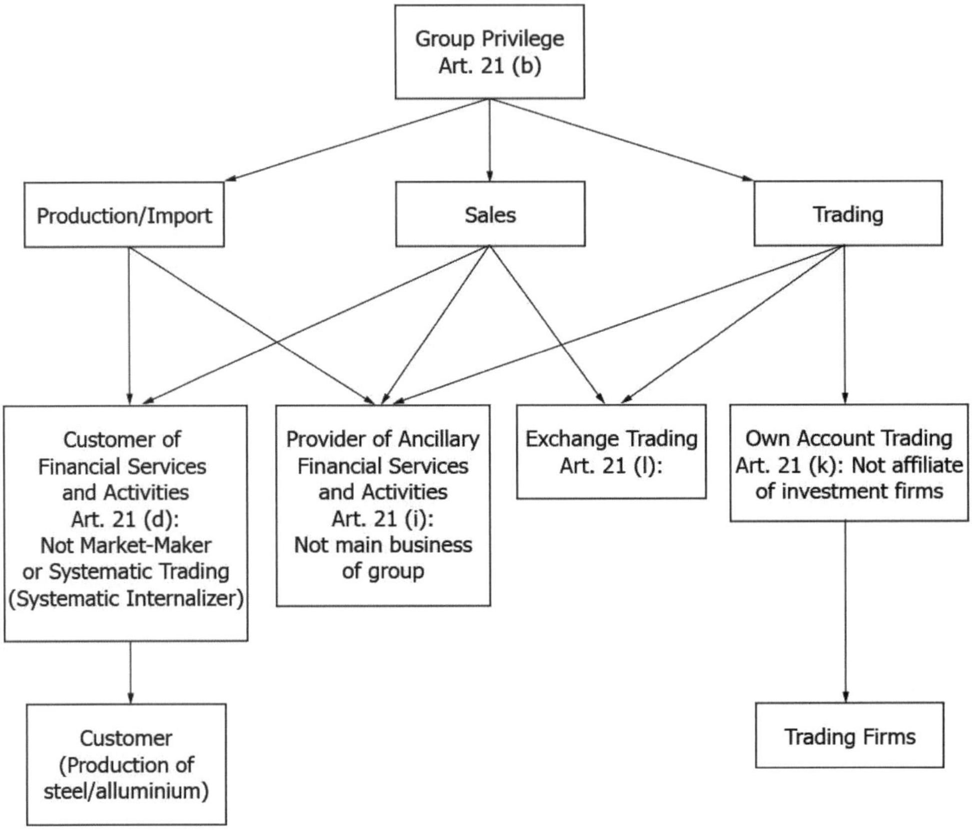

```
                        Group Privilege
                          Art. 21 (b)
                   ┌──────────┼──────────┐
           Production/Import  Sales    Trading
```

- Customer of Financial Services and Activities Art. 21 (d): Not Market-Maker or Systematic Trading (Systematic Internalizer)
- Provider of Ancillary Financial Services and Activities Art. 21 (i): Not main business of group
- Exchange Trading Art. 21 (l):
- Own Account Trading Art. 21 (k): Not affiliate of investment firms

→ Customer (Production of steel/alluminium)

→ Trading Firms

Source: RWE Supply & Trading.

The financial crisis. The recent increase in market prices and volatility of such goods has diverted attention away from a potential link between prices on spot markets and volumes and prices of transactions done on underlying future markets. The alleged 'financialisation' of commodities and their prices formation process has put many derivatives transactions under the regulatory spotlight, in an attempt to address the historical high price volatility in commodity markets. It needs to be said that derivative markets (in particular, future markets) are just one of the variables that may affect the price formation processes of commodities. Amongst other variables, there are fundamental aspects such as: demand (e.g. the GDP is a valid measure); supply constraints; transportation costs; storage costs; and other exogenous factors (weather, political stability, etc). Uncertainty about the global economic outlook, testified by the rise in the prices of commodities such as gold, does not help to control volatility either. The growing uncertainty has increased producers' needs to find protection by increasingly accessing sophisticated financial transactions, particularly in derivatives markets. These markets provide a formidable mean of hedging against price changes in the physical product. Since markets, however, would not be liquid with only investors hedging in the same direction (there would be no counterparty to their trades), speculation, intended as a way of trading by investing in gathering private information, becomes indispensable to create a buffer of 'noise' trading that can give markets enough liquidity.

New proposals. Besides fragmented and conflicting views on the role of financial markets on commodity prices, regulators are asking for more powers and transparency over positions in commodity derivatives in order to avoid risks of manipulation and better control market participants' positions (EU COM, 2010b, pp. 37-39). One option to reach these objectives implies a partial or total removal of exemptions under MiFID. This situation would extend the scope of MiFID and bring the energy and energy trading markets into the scope of financial market regulation for the first time. Additional regulatory and capital requirements will apply to business firms that will need to get authorisation as MiFID investment firms. For instance, energy companies running a trading desk internally will have to set up a licensed investment firm. Such firms would be then subject to the full regime of the Capital Requirements Directive ("CRD") and need to hold regulatory capital if the parallel exemption for commodity firms under the CRD is not extended beyond 2014 (capital requirements applying to commodities firms will be most likely subject to a separate review under CRD).

Instead of regulating market participants, another viable option would be to strengthen regulation on trading activities through new market integrity and transparency rules (e.g. transaction and trade reporting).

The Commission (2010b) has suggested introducing new reporting obligations for positions in commodity derivatives, covering all official venues (RMs, MTFs, OTFs). The proposal – in line with the review requested by MiFID in Art. 65.3 – requires investment firms and banks to disclose the counterparty, which can be an entity classified under EU legislation (such as UCITS, credit institution, etc) or a commercial trader (not classified under any EU legislation), and then decide if more information is needed. An alternative option would require reporting only for transactions not qualifying as 'hedges', using current international accounting standards such as IFRS IAS 39. A combination of the previous two options is also on the table.

In line with the approach to the review, the Commission will most probably narrow the breadth of the exemptions in order to cover commercial firms that are not sophisticated clients under MiFID ORs and CoB rules. To achieve this, Art. 2.1(i) and 2.1(d) would clarify that the exemption should be granted only to the business of "hedging physical and price risks" (EU COM, 2010b, p. 41). To verify if activities are "ancillary" to the main business, quantitative (e.g. a certain percentage of the main business) and qualitative measures should be introduced (e.g. dedicated personnel). Finally, the exemption of Art. 2.1(k) seems to overlap with the others, so it could be deleted. However, the original intention of this exemption was to enable a review of the capital requirements for investment firms dealing with commodities before applying any MiFID rules and CRD regime, and giving the time to define an appropriate prudential regime for this business. Finally, the Commission decided that capital requirements for these firms will be consistently defined in a specific review of the Directive 2006/49 (EU COM, 2010b, p. 41).

As a result of these multiple changes, investment firms dealing with commodities not for hedging purposes will need to apply licensing, transparency, conduct of business rules and organisational rules as well as potential requirements under the CRD regime.[218] They will therefore need to set up MiFID licensed firms and apply organisational requirements and CoB rules.

Market views. On transparency and legal exemptions, market views are split between those who believe that exemptions should be kept as they now stand or allow for a less onerous regime for these companies, and those who favour a comprehensive harmonisation of rules in this area. On the one hand, some market participants (in particular, energy companies) believe that the removal of the exemption will harm their business

---

[218] This approach does not seem to be in line with the legal text proposed for central counterparty (CCP) clearing of over-the-counter derivatives in the recent proposal of European Market Infrastructure Regulation (EMIR; COM (2010), 484/5). In that proposal, non-financial counterparties are not in principle covered by the scope of the regulation if they do not breach a certain clearing threshold.

(especially for small companies) and indirectly affect underlying prices (e.g. energy prices). The inclusion of these companies in the MiFID original regime will mean:

1) Treating specialised commodity firms as financial institutions, even though they do not access central bank money or other credit facilities at favourable terms, do not offer products to retail investors (or are not retail investors themselves), and do not add up to the systemic risk of the financial system U;[219]

2) Imposing commodity firms to transfer their business to a MiFID-licensed firm (high compliance costs); and

3) Complying with all MiFID requirements (CoB and ORs).

In their view, the potentially positive effects of being classified as a MiFID-licensed firm may not offset the actual costs of this proposal. In particular, benefits would include:

i) The availability of an EU passport for MiFID investment firms, which may not be useful for some participants, such as energy trading companies, as they do not offer cross-border investment services;

ii) The assurance of continuity of the trading business under the MiFID framework (ORs); and

iii) A harmonised set of rules for investor protection (CoB).

As a result, the imbalance between benefits and costs may boost hedging costs, either causing energy price for end-consumers to go up or reducing the overall use of hedging tools. The proposal may also reduce liquidity and competition by raising barriers to entry, in contrast with widespread processes of market liberalisation in many sectors (e.g. energy).

On the other hand, some market participants and regulators stress the importance of levelling the playing field in terms of market transparency among different classes of traders (also for financial stability purposes).

---

[219] The joint advice of the Committee of European Banking Supervisors ('CEBS') to the EU Commission ("CEBS-Advice") in 2008 clearly states that "... systemic risk concerns [of commodities business firms]... appear significantly smaller relative to the systemic risks posed by banks and ISD financial investment firms. In the commodities case studies examined in this report, systemic concerns were limited and contained." See, joint CESR-CEBS Advice (ref. CESR/08-752), 15 October 2008, see ref. 12, ref. 38 et seq., 213 et seq., 282 et seq., (http://www.c-ebs.org/getdoc/ee9b85fa-4d64-48dc-9f45-a7350881ddac/2008-15-10-CESR-CEBS-advice-on-Commodities.aspx).

Greater transparency may also improve price formation processes in commodity related markets (such as future markets), ultimately ensuring better price formation in the underlying commodity market. Finally, small firms (e.g. farmers) whose main business is not the provision of investment services, will in this way be granted a greater set of investor protection rules, which should reduce the possibilities of fraud and market manipulation.

Definition under MiFID. Furthermore, the definition of a commodity derivative as a financial instrument under MiFID is also under discussion in order to have a larger coverage of over-the-counter derivatives (EU COM, 2010b, pp. 41-42). In addition to the requirement for the physical delivery of the commodity to take place on at least two trading days, an OTC derivative contract would be considered MiFID financial instrument if:

(1) Traded or equivalent to a contract traded on RMs, MTFs, or similar facility and

(2) Standardised in terms of price, lot, date of delivery, etc.

A third requirement concerning the need to be cleared on a CCP or being subject to the payment of margins is currently under discussion. However, the requirement to be centrally cleared would restrict the number of OTC derivatives that would fall under MiFID rules. In addition, by doing so, the eligibility requirements for CCP-clearing would be indirectly applied to trading, where different conditions and a regulatory approach under MiFID applies. Moreover, current legal text may diverge from the US Dodd-Frank Act, which exempts physically settled OTC forward transactions from the definition of a 'swap'. The level playing field between the EU and US regulation should be preserved.

Position limits and management. With the review of MiFID, regulators and competent authorities advocate strengthening and harmonising supervisory powers to control the build-up of systemic risk and disorderly markets arising from market manipulation. These powers should allow setting position limits to minimise the risks of price and market manipulation (Langen, 2010; EU COM, 2010b, pp. 82-83).[220]

'Curbing speculation' is a vague objective, since how someone can actually distinguish between hedging and speculative trading remains

---

[220] In line also with the US 'Dodd-Frank' Wall Street Reform and Consumer Protection Act, P.L. 111-203, H.R. 4173.

highly controversial. 'Speculation' involves the use of private information based on greater market knowledge, which is different from inside information (manipulation).[221] Informed trading activities – based on more or less sophisticated expectations that market prices may go in a specific direction – may be also done for hedging purposes. For instance, an electricity company willing to cover its future exposure by purchasing a future price contract based on the expectation that prices may go up/down, even though the company does not currently own the commodity (energy is not storable), which would be hardly defined as speculation, even though it looks that way. In addition, with no investors investing in information there would be no space for hedgers to find a counterparty that actually prices and is willing to trade the probability that the event to be hedged in the end will not occur. Regulators, therefore, should shed light on the risks of price and market manipulation in commodity markets, potentially arising from the accumulation of dominant net positions in derivatives markets (in particular, futures markets). The attempt to squeeze the market by collecting a dominant share of a commodity future for a specific settlement date may have disruptive effects on spot prices, since the dominant owner of a long position for that date may exercise unreasonable upward pressure on futures prices and thereby indirectly on spot market prices as well.

To reduce the harmful effects of settlement squeezes, regulators and supervisors typically adopt two tools: position limits and position management. Position limits may be imposed not only for exchange-traded products but also for OTC contracts. In addition, counterparties entering the derivative contract could be asked to provide a full explanation of the position and other relevant documentation, besides the regulatory requirements currently in place. Position limits may need to be further investigated to determine the size of a position that can be deemed to be manipulative. It is essential to ensure that limits are neither set at unsustainable (too low) nor at irrelevant levels (too high), which would mean either an excessive shift in market structure or no impact at all. In addition, the extension to OTC contracts, on the one side, may reduce the incentives to move some of the trading activities from open markets to

---

[221] The border between private 'legal' information and 'inside' information is often so unclear that regulators may be willing to ban trading a product rather than monitoring activities on an ongoing basis. See Art. 1, Market Abuse Directive 2003/124/EC.

OTC. On the other side, position limits for OTC contracts may increase the number of trades and eventually the costs that the 'requesting' counterparty should pay, since it could not benefit from the freedom to privately negotiate an important risk exposure. However, it greatly depends on how the position limit would be formulated, whether or not it would be an obligation to reduce size of the position below the limit, or whether it would only require disclosure to regulators. Position limits generally impose on commodity traders a cap on the size of transactions based on broader indicators. Some argue that these measures may be easily circumvented by trading more frequently with smaller sizes, which makes supervision a more complex and costly activity. By contrast, the use of position limits may be indispensable in markets where the single transaction can directly manipulate prices, such as physical markets or markets for non-storable commodities (e.g. electricity exchanges).

Position management allows the detection of dominant net positions at the end of the trading day and a more accurate monitoring of systemic risk. If positions create unreasonable upward or downward pressures on prices, market operators can require traders, at the beginning of the next trading day, to reduce their positions. Position management may thus be a more effective tool for tackling this issue, since manipulation in commodity markets does not usually come from the impact on prices of the availability of investors to transact a security at a specific price, but from the availability of counterparties to bargain a future position. Since the availability of settlement dates is actually quite limited, it would be more meaningful to collect all trading reports and calculate the total net position of an investor in that specific market. In securities markets, however, the availability of securities is typically wider and manipulation comes frequently from the misuse of a single or multiple transactions by exploiting inside information or the accumulated size (trading with knowledge). Some have also cast doubt on the improper use of leverage. These worries also concern securities markets, but the issue itself should be confined to the reforms on capital requirements for financial institutions (Basel III), as it may be more appropriate to tackle them in that context.

Conclusion # 23

Narrowing exemptions for commodity derivatives under MiFID may have a substantial impact on the business of non-financial companies. Some market participants advocate the need for a level playing field between financial and non-financial firms when they come to trade financial instruments. In their view, it would represent an important step towards greater transparency and investor protection, while others ask for further investigation of the unintended consequences in terms of higher costs of hedging relevant exposures in the market, as well as lower competitiveness, liquidity, and competition. The need for consistency across several regulations in the commodity business may need a more fully articulated answer and coordination with initiatives to define capital requirements for investment firms.

'Curbing speculation' is a vague objective, since how someone can actually distinguish between hedging and speculative trading remains highly controversial. Regulators instead should shed light on the risks of price manipulation potentially arising from the accumulation of dominant net positions in derivatives markets (futures). Strengthening supervisory powers may in principle be effective to control price manipulation, but its role in controlling systemic risk may be doubtful, in particular through position limits. The use of position management tools to monitor the size of net positions would be more effective.

8. CONCLUSIONS

The MiFID review is an opportunity to boost investor confidence and strengthen the resilience, efficiency and transparency of financial markets and instruments. Investor protection and market efficiency should remain the guiding principles of the Directive but be reconciled with broader goals brought about by the financial crisis, such as market safety and financial stability. Regulation, as a consequence, will become more prescriptive so the market will be left with less freedom to self-regulate. Supervisors will carry on the difficult task to keep rules up-to-date with fast-changing market developments. Regulators should also make sure that the revised text will be coherent with other forthcoming legislations, which will also touch upon areas primarily falling under MiFID.

MiFID has changed the landscape of European capital markets for the better in many ways. Most notably, the Directive has led to a more competitive environment, huge investments in technologies, and greater investor protection. The revision of the Directive, however, should clarify intended scopes and fill regulatory gaps in the legal text, as well as create a more harmonised framework of supervisory practices among member states. It should make sure that the benefits of a new competitive environment are spread along the value chain and passed on to final users, retail and wholesale investors, as appropriate.

Transparency plays a crucial role in the smooth functioning of financial markets and the monitoring of systemic risk. It also ensures that the process of price formation works well, through efficient price discovery mechanisms. However, transparency is not a panacea for market failures. Ill-defined transparency requirements would harm market efficiency in less-liquid markets with no increase in investor protection or reduction of systemic risk. Hence, regulatory intervention should be proportional to the nature of each market, whether auction or bilateral, and take into account the dynamics through which orders find their market clearing price.

Pre-trade transparency supports the functioning of venues' trading mechanisms, as well as efficient price discovery and the implementation of best execution policies. Under certain conditions, however, pre-trade transparency may impair market liquidity.

For equity financial instruments, waivers of pre-trade transparency should be retained. A move towards a sounder rule-based approach, however, should be balanced with flexible application and ongoing supervision in order to meet market needs. Conflicting views in the market emerge when discussing the breadth of these exemptions. Regulators need to devise a new set of rules that promotes the efficient and stability of Europe's capital markets and meets investors' needs with no adverse impact on market structure, market liquidity, efficiency, or investor confidence. In addition, the consistent and uniform application across Europe should be ensured.

For non-equity financial instruments, a strong push towards more pre-trade public disclosure would require, in some cases, a rethink of the current market structure for less-liquid asset classes, and a shift from its mainly institutional demand to a more retail and smaller professional one. Clashing positions in this area emerge as a result of different views around the most efficient market structure for these products.

Liquidity in non-equity markets, such as markets for bonds, derivatives and structured products, is mostly handled through quote-driven auction markets, inter-dealer platforms or purely bilateral negotiations through the direct commitment of dealers' capital. For auction markets, whether led by dealers/market-makers (quote-driven) or directly by demand (order-driven), pre-trade transparency is strictly needed. For inter-dealer platforms (request-for-quotes model) or bilateral negotiations, where dealers commit capital by being non-neutral counterparties, less pre-trade transparency than in order-driven ones (e.g. equity) could enable them to function properly. Executable prices might thus not always be consistently available. Current market structure, however, does not impede future market developments in the years to arrive at a different structure of intermediation and nature of the demand.

The alternative to a shift in market structure and demand, which may not necessarily occur, is to design a different transparency regime from the one applied to equities. However, an appropriate level of pre-trade transparency may also be beneficial for non-auction markets, as it reduces investors' search costs and promotes greater competition among dealers.

Turning to post-trade disclosure, the financial crisis called for a further layer of transparency requirements. A new regime should include the disclosure of aggregate data on capital markets to monitor systemic risk and increase market integrity and efficiency. The extension of trade reporting to both shares admitted to trading only on MTFs, or to organised trading facilities and to equity-like instruments would be helpful, since all these instruments serve similar purposes. However, for financial instruments other than shares and the like, the mere extension of the rules for equities would most probably generate inconsistencies, given their diverse nature.

For equity markets, transparency issues remain with the quality of OTC market data and the costs of consolidated solutions. In the post-MiFID environment, several aspects have contributed to reduce the quality of data and hindered its consolidation. The MiFID review should promote a greater standardisation of both data formats (code identifiers, etc) and flags. Market initiatives should consistently reduce the number of trade flags, currently around 50, to fewer than 10 across Europe. In this regard, ESMA should rather support current industry-led initiatives to improve standardisation and reduce inconsistencies. However, either the Commission or ESMA should be able to impose consistency if commercial initiatives do not lead to a satisfactory solution in a reasonable timeframe.

Finally, on time limits for trade reporting, reducing the maximum allowed delay for equity transactions from three minutes to one may prove immaterial since this delay cannot be exploited by trading platforms in favour of their members. In any case, the legal obligation is to report 'as close to real time as possible' and this duty should be duly enforced. All market data that is not subject to delays should be freely available after 15 minutes, in line with ESMA's recommendations. Delays should be permitted in specific circumstances, with appropriate calibration for trades done at the end of the day.

For non-equity markets, post-trade transparency should be consistently applied both to auction markets and purely over-the-counter bilateral transactions. For this purpose, the post-trade transparency regime for equities should be extended, with appropriate changes, to all financial instruments admitted to trading on regulated markets, multilateral trading facilities or organised trading facilities. A transparency regime disclosing meaningful information would stimulate price discovery.

Exemptions and due calibrations should be based on 'dynamic' liquidity measures, to be defined at Level 2, in order to preserve efficient price formation and to guarantee an effective monitoring of systemic risk. Calibrations should take into account the nature of these markets and of each financial instrument, rather than a division into broader categories (e.g. by asset classes). Finally, dynamic measures of liquidity can be designed around aspects such as frequency of trades, overall turnover or prospective liquidity, product standardisation, or transaction size.

Confidential disclosure to regulators (transaction reporting) should be extended to all financial instruments admitted to trading on RMs, MTFs or OTFs. In addition, to monitor the build-up of systemic risk, aggregate data on net exposures, in particular for financial instruments whose value is linked to an underlying asset (e.g. structured financial products or OTC derivatives) should be disclosed, leveraging current infrastructures such as trade repositories.

Priority should be given to removing obstacles to the use of consolidated post-trade data solutions in terms of costs and lack of data quality. Unbundling of data services and fees would reduce costs and increase the accessibility to consolidated data solutions. Broader actions by competition authorities to identify potentially unfair and anticompetitive practices in the market for data should also be undertaken. Further positive contribution may come from the standardisation of data formats and the use of harmonised flags. Consolidated tapes, therefore, can be designed and offered by competing data operators once the 'rules of the game' have been clearly defined and duly enforced. These tapes could potentially cover not only shares but also other financial instruments admitted to trading on RMs, MTFs or organised trading facilities, once an appropriate post-trade transparency regime is in place. Only if the industry fails to deliver, should ESMA adopt the necessary arrangements to set a single consolidated tape in the EU.

Narrowing exemptions for commodity derivatives under MiFID is an action coherent with the post-crisis approach to regulation. However, this action may have a substantial impact on the business of non-financial companies by requiring them to become MiFID-licensed investment firms and eventually to be subject to capital requirements. The consequences in terms of the cost of hedging relevant exposures under narrower exemptions should be further investigated.

'Curbing speculation' is a vague objective, since how to distinguish between hedging and speculative trading remains highly controversial. Regulators should instead shed light on the risks of price manipulation that arise from the accumulation of dominant net positions in future and derivatives markets. Supervisory powers should be strengthened through position limits, for physical markets or markets for non-storable commodities (e.g. electricity). There should also be position management mechanisms to monitor whether operators reach a net dominant position in the market, which may lead to manipulative actions.

MiFID should ensure a harmonised approach in the application of regulatory requirements for official trading venues. Regulated markets and multilateral trading facilities should be subject to convergent legal obligations and supervisory oversight across member states.

On the classification of broker-dealer crossing networks (BCNs), there is no agreement between market participants on prospected proposals. However, the review should clarify what kind of trades are subject to OTC requirements under MiFID (e.g. 'child' or 'parent' orders). Current proposals would bring further confusion to current definitions. For instance, 'multilateral' does not mean that third parties can enter an order; t it rather means that the platform does not act on its 'own account' where matching transactions, and therefore does not exercise any discretion on how trading interests should interact.

Financial market infrastructures, e.g. trading venues, are competing networks. Stronger action by competent authorities is needed to keep barriers to entry and exit low, giving due attention to economies of scale and scope. Legislation and supervisory practice should work together to realise a more open market architecture. The industry's Code of Conduct was a positive first step in this direction. However, more needs to be done to solve existing commercial and technical challenges. Increased accessibility to the post-trading infrastructure could be achieved through unbundling and better interoperability of services, together with clearer legal definitions (e.g. 'legitimate commercial ground').

The systemic importance of modern capital markets highlights the inner tensions among financial stability, market efficiency and technological innovation. A well-functioning market must balance efficiency and safety. A coherent set of emergency procedures in case of market disruptions should be designed in consultation with market participants (e.g. circuit breakers). There are a several efficient monitoring systems already in place, which could serve as model systems.

Best execution duties lie at the foundation of the fiduciary relationship between service providers and clients. MiFID should clarify if execution policies should follow an obligation of 'means' or a more general obligation of 'results'. More accurate execution policies and better quality for execution data should allow sufficient verifiability of execution.

Investment advice must always be 'suitable' under MiFID. However, conflicts of interest may affect the quality of investment advice. These can arise from the remuneration structure and/or from disclosure levels. Mandating a purely fee-based remuneration structure, however, may increase service costs and reduce access to advice by investors, with unclear long-term effects. It might be preferable—to make both remuneration solutions available and, in addition, to mandate disclosure of all adviser fees. In this way, investors themselves would be able to choose one that best suits their needs.

The distinction between complex and non-complex financial instruments should be reviewed under the caveat that complexity does not necessarily mean more risk. The objective should be to distinguish products according to the investors' ability to understand the ultimate risk they carry. Regulation should not decide the level of risk investors ultimately want to take.

MiFID rules on conflicts of interest are not only disclosure requirements but provide rules for the identification and management of these conflicts. However, this set of rules should be coupled with harmonised supervisory practices and a strong common set of sanctions that would allow some flexibility to member states to adapt rules and procedures in line with their national contexts.

REFERENCES

AFM (Authority for the Financial Markets) (2010), *High frequency trading. The application of advanced trading technology in the European marketplace*, Report, December (http://www.afm.nl/en/professionals/afm-actueel/rapporten/2010/hft-rapport.aspx).

Akerlof, G.A. (1970), "The market for lemons. Qualitative uncertainty and the market mechanism", *Quarterly Journal of Economics*, Vol. 84, No. 3, August, pp. 488-500.

Amihud, Yakov and Haim Mendelson (1996), "A New Approach to the Regulation of Trading across Securities Markets", *New York University Law Review*, Vol. 71, No. 6, December.

Amihud, Yakov, Haim Mendelson and Beni Lauterbach (1997), "Market microstructure and securities values: Evidence from the Tel Aviv Stock Exchange", *Journal of Financial Economics*, Vol. 45, No. 3, September, pp. 365-390.

Angel, James J., Lawrence E. Harris and Chester Spatt (2010), *Equity Trading in the 21st Century*, Working Paper (www.ssrn.com).

Areeda, Phillip (1990), "Essential Facilities: An Epithet in Need of Limiting Principles", *58 Antitrust L.J.*

Armstrong, Mark (2006), "Competition in two-sided markets", *RAND Journal of Economics*, Vol. 37, No. 3, Autumn.

Atradia (2010), *The cost of access to real time pre- and post-trade order book data in Europe. A review of content fees within the wider context of data product, delivery and infrastructure costs*, Research Study, August.

Baruch, Shmuel (2005), "Who Benefits from an Open Limit-Order Book?", *Journal of Business*, Vol. 78, No. 4, July, pp. 1267-1306.

Battalio, Robert H. (1997), "Third Market Broker-Dealers: Cost Competitors or Cream Skimmers?", *The Journal of Finance*, Vol. 52, No. 1, March.

Battalio, Robert H., Jason Greene and Robert Jennings (1997), "Do Competing Specialists and Preferencing Dealers affect Market Quality?", *The Review of Financial Studies*, Vol. 10, No. 4, October, pp. 969-993.

Baumol, William J., John C. Panzar, and Robert D. Willig (1982), *Contestable Markets and the Theory of Industry Structure*, New York, NY: Harcourt Brace Jovanovich, June.

Bessembinder, Hendrik, William Maxwell and Kumar Venkataraman (2006), "Market transparency, liquidity externalities, and institutional trading costs in corporate bonds", *Journal of Financial Economics*, Vol. 82, May, pp. 251-288.

Biais, Bruno (2010), "Algorithmic Trading. Equilibrium, efficiency and stability", presentation at Market Microstructure Conference, Institut Louis Bachelier (ILB), Paris, 6 December.

Biais, Bruno and Fany Declerk (2007), *Liquidity, Competition and Price Discovery in the European Corporate Bond Market*, IDEI Working Papers, Institut d'Economie Industrielle, University of Toulouse (http://idei.fr/doc/wp/2007/liquidity_competition.pdf).

Biais, Bruno, Fany Declerck, James Dow, Richard Portes and Ernst-Ludwig von Thadden (2006), *European Corporate Bond Markets: Transparency, liquidity, efficiency*, CEPR Working Paper for the City of London, Centre for Economic Policy Research, London, May (http://www.cepr.org/PRESS/TT_CorporateFULL.pdf).

Biais, Bruno and Richard C. Green (2007), *The Microstructure of the Bond Market in the 20th Century*, IDEI Working Paper, Institut d'Economie Industrielle, University of Toulouse, 29 August (http://neeo.univ-tlse1.fr/502/1/bondmarket.pdf).

Bloomfield, Robert and Maureen O'Hara (1999), "Market Transparency: Who Wins and Who Loses?", *The Review of Financial Studies*, Vol. 12, No. 1, Spring, pp. 5-35.

Boehmer, Ekkehart, Gideon Saar and Lei Yu (2005), "Lifting the Veil: An Analysis of Pre-Trade Transparency at the NYSE", *The Journal of Finance*, Vol. 60, No. 2, April, pp. 783-815.

Brogaard, Jonathan A. (2010), "High-frequency Trading and Its Impact on Market Quality", Working Paper, Northwestern University, July (www.ssrn.com).

Buccirossi, Paolo (ed.) (2008), *Handbook of Antitrust Economics*, Cambridge, MA: The MIT Press.

Burton-Taylor LLC (2010), "Financial Market Data/Analysis Global Share and Segment Sizing 2010" (http://www.burton-taylor.com/samples/B-T_Global_Market_Data-

Analysis_3_Year_Segment_and_5_Year_Competitor_Analysis_2010-Information_Kit.pdf).

Buti, Sabrina, Barbara Rindi and Ingrid M. Werner (2010a), *Dynamic Dark Pool Trading Strategies in Limit Order Markets*, Dice Centre Working Paper, 2010-6, Charles A. Dice Center for Research in Financial Economics, Ohio State University, March.

----------- (2010b), *Diving into Dark Pools*, Dice Centre Working Paper, 2010-10, Charles A. Dice Center for Research in Financial Economics, Ohio State University, June.

Caglio, Cecilia and Stewart Mayhew (2009), "Equity Trading and the Allocation of Market Data Revenue", draft Working Paper (http://business.rutgers.edu/files/caglio_mayhew_may272009.pdf).

Casey, Jean-Pierre (2006), *Bond Market Transparency: To Regulate or not to Regulate*, ECMI Policy Brief, No. 4, December.

Casey, Jean-Pierre and Karel Lannoo (2009), *The MiFID Revolution*, Cambridge: Cambridge University Press.

Celent (2008), "The Evolution of Direct Market Access (DMA) Trading Services in the US and Europe Report", March (http://reports.celent.com/PressReleases/20080313/DMA.htm).

----------- (2009), "Demystifying and Evaluating High Frequency Equities Trading", Report, December.

CESAME Group (Clearing and Settlement Advisory and Monitoring Experts Group) (2008), *Solving the industry Giovannini Barriers to Post-Trading within the EU*, Group Report, 28 November (http://ec.europa.eu/internal_market/financial-markets/clearing/index_en.htm).

CESR (Committee of European Securities Regulators) (2007), "Best Execution under MiFID. Questions and Answers", Ref CEST/07-320.

----------- (2008), *Transparency of corporate bond, structured finance product and credit derivatives markets*, Consultation Paper CESR/08-1014, 19 December.

----------- (2009a), *Impact of MiFID on equity secondary markets functioning*, Report 09/355, 10 June.

----------- (2009b), *Transparency of corporate bond, structured finance product and credit derivatives markets*, Report CESR/09-348, 10 July.

——————— (2010a), "CESR Technical Advice to the European Commission in the context of MiFID Review – Transaction Reporting", Technical Advice CESR/10-808, 29 July.

——————— (2010b), "CESR Technical Advice to the European Commission in the context of the MiFID Review – Equity Markets", Technical Advice CESR/10-802, 29 July.

——————— (2010c), "CESR Technical Advice to the European Commission in the context of the MiFID Review – Investor Protection and Intermediaries", Technical Advice CESR/10-859, 29 July.

——————— (2010d), "Micro-structural issues of the European equity markets", Call for Evidence, *CESR/10-142,* 1 April.

——————— (2010e), "Waivers from Pre-trade Transparency Obligations under the Markets in Financial Instruments Directive (MiFID). Update.", CESR/09-324, 6 January.

——————— (2010f), "CESR Technical Advice to the European Commission in the Context of the MiFID Review: Non-equity markets transparency", Technical Advice CESR/10-799, 29 July.

——————— (2010g), "CESR Technical Advice to the European Commission in the Context of the MiFID Review – Equity Markets. Post-trade Transparency Standards", Technical Advice CESR/10-882, October.

——————— (2010h), "Summary of responses from investment firms and execution venues to CESR's 2009 Best Execution Questionnaire (Sections 1-4)", Report, 19 November.

——————— (2010i), "Inducements: good and poor practices", Feedback Statement, *CESR/10-296,* 19 April.

CFA Institute (Chartered Financial Analysts) (2009), *Market Microstructure: The Impact of Fragmentation under the Markets in Financial Instruments Directive* (http://www.cfapubs.org/toc/ccb/2009/2009/13).

Chaboud, Alain, Erik Hjalmarsson, Clara Vega and Ben Chiquoine (2009), *Rise of the Machines: Algorithmic Trading in the Foreign Exchange Market*, Federal Reserve Board International Finance Discussion Paper, No. 980, October (http://ssrn.com/abstract=1501135).

Cheuvreux (2010), "Micro-structural issues of the European equity markets", Call for evidence CESR/10-142, 30 April (http://www.cesr-eu.org/index.php?page=responses&id=158).

Chi-X (2010), "Response to CESR call for evidence on market microstructure issues of the European equity markets" (http://www.cesr-eu.org/index.php?page=responses&id=158).

Chowdhry, B. and V. Nanda (1991), "Multi-market trading and market liquidity", *Review of Financial Studies 4*, 483–511.

Cici, Gjergji, Scott Gibson and John J. Merrick (2008), *Missing the Marks: Dispersion in Corporate Bond Valuations across Mutual Funds*, Working Paper, July (www.ssrn.com/abstract=1104508).

Coase, Ronald (1960), "The Problem of Social Cost", *Journal of Law and Economics*, Vol. 3, October.

Comerton-Forde Carole and James Rydge (2004), "A Review of Stock Market Microstructure", *Equity Market Microstructure Review*, CMCRC Limited and SIRCA, April.

Cooter, Robert D. and Bradley J. Freedman (1991), "The Fiduciary Relationship: Its Economic Character and Legal Consequences", *NYU. Law Review*, Vol. 66, pp. 1045-1075.

CRA (Charles River Associates) International (2009), *Evaluation of the Economic Impacts of the FSAP*, Study for the European Commission, 7 July.

Credit Suisse (2011), "Measuring Dark Pools' Impact", Market Commentary, Portfolio Strategy, 31 January.

David S. Evans and Michael Salinger (2002), "Competition Thinking at the European Commission: Lessons from the aborted GE-Honeywell Merger", *George Mason Law Review*, Vol. 10.

De Winne, Rudy and Catherine D'Hondt (2007), "Hide-and-Seek in the Market: Placing and Detecting Hidden Orders", *Review of Finance*, Vol. 11, No. 4, pp. 663-692.

Degryse, Hans, Frank de Jong and Vincent van Kervel (forthcoming 2010), "Impact of OTC trading on invisible market depth of large Dutch firms", preliminary results.

Degryse, Hans, Mark Van Achter and Gunther Wuyts (2008), *Shedding Light on Dark Liquidity Pools*, TILEC Discussion Paper, DP 2008-039, November.

----------- (2009), "Dynamic order submission with competition between a dealer market and a crossing network", *Journal of Financial Economics*, Vol. 91, pp. 319-338.

Demarigny, Fabrice (2010), *An EU-Listing Small Business Act*, Report for the French Ministry, March (http://www.eurocapitalmarkets.org/node/455).

Demsetz, Harold (1968), "The Cost of Transacting", *Quarterly Journal of Economics*, Vol. 82, No. 1, February, pp. 33-53.

Di Noia, Carmine (2001), "Competition and Integration among Stock Exchanges in Europe: Network Effects, Implicit Mergers and Remote Access", *European Financial Management*, Vol. 7, No. 1, March, pp. 39-72.

Domowitz, Ian (1990), "The Mechanisms of Automated Trade Execution Systems", *Journal of Financial Intermediation*, Vol. 1, pp. 167-194.

––––––––––– (1996), "The Classification and Regulation of Automated Trading Systems", in Andrew W. Lo (ed.), *The Industrial Organisation and Regulation of the Securities Industry*, National Bureau of Economic Research Conference Report, Chicago, IL: University of Chicago Press.

Domowitz, Ian and Benn Steil (1999), *Automation, Trading Costs, and the Structure of the Securities Trading Industry*, Brookings-Wharton Papers on Financial Services (http://www.cfr.org/content/publications/attachments/Brookings-Wharton.pdf).

Dow, James and Gary Gorton (2006), *Noise Traders*, NBER Working Paper, No. W12256, National Bureau of Economic Research, Cambridge, MA, May.

DTCC Deriv/Serv, CDS Data warehouse (www.dtcc.com/products/derivserv/data/index.php).

Easley, David, Nicholas M. Kiefer, Maureen O'Hara (1996), "Cream-Skimming or Profit-Sharing? The Curious Rule of Purchased Order Flow", *The Journal of Finance*, Vol. 51, No. 3, July, pp. 811-833.

Easterbrook, Frank H. and Daniel R. Fischel (1993), "Contract and Fiduciary Duty", *Journal of Law and Economics*, Vol. XXXVI, April.

Economides, Nicholas (1993), "Network Economics with Application to Finance", *Financial Markets, Institutions and Instruments*, Vol. 2, No. 5, December, pp. 89-97.

––––––––––– (1996), "The Economics of Networks", *International Journal of Industrial Organization*, Vol. 14, pp. 673-699.

———————— (2008), "Public Policy in Network Industries", in Paolo Buccirossi (ed.), *Handbook of Antitrust Economics*, Cambridge, MA: MIT Press.

Economides, Nicholas and Robert A. Schwartz (1995), "Electronic Call Market Trading", *Journal of Portfolio Management*, Vol. 21, No. 3, Spring.

Edwards, Amy K., Lawrence Harris and Michael S. Piwowar (2007), "Corporate Bond Market Transaction Costs and Transparency", *Journal of Finance*, Vol. 62, No. 3, June.

EFAMA (European Fund and Asset Management Association) (2010), *Revisiting the landscape of European long-term savings – A call for action from the asset management industry*, Report (sponsored by EFAMA), March.

Ende, B., P. Gomber and M. Lutat (2008), *Smart order routing technology in the new European equity trading landscape*, Working Paper E-Finance Lab, Goethe University, Frankfurt.

Engel, Kathleen C. and Patricia A. McCoy (2002), "A Tale of Three Markets: The Law & Economics of Predatory Lending", *Texas Law Review*, Vol. 80, No. 6, May.

Engelen Peter and Karel Lannoo (eds) (2009), *Facing New Regulatory Frameworks in Securities Trading in Europe*, Mortsel, Belgium: Intersentia.

Enriques, Luca (2006), "Conflicts of Interests in Investment Services: The Price and Uncertainty Impact of MiFID's Regulatory Framework", in Ferrarini Guido and Eddy Wymeersch (eds), *Investor Protection in Europe*, Oxford: Oxford University Press.

ESME (European Securities Markets Expert Group) (2009a), "Fact-finding regarding the availability of post-trade data in equities in the EU", 19 March (http://ec.europa.eu/internal_market/securities/docs/esme/report-data-availability_en.pdf).

———————— (2009b), "Fact-finding regarding the developments of certain aspects of pre-trade transparency in equities under MiFID", 27 July (http://ec.europa.eu/internal_market/securities/docs/esme/report_pretrade_11_full_esme_20090727_en.pdf).

EuroCCP (2010), "Reducing Risk Among Interoperating CCPs", *Interoperability Update Briefing*, 14 January (http://www.euroccp.co.uk/leadership/index.php).

ECMI (European Capital Markets Institute) (2010), *2010 Statistical Package*, October, (www.eurocapitalmarkets.org).

European Commission (2008), *Report on non-equities markets transparency pursuant to Article 65(1) of Directive 2004/39/EC on markets in financial instruments ('MiFID')*, DG Internal Market and Services Working Document, 3 April, (http://ec.europa.eu/internal_market/securities/docs/isd/nemt_report_en.pdf).

----------- (2009a), Commission Communication on ensuring efficient, safe and sound derivatives markets: future policy actions, COM (2009) 563 final, October.

----------- (2009b), *The Code of Conduct on Clearing and Settlement: Three Years of Experience*, Commission Staff Working Document to the ECOFIN, 6 November.

----------- (2010a), "Europe 2020. A European strategy for smart, sustainable and inclusive growth", COM (2010) 2020, 3 March.

----------- (2010b), Public Consultation. Review of the Markets in Financial Instruments Directive (MiFID), Consultation Report, 8 December, (http://ec.europa.eu/internal_market/securities/isd/mifid_en.htm).

Fabozzi, Frank J. (2007), *Fixed Income Analysis*, CFA Institute, New Jersey: John Wiley & Sons.

Ferrarini, Guido (2009), "Market transparency and best execution: Bond trading under MiFID", in M. Tison et al. (eds), *Perspectives in company law and financial regulation,* Cambridge: Cambridge University Press.

Ferrarini, Guido and Eddy Wymeersch (eds) (2006), *Investor Protection in Europe. Corporate Law Making, the MiFID and Beyond,* Oxford: Oxford University Press.

FESE, EACH, ECSDA (2006), "European Code of Conduct for Clearing and Settlement", 7 November (http://ec.europa.eu/internal_market/financialmarkets/docs/code/code_en.pdf).

----------- (2007), "Access and Interoperability Guideline", 28 June (http://ec.europa.eu/internal_market/financialmarkets/docs/code/guideline_en.pdf).

Financial Stability Board (2010), "Implementing OTC Derivatives Market Reforms", 25 October (http://www.financialstabilityboard.org).

Fleuriot, Pierre (2010), *The Review of the Markets in Financial Instruments Directive (MiFID)*, Working Group Report to the French Minister for the Economy, Industry and Employment, February.

Flood, Mark D., Ronald Huisman, Kees G. Koedijk and Ronald J. Mahieu (1999), "Quote Disclosure and Price Discovery in Multiple-Dealer Financial Markets", *The Review of Financial Studies*, Vol. 12, No. 1, Spring , pp. 37-59.

Foucault, Thierry (1999), "Order flow competition and trading costs in a dynamic limit order market", *Journal of Financial Markets*, Vol. 2, pp. 99-134.

Foucault, Thierry and Albert Menkveld (2008), "Competition for Order Flow and Smart Order Routing Systems", *The Journal of Finance*, Vol. LXIII, No. 1, February.

G20, (2009a), "Declaration on strengthening the financial system", London Summit, 2 April (http://www.londonsummit.gov.uk/resources/en/PDF/annex-strengthening-fin-sysm).

---------- (2009b), "Leaders' Statement: The Pittsburgh Summit", Pittsburgh Summit, 24-25 September (http://www.pittsburghsummit.gov/mediacenter/129639.htm).

Francioni, Reto and Robert A. Schwartz (2004), *Equity Markets in Action. The Fundamentals of Liquidity, Market Structure and Trading*, John Wiley & Sons, Inc.

Francioni, Reto, Sonali Hazarika, Maritn Reck and Robert A. Schwartz (2008), "Equity Market Microstructure: Taking Stock of What We Know", *The Journal of Portfolio Mangagement*, Vol. 35, No. 1, pp. 57-71.

Frankel, Tamar (1983), "Fiduciary Law", *71 CAL. L. REV.*, p. 795.

FSA (Financial Services Authority) (2006a), *Implementing MiFID's best execution requirements*, Discussion paper DP06/3, May.

---------- (2006b), *The Overall Impact of MiFID*, Report, November.

---------- (2008), "Sponsored Access (SA)", *Market Watch*, No. 30, November.

---------- (2010a), "Distribution of retail investments: delivering the RDR", Feedback to CP09/18 and final rules, March.

---------- (2010b), "Trading venue outages", *Market Watch*, No. 36, August.

Gajewsky, Jean-François and Carole Gresse (2007), "Centralised order books versus hybrid order books: A paired comparison of trading costs on NSC (Euronext Paris) and SETS (London Stock Exchange)", *Journal of Banking and Finance,* Vol. 31, No. 9, September, pp. 2906-2924.

Giovannini Group (2001), "Cross-Border Clearing and Settlement Arrangements in the European Union", Brussels, November (http://ec.europa.eu/internal_market/financial-markets/clearing/index_en.htm).

----------- (2003), "Second report on EU Clearing and Settlement Arrangements", April (http://ec.europa.eu/internal_market/financial-markets/clearing/index_en.htm).

Giraud, Jean-René and Catherine D'Hondt (2006), *MiFID. Convergence towards a unified European capital markets industry,* London: Risk Books.

Glosten, Lawrence R. (1989), "Insider Trading, Liquidity, and the Role of the Monopolist Specialist", *Journal of Business,* No. 62, pp. 211-236.

----------- (1994), "Is the Electronic Open Limit Order Book Inevitable?", *The Journal of Finance,* Vol. XLIX, No. 4, September.

Goldstein, Michael A., Edith S. Hotchkiss and Erik R. Sirri (2006), *Transparency and Liquidity: A Controlled Experiment on Corporate Bonds,* Working Paper, 2 March (www.ssrn.com).

Gomber, Peter and Axel Pierron (2010), *MiFID. Spirit and Reality of a European Financial Markets Directive,* Report, Goethe University Frankfurt and Celent, September.

Gomber, Peter, Gregor Pujol and Adrian Wranik (2009), "The Implementation of European Best Execution Obligations. An Analysis for the German Market", Proceedings of the 4th International Workshop on Enterprise Applications and Services in the Finance Industry, Springer LNBIP, pp. 126-144.

Graf, Raoul, Fabien Durif and Mario Belzile (2008), "'Echo Generation': Switching costs and the relational approach in the banking industry", *Innovative Marketing,* Vol. 4, Issue 1, pp. 77-86.

Gresse, Carole (2010), "Multi-Market Trading and Market Quality", Working Paper, University Paris Dauphine (http://basepub.dauphine.fr/handle/123456789/3148).

Group of Thirty (2010), "Enhancing Financial Stability and Resilience. Macroprudential Policy, Tools, and Systems for the Future", Special Report, August.

Hagerty, Kathleen and Robert L. McDonald (1996), "Brokerage, Market Fragmentation, and Securities Market Regulation", in Andrew W. Lo (ed.), *The Industrial Organisation and Regulation of the Securities Industry*, National Bureau of Economic Research, The University of Chicago Press.

Harris, Lawrence E. (1996), *The Economics of Best Execution*, USC Working Paper, University of Southern California, Los Angeles, CA, 9 March.

----------- (1997), Order Exposure and Parasitic Traders, Report prepared for Deutsche Boerse AG Symposium "Equity Market Structure for Large and Mid-Cap Stocks", Frankfurt, 12 December.

----------- (2002), *Trading and Exchanges: Market Microstructure for Practitioners*, Oxford: Oxford University Press.

----------- (ed.), (2010), *Regulated Exchanges: Dynamic Agents of Economic Growth*, 50th Yearbook, World Federation of Exchanges, in cooperation with the Centre for European Policy Studies, Oxford: Oxford University Press.

Hazen, Thomas Lee (2006), *Principles of Securities Regulation*, Second Edition, Thomas/West.

Hendershott, Terrence and Charles M. Jones (2005), "Island Goes Dark: Transparency, Fragmentation, and Regulation", *The Review of Financial Studies*, Vol. 18, No. 3, Autumn, pp. 743-793.

Hendershott, Terrence, Pamela C. Moulton and Mark S. Seasholes (2007), "Market Maker Inventories and Liquidity", AFA 2008 New Orleans Meetings Paper, 9 May (www.ssrn.com).

Hendershott, Terrence, Charles M. Jones, and Albert J. Menkveld (2008), "Does Algorithmic Trading Improve Liquidity?", WFA 2008 Paper, March.

Hendershott, Terrence and Ryan Riordan (2009), *Algorithmic Trading and Information*, NET Institute Working Paper No. 09-08, September.

Hermalin, Benjamin E., Avery W. Katz, and Richard Craswell, "Contract Law", in Mitchell Polinsky and Steven Shavell (eds.), *Handbook of Law and Economics*. Volume 1, Elsevier.

Holmstrom, Bengt (1979), "Moral Hazard and Observability", *The Bell Journal of Economics*, Vol. 10, No. 1, Spring, pp. 74-91.

Hynes Richard and Eric A. Posner (2001), *The Law and Economics of Consumer Finance*, John Olin Law and Economics WP No. 117, 20 February (www.ssrn.com).

IOSCO (International Organization of Securities Commissions) (2004), *Transparency of Corporate Bond Markets*, Report of the Technical Committee of the International Organisation of Securities Commission, May.

─────────── (2007), "Market Intermediary Management of Conflicts that Arise in Securities Offerings", Consultation Report, Technical Committee, February.

─────────── (2009a), "Policies on Direct Electronic Access", Consultation Report, Technical Committee of the IOSCO, February.

─────────── (2010a), "Objectives and Principles of Securities Regulation", Report, June.

─────────── (2009b), "Transparency of Structured Finance Products", Consultation Report, Technical Committee, September.

─────────── (2010b), "Principles for Direct Electronic Access to Markets", Final Report FR08/10, August.

─────────── (2010c), "Issues Raised by Dark Liquidity", Consultation Report CR05/10, October.

─────────── (2010d), "Guidance for Efficient Regulation of Conflicts of Interest Facing Market Intermediaries", Final Report, October.

International Swaps and Derivatives Association (2003): "ISDA Credit Derivatives Definitions", Supplements and Commentaries.

Jolls, Christine (2007), *Behavioral Law and Economics*, WP No. 12879, National Bureau of Economic Research, Cambridge, MA, January.

Jolls, Christine, Cass R. Sunstein and Richard Thaler (2000), "A Behavioral Approach to Law and Economics", in Cass R. Sunstein (ed.), *Behavioral Law and Economics*, Cambridge: Cambridge University Press.

Klemperer, Paul (1995), "Competition When Consumers Have Switching Costs: An Overview with Applications to Industrial Organisation, Macroeconomics and International Trade", *Review of Economic Studies*, 62, pp. 515-539.

Korobkin, Russel B. and Thomas S. Ulen (2000), "Law and Behavioral Science: Removing the Rationality Assumption from Law and Economics", *California Law Review*, Vol. 88.

Kovtunenko, Boris (2002), "Post-Trade Transparency: The More the Better?", May (www.ssrn.com).

Kraakman, Reinier H. (1986), "Gatekeepers: The Anatomy of a Third-Party Enforcement Strategy", *Journal of Law, Economics and Organization*, Vol. 2, No. 1, Spring.

Kumar, Kiran K., Ramabhadran S. Thirumalai and Pradeep K. Yadav (2009), "Hiding behind the Veil: Pre-trade Transparency, Informed Traders and Market Quality", Working Paper (www.ssrn.com).

Kyle, Albert S. (1985), "Continuous Auctions and Insider Trading", *Econometrica*, Vol. 53, No. 6, November, pp. 1315-1335.

Laganá, Marco, Martin Peřina, Isabelle von Köppen and Avinash Persaud (2006), *Implications for liquidity from innovation and transparency in the European corporate bond market*, ECB Occasional Paper No. 50, European Central Bank, Frankfurt, August.

Langen, Werner (2010), *Report on derivatives markets: future policy options*, Committee on Economic and Monetary Affairs 2010/2008 (INI), European Parliament, 7 June.

Lannoo, Karel and Diego Valiante (2009), "Integrating Europe's Back Office: 10 Years of Turning in Circles", in Peter Engelen and Karel Lannoo (eds) (2009), *Facing New Regulatory Frameworks in Securities Trading in Europe*, Intersentia, pp. 31-53.

----------- (2011), "*The MiFID Metamorphosis: A new paradigm for market structure*", *Journal of Securities and Custody*, Vol. 3, No. 4, January.

Lee, Ruben (1998), *What is an exchange? The Automation, Management, and Regulation of Financial Markets*, Oxford: Oxford University Press, New York.

----------- (2002), *Capital Markets that Benefit Investors. A Survey of the Evidence on Fragmentation, Internalisation and Market Transparency*, Oxford Finance Group, 30 September.

Levin, Mattias (2003), *Competition, Fragmentation and Transparency. Providing the Regulatory Framework for Fair, Efficient and Dynamic European Securities Markets. Assessing the ISD*, CEPS Task Force Report No. 46, CEPS, Brussels, April.

Llewellyn, David T. (1995), "Regulation of Retail Investment Services", *Economic Affairs*, Vol. 15, No. 2, pp. 12-17.

Lo, Andrew W. (ed.) (1996), *The Industrial Organisation and Regulation of the Securities Industry*, National Bureau of Economic Research, The University of Chicago Press.

London Economics (2010), *Understanding the impact of MiFID in the context of global and national regulatory innovations*, Report prepared for the City of London, October.

London Stock Exchange (2010), "Response to CESR MiFID Consultation Paper 10-394 – equity markets" (www.cesr.org).

Macey, Jonathan R. and Maureen O'Hara (1997), "The Law and Economics of Best Execution", *Journal of Financial Intermediation*, No. 6, pp. 188-223.

─────────── (2005), "From Orders to Markets", *Regulation*, Vol. 28, No. 2, pp. 62-70, Summer.

Madhavan, Ananth (1992), "Trading Mechanisms in Securities Markets", *The Journal of Finance*, Vol. 47, No. 2, June, pp. 607-641.

─────────── (1995), "Consolidation, Fragmentation, and the Disclosure of Trading Information", *Review of Financial Studies*, No. 8, pp. 579-603.

─────────── (1996), "Security Prices and Market Transparency", *Journal of Financial Intermediation*, No. 5, pp. 255-283.

─────────── (2000), "Market Microstructure: A Survey", *Journal of Financial Markets*, Vol. 3, pp. 205-258.

Madhavan, Ananth, David Porter and Daniel Weaver (2005), "Should securities markets be transparent?", *Journal of Financial Markets*, No. 8, July, pp. 266-288.

Malinova, Katya and Andreas Park (2008), "Liquidity, Volume, and Price Behaviour: The Impact of Order vs. Quote Based Trading", 11th Symposium on Finance, Banking, and Insurance, University of Karlsruhe, December.

Matthews, Barbara (2010), "MiFID Review and Best Execution Cross-Border Macro-Trend Analysis", Presentation to CEPS/ECMI MiFID Review Task Force, BCM International Regulatory Analytics LLC, October.

McCleskey, Scott (2004), *Achieving Market Integration: Best Execution, Fragmentation and the Free Flow of Capital*, Butterworth-Heinemann.

McInish, Thomas H. and Robert A. Wood (1996), "Competition, Fragmentation, and Market Quality", in Andrew W. Lo (ed.), *The Industrial Organisation and Regulation of the Securities Industry*, National Bureau of Economic Research, The University of Chicago Press.

Mendelson, Haim (1987), "Consolidation, Fragmentation and Market Performance", *Journal of Financial and Quantitative Market Analysis,* Vol. 22, No. 2, pp. 189-207.

Milgrom, Paul and John Roberts (1992), *Economics, Organization and Management,* New Jersey: Prentice Hall Inc.

Moinas, Sophie (2010), *Hidden limit orders and liquidity in order driven markets,* Working Paper, Toulouse University and IDEI (http://idei.fr/doc/wp/2010/hidden_sm_03_2010.pdf).

Moloney, Niamh (2008), *EC Securities Regulation* (2nd ed), Oxford: Oxford University Press

Monti, Mario (2010), *A New Strategy for the Single Market: At the Service of Europe's Economy and Society,* Report to the Present of the European Commission, José Manuel Barroso, 9 May.

Naik, Narayan Y., Anthony Neuberger and S. Viswanathan (1999), "Trade Disclosure Regulation in Markets with Negotiated Trades", *The Review of Financial Studies,* Vol. 12, No. 4, pp. 873-900.

Nasdaq OMX (2010), "Automated Gains: How to adapt to a High-Speed Environment", presentation by Hans-Ole Jochumsen, President, October.

Nelson, Phillip (1970), "Information and Consumer Behavior", *The Journal of Political Economy,* Vol. 78, No. 2, March - April, pp. 311-329.

Nomura (2010), "Market Structure. European Equity Market Structure Update", *Nomura Market Structure Newsletter,* October.

Office of Fair Trading (OFT) (2008), "Assessing the effectiveness of potential remedies in consumer markets", OFT 994, April.

O'Hara, Maureen (1995), *Market Microstructure Theory,* Cambridge: Blackwell Publishing.

O'Hara, Maureen and Mao Ye (2009), "Is Market Fragmentation Harming Market Quality?", Working Paper, Cornell University (www.ssrn.com).

Oxera (2009), *Monitoring prices, costs and volumes of trading and post-trading services,* Report prepared for the European Commission, MARKT/2007/02/G, July (http://www.oxera.com/cmsDocuments/Trading%20and%20post%20trading%20report.pdf).

------------ (2010), "Retail Distribution Review Proposals: Impact on market structure and competition", March (http://www.fsa.gov.uk/pubs/policy/oxera_rdr10.pdf).

Pagano, Marco (1989), "Trading Volume and Asset Liquidity", *The Quarterly Journal of Economics*, Vol. 104, No. 2, May, pp. 255-274.

Pagano, Marco and Ailsa Roëll (1993), "Auction markets, dealership markets and execution risk", in Vittorio Conti and Rony Hamaui (eds), *Financial Markets Liberalisation and the role of Banks*, Cambridge: Cambridge University Press.

——————— (1996), "Transparency and liquidity: a comparison of auction and dealer markets with informed trading", *Journal of Finance*, No. 51, pp. 579-612.

Parlour, Christine A. (2010), "Limit Order Markets: An Economic Perspective", presentation at Market Microstructure Conference, Institut Louis Bachelier (ILB), Paris, 6 December.

Pistor, Katharina and Chenggang Xu (2002), *Fiduciary Duty in Transitional Civil Law Jurisdictions. Lessons from the Incomplete Law Theory*, Law Working Paper, No. 01/2002, European Corporate Governance Institute.

Posner, Richard A. (1998), "Economic Analysis of Law", *Aspen Law and Business*, 5th ed., January.

Ready, Mark J. (2009), "Determinants of Volume in Dark Pools", AFA 2010 Atlanta Meeting Papers, 12 December (www.ssrn.com).

Renda, Andrea and Diego Valiante (2010), *Legal and Economic Approach to Tying and Other Potentially Unfair and Anticompetitive Commercial Practices: Focus on Financial Services*, Working Paper Series, February (www.ssrn.com).

Riordan, Ryan, Andreas Storkenmaier, Martin Wagener (2009), *Fragmentation, Competition and Market Quality: A Post-MiFID Analysis*, Working Paper, Karlsruhe Institute of Technology (www.ssrn.com).

Rochet, Jean-Charles and Jean Tirole (2003), "Platform Competition in Two-Sided Markets", *Journal of the European Economic Association*, Vol. 1, No. 4, pp. 990-1029.

——————— (2004), "Defining Two-Sided Markets", mimeo, University of Toulouse.

——————— (2006), "Two-Sided Markets: A Progress Report", *The RAND Journal of Economics*, Vol. 37, No. 3, Autumn, pp. 645-667.

Sabatini, Giovanni and Isadora Tarola (2002), "Transparency on Secondary Markets. A Survey of Economic Literature and Current Regulation in Italy", *Quaderni di Finanza CONSOB*, No. 50, May.

Schmiedel, Heiko, Markku Malkamäki and Juha Tarkka (2006), "Economies of scale and technological development in securities depository and settlement systems", *Journal of Banking and Finance*, No. 30, pp. 1783-1806.

Schmiedel, Heiko (2002), *Total factor productivity growth in European stock exchanges: A non-parametric frontier approach*, Bank of Finland Discussion Paper, November.

Schmiedel, Heiko and Andreas Schönenberger (2005), *Integration of securities market infrastructures in the Euro area*, Occasional Paper Series No. 33, July.

Segré, Claudio (1966), *The development of a European capital market*, Report of a Group of Experts appointed by the European Commission.

----------- (2009), "Regulation of Non-Public Trading Interest", Release No. 34-60997, File No. S7-27-09, 13 November.

----------- (2010a), "Concept Release on Equity Market Structure", Release No. 34-61358, File No. S7-02-10, 14 January.

----------- (2010b), *Findings Regarding The Market Events of May 6, 2010*, Report of the Staffs of the CFTC and SEC to the Joint Advisory Committee on Emerging Regulatory Issues, September 30.

Shim, Ilhyock and Haibin Zhu (2010), *The Impact of CDS trading on the bond market: Evidence from Asia*, BIS Working Papers No. 332, Bank for International Settlements, November.

Simon, Herbert (1957), "A Behavioral Model of Rational Choice", in *Models of Man, Social and Rational: Mathematical Essays on Rational Human Behavior in a Social Setting*, New York, NY: John Wiley.

Smith, Reginald (2010), *Is High-frequency Trading Inducing Changes in Market Microstructure and Dynamics?*, Working Paper Series, MIT – Sloan School of Management, MIT, Cambridge, MA, June (www.ssrn.com).

Stoll, Hans R. (1978), "The Supply of Dealer Services in Securities Markets", *The Journal of Finance*, Vol. 33, No. 4, September, pp. 1133-1151.

Swinburne, Kay (2010), *Report on Regulation of trading in financial instruments – 'dark pools' etc.*, Committee on Economic and Monetary Affairs, 2010/2075(INI), European Parliament, November.

Valiante, Diego (2010), *Shaping Reforms and Business Models for the OTC Derivatives Market: Quo vadis?*, ECMI Research Report No. 5, ECMI, Brussels, April (www.eurocapitalmarkets.org).

Van Cayseele, Patrick and Jo Reynaerts (2010), "Complementary Platforms", under revision, *Journal of Network Economies*.

Van Cayseele, Patrick and Christophe Wuyts (2006), *Measuring Scale Economies in a Heterogeneous Industry: The case of European Settlement Institutions*, SUERF – The European Money and Finance Forum, Vienna.

─────────── (2007), "Cost Efficiency in the European Securities Settlement and Depository Industry", *Journal of Banking and Finance*, Vol. 31.

Varian, Hal R. (2006), *Intermediate Microeconomics. A Modern Approach*, New York, NY: W.W. Norton and Company Inc.

Walter, Ingo (2004), "Conflicts of Interest and Market Discipline Among Financial Services Firms", *European Management Journal*, Vol. 22, No. 4, pp. 361-376.

─────────── (2006), *Reputational Risk and Conflicts of Interest in Banking and Finance: The Evidence So Far*, Working Paper, Stern School of Business, NYU, New York, NY, 9 December.

Williamson, Oliver E. (1975), *Markets and Hierarchies: Analysis and Antitrust Implications – A Study in the Economics of Internal Organization*, New York, NY: Free Press.

ANNEX I. LIST OF ACRONYMS

ABCP	Asset-Backed Commercial Paper
ABS	Asset-Based Security
ADT	Average Daily (order book) Turnover
ASO	Average Size of Orders
ATS	Alternative Trading System
BBO	Best Bid Offer
BCS	Broker-dealer Crossing System
BCN	Broker-dealer Crossing Network
CATS	Computerised Automated Trading System
CCP	Central Counterparty Clearing
CDO	Collateralised Debt Obligation
CDS	Credit Default Swap
CEBS	Committee of European Banking Supervisors
CESR	Committee of European Securities Regulators
CFTC	Commodity Futures Trading Commission
CoB	Conduct of Business
CoI	Conflict of Interest
CRD	Capital Requirements Directive
CSD	Central Securities Depositories
CSDR	Central Securities Depositories Regulation
CUA	Customised Unilateral Access
DA	Direct Access
DEA	Direct Electronic Access
DMA	Direct Market Access
DTCC	Depository Trust and Clearing Corporation
EACH	European Association of CCP Clearing Houses
EBBO	European Best Bid and Offer
ECSDA	European Central Securities Depositories Association
EEA	European Economic Area
EFAMA	European Fund and Asset Management Association
EMIR	European Market Infrastructure Regulation
ECP	Eligible Counterparty
ETD	Exchange-Traded Derivative
ESMA	European Securities and Markets Authority
ESME	European Securities Markets Expert Group

FESE	Federation of European Securities Exchanges
FINRA	Financial Industry Regulatory Authority
HFT	High-Frequency Trading
IMD	Insurance Mediation Directive
IOI	Indication of Interest
IOSCO	International Organization of Securities Commissions
IPO	Initial Public Offer
IRS	Interest Rate Swap
ISD	Investment Services Directive
LISO	Large In-Scale Order
MAD	Market Abuse Directive
MiFID	Markets in Financial Instruments Directive
MTF	Multilateral Trading Facility
NASDAQ	National Association of Securities Dealers Automated Quotations Systems
NBBO	National Best Bid and Offer
NYSE	New York Stock Exchange
OLOB	Open Limit-Order Book
OTF	Organised Trading Facility
PRIP	Packaged Retail Investment Product
RFQ	Request For Quote
RM	Regulated Market
SA	Sponsored Access
SEC	Securities and Exchange Commission
SEF	Swap Execution Facility
SFP	Structured Financial product
SI	Systematic Internaliser
SLD	Securities Law Directive
SMS	Standard Market Size
SPV	Special Purpose Vehicle
STP	Straight-Through Processing
TFA	Transaction Feed Access
UCITS	Undertakings for Collective Investments in Transferable Securities
VWAP	Volume Weighted Average Price

ANNEX II.
THE OBJECTIVES OF THE TASK FORCE

Mandate

The Task Force was composed of 31 members, who represented most segments of European capital markets.[222] It aims at increasing knowledge around new economic and regulatory issues brought about by MiFID and to include – where agreement was found – recommendations that may support the regulatory and policy-making process. This report, in effect, offers its contribution based on a coherent and – wherever possible – agreed approach to relevant regulatory and economic issues, aimed at avoiding haphazard or ill-informed decisions.

The Task Force is an independent and non-political group representing major segments of the industry (see list of participants). The report is built on the basic tenets of financial markets and it has been drafted to be understandable not just by technical experts and to address readers on issues and technicalities of European capital markets. Official papers of the CESR and the European Commission provided background documents for each of the five meetings held from June to November 2010.

Priorities

The members acknowledges that the scope of the Task Force is fairly broad, and hence priority has been given to three main areas:

1. Pre- and post-trade transparency (including extension of post-trade requirements to non-equity markets, and improved over-the-counter trade transparency and reporting);
2. Trading venues classification (including regulated markets, multilateral trading facilities and other trading venues[223]) and market microstructure; and
3. Conduct of business rules (selling practices and best execution).

---

[222] No representatives of issuers associations were formally involved in the work of the Task Force.

[223] In particular, organised trading facilities, so-called 'OTFs' (EU COM, 2010b).

The approach taken aimed to combine theoretical aspects from diverse disciplines (e.g. competition policy, economics, financial regulation, etc.) with more empirical aspects (such as market data) and members' direct contributions. One of the objectives of the Task Force report therefore is to clarify where differences of views are due to the use of different definitions and also, most notably, to provide data in order to give issues their real value.

The report will present as many recommendations as possible but it is intended to include recommendations only when there is general consensus between all the segments represented in the Task Force, including both members and observers. Recommendations will represent the views of the Task Force participants only, and not those of the rapporteurs, while the content of the Report is mainly their work. The role of the rapporteurs thus is to set out the views of the Members in a proper and neutral manner.

The final report takes into account all different views – including minority ones – explaining them in a fair and, where possible, neutral manner. The report aims at having a balanced and well-documented set of facts. The intention was not to seek to force consensus when views clearly differed.

Activities and meetings of the Task Force have followed a tight timeline from June to December 2010. As shown below, the Group held five meetings, three of which were devoted to a discussion of the core issues of the MiFID Review.

Figure AII.1 Task Force timeline

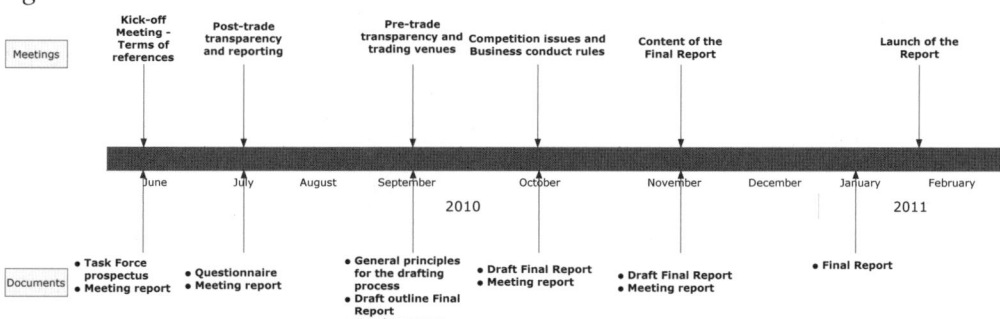

Materials and members' contributions/presentations have been circulated in order to enrich the content of each session. Meeting reports have been a helpful tool to crystallise recommendations in the aftermath of each meeting.

Annex III. Overview of Regulated Markets[224] and Pan-European MTFs[225] Infrastructure (SEE NOTES AT END OF THE TABLE)

	Trading Services		Clearing Services	Settlement Services	Market Model
	Platform	Type[226]			
LSE	TradElect (Electronic)	SETS (Order-driven) SETSqx (Hybrid) SEAQ (Quote-driven)	LCH.Clearnet Ltd SIX X-clear *Eurex Clearing*[227]	Euroclear UK & Ireland	Horizontal
NYSE Euronext[228]	Universal Trading Platform (Electronic)	Order-driven	LCH.Clearnet[229] SA Interbolsa (Lisbon) *Eurex Clearing*[230]	Euroclear Group[231] Interbolsa (Lisbon)	Semi-Horizontal
Deutsche Börse	Xetra 11.0 (Electronic) Frankfurter Wertpapierbörse Frankfurt Stock Exchange (Floor Trading)	Order-driven	Eurex Clearing[232]	Clearstream Banking Frankfurt[233] *Euroclear Bank*[234] *SIS SegaInterSettle*[235]	Vertical

MiFID 2.0: Casting New Light on Europe's Capital Markets | 243

Exchange	Trading System	Type	CCP	CSD	Structure
BME Spanish Exchanges	SIBE (Electronic)	Order-driven	*Iberclear*[236]	Iberclear[237]	Vertical
Borsa Italiana	TradElect (Electronic)	Order-driven	CC&G	Monte Titoli *Euroclear Bank*[238]	Vertical
Nasdaq OMX Nordic[239]	INET Nordic (Electronic)	Order-driven	EMCF[240] *EuroCCP*[241] *SIX X-clear*[242]	Euroclear Sweden and Finland, VP Securities (DK)[243]	Vertical
SIX Swiss Exchange	SIX Platform (Electronic)	Order-driven	SIX X-clear LCH. Clearnet *Eurex Clearing*[244] *EMCF*[245]	SIS SegaInterSettle[246] *Clearstream*[247] *Euroclear Bank*[248]	Vertical
Oslo	TradElect (Electronic)	Order-driven	Oslo Clearing *LCH.Clearnet*[249]	VPS[250]	
Athens	OASIS (Integrated Automatic System for Electronic Trading) (Electronic)	Order-driven	ATHEXClear S.A.	Hellenic Exchanges S.A.[251]	Vertical
Warsaw	WARSET (WARsaw Stock Exchange Trading System) (Electronic)	Order-driven	National Depository for Securities	National Depository for Securities	Vertical
Vienna	Xetra (Electronic)	Order-driven	Central Counterparty Austria (CCP.A)	Oesterreichische Kontrollbank AG (OeKB)[252]	Vertical

Budapest	MMTS (Multi Market Trading System)	Order-driven	Central Clearing House & Depository Rt. (KELER)	Central Clearing House & Depository Rt. (KELER)	Vertical
Prague	-	Order-driven	Central Securities Depository Prague	Central Securities Depository Prague	Vertical
Irish SE	ISE Xetra 11.0 (electronic)	Order-driven	Eurex Clearing	Euroclear UK & Ireland	Horizontal
Bucharest	BSE Horizon – EFA Software Services (electronic)	Order-driven	BSE Equator	BSE Equator	Vertical
Cyprus	OASIS (Integrated Automatic System for Electronic Trading) (Electronic)	Order-driven	Cyprus Stock Exchange CSD	Cyprus Stock Exchange CSD[253]	Vertical
Ljubljana	BTS (Electronic)	Order-driven	KDD (Central Securities Clearing Corporation)	KDD (Central Securities Clearing Corporation)	Vertical
Nasdaq OMX Baltic[254]	INET Baltic (Electronic)	Order-driven	National CSDs	National CSDs	Horizontal
Bulgarian SE	Xetra (Electronic)	Order-driven	Central depository	Central depository	Vertical
Belgrade	BELEXFIX (Electronic)	Order-driven	Central Securities Depository and Clearing House a.d. Beograd	Central Securities Depository and Clearing House a.d. Beograd	Vertical

MiFID 2.0: Casting New Light on Europe's Capital Markets | 245

		Trading Services		Clearing Services	Settlement Services	Market Model
Luxembourg		UTP (Universal Trading Platform SM) (Electronic)	Order-driven	LCH.Clearnet	Bank's and ICSD's books	Horizontal
Bratislava		EBOS (Electronic Stock Exchange Trading System) (Electronic)	Order-driven	Central Securities Depositary of the Slovak Republic (CSD SR)	Central Securities Depositary of the Slovak Republic (CSD SR)	Vertical
Malta SE		Horizon (Electronic)	Order-driven	Malta Stock Exchange CSD	Malta Stock Exchange CSD	Vertical
		Trading Services		**Clearing Services**	**Settlement Services**	**Market Model**
Lit Pan-European Venues[255]						
Chi-X		Chi-X Platform (Electronic)	Order-driven	EMCF SIX X-clear LCH.Clearnet[256]	National CSDs	Horizontal
Turquoise		Millennium Exchange platform (Electronic)	Order-driven	EuroCCP SIX X-clear[257] LCH.Clearnet[258]	National CSDs Euroclear Bank[259]	Horizontal
BATS Europe		BATS MTF (Electronic)	Order-driven	LCH.Clearnet[260] EMCF SIX X-clear[261]	National CSDs	Horizontal
NYSE Arca Europe		Universal Trading Platform - NYSE Euronext systems	Order-driven	LCH.Clearnet[262] EuroCCP	National CSDs	Horizontal

Xetra International	(Electronic)	Order-driven	Eurex Clearing	National CSDs Clearstream Banking Frankfurt	Vertical
	Xetra 11.0 (Electronic)	Order-driven	Nomura NX	Nomura NX	Vertical
Nomura NX	Nomura NX (Electronic)	Order-driven	LCH.Clearnet Depending on home market[263]	National CSDs	Horizontal
Equiduct	Equiduct (Electronic)	Order-driven	EMCF	Euroclear Sweden and Finland, VP Securities Denmark	Horizontal
Burgundy	BTP (Burgundy Trading Platform) (Electronic)	Order-driven	Six X-clear *EuroCCP*[264]	National CSDs	Horizontal
UBS MTF	UBS MTF	Order-driven	Six X-clear *EuroCCP*[264]	National CSDs	Horizontal

[224] For latest developments in access and interoperability for clearing and settlement of cash equities between trading platform and CCPs/CSDs and between CCPs and/or CSDs, please see FESE, EACH & ECSDA, "Joint Status Update of the Code of Conduct", (http://ec.europa.eu/internal_market/financial-markets/docs/code/mog/20100315_fese_each_ecsda_en.pdf). There are three types of access to the infrastructure: standard access (SA); customized unilateral access (CUA or CA); and transaction feed access (TFA). 'Interoperability' between infrastructures means "advanced forms of relationships amongst Organisations where an Organisation is not generally connecting to existing standard service offerings of the other Organisations but where Organisations agree to establish customised solutions. Amongst its objectives, Interoperability will aim to provide a service to the customers such that they have choice of service provider. Such agreement will require Organisations to incur additional technical development". Please, see FESE, EACH and ECSDA, "European Code of Conduct for Clearing and Settlement", § 23-24 (http://ec.europa.eu/internal_market/financial-markets/docs/code/code_en.pdf).

[225] Firms that showed interest in entering the market (potential competitors) but have not yet been granted the link with incumbent infrastructures are represented in *Italics*.

[226] According to different rules, the vast majority of these order-driven markets are supported by liquidity providers, i.e. market-makers

allowed to submit quotes if needed.

227 Requested a TFA to LSE.

228 Includes Paris (CAC 40), Amsterdam (AEX), Brussels (BEL 20), and Lisbon (PSI 20).

229 NYSE Euronext has recently decided to terminate its contract with LCH.Clearnet and it will start soon clearing trades in-house; (http://www.efinancialnews.com/story/2010-05-24/nyse-euronext-challenges-cme).

230 Requested a TFA to Euronext Lisbon, Paris, Amsterdam and Brussels and a TFA to Euroclear Belgium, France and Netherlands, and Interbolsa.

231 Euroclear Group comprises International Central Securities Depository (ICSD) Euroclear Bank in Brussels and Central Securities Depositories (CSDs) Euroclear Belgium, Euroclear Finland, Euroclear France, Euroclear Nederland, Euroclear Sweden and Euroclear UK & Ireland.

232 TFA request from SIX x-clear not live.

233 Part of Link Up Markets, a joint venture by ten leading Central Securities Depositories (CSDs) – Clearstream Banking AG Frankfurt (Germany), Cyprus Stock Exchange (Cyprus), Hellenic Exchanges S.A. (Greece), IBERCLEAR (Spain), MCDR (Egypt), Oesterreichische Kontrollbank AG (Austria), SIX SIS AG (Switzerland), STRATE (South Africa), VP SECURITIES (Denmark) and VPS (Norway). Its key objective is to improve efficiency and reduce costs of post-trade processing of cross-border securities transactions by streamlined interoperability on the CSD layer.

Launched on 30 March 2009, Link Up Markets has established a common infrastructure allowing for streamlined interoperability between CSD markets and introducing efficient cross-border processing capabilities. The solution enables CSD customers to significantly reduce the cost gap between settling and safekeeping domestic and foreign securities.

234 TFA with Eurex Clearing requested.

235 Requested TFA with FWB and Eurex, and SA or CA with Clearstream.

236 Iberclear provides risk management services. A project to set up a CCP is in progress, with a consultation open by the Spanish Supervisor (CNMV).

237 Part of Link Up Markets. See footnote 233 above.

238 Requested a TFA with CC&G.

239 Includes Copenhagen (OMX Copenhagen 20, or OMXC20), Stockholm (OMX Stockholm 30 Index, or OMXS30), Helsinki (OMX Helsinki 25, or OMXH25), and Iceland (OMX Iceland 6 PI ISK, or OMXI6ISK).

240 European Multilateral Clearing Facility; EMCF is owned 78% by ABN AMRO Bank N.V. and 22% by NASDAQ OMX AB.

248 | ANNEXES

241 Not live yet. MoU with Nasdaq OMX to clear equities for Copenhagen, Stockholm and Helsinki.
242 Not live yet. Interoperability between CCPs dealing with trades executed on Nasdaq OMX Nordic (EMCF).
243 Part of Link Up Markets. See footnote 233 above.
244 It requested: TFA and Interoperability with SIX X-clear; interoperability with LCH.CLearnet; and TFA with SIX Platform and SIS SegaInterSettle.
245 TFA requested.
246 Part of Link Up Markets. See footnote 233 above.
247 SA or CA with SIS SegaInterSettle and SIX Platform requested.
248 TFA with X-Clear requested
249 Interoperability with Oslo Clearing requested.
250 Part of Link Up Markets. See footnote 233 above.
251 Part of Link Up Markets. See footnote 233 above.
252 Part of Link Up Markets. See footnote 233 above.
253 Part of Link Up Markets. See footnote 233 above.
254 Includes Tallinn (OMX Tallinn, or OMXT), Riga (OMX Riga, or OMXR), and Vilnius (OMX Vilnius, or OMXV).
255 The biggest 11 venues by turnover (Thomson Reuters data; January - May 2010).
256 Requested a TFA to Chi-X and Interoperability with EMCF.
257 Requested a TFA to Turquoise and Interoperability with EuroCCP.
258 TFA to Turquoise requested.
259 TFA to EuroCCP requested.
260 TFA to BATS Europe requested (for all Irish securities).
261 Not live yet.
262 TFA to NYSE Arca requested.
263 SIX x-clear for German stocks.
264 To be activated when interoperability models have been approved by national authorities.

ANNEX IV. FIGURES AND TABLES ILLUSTRATING EQUITY MARKETS

Figure AIV.1 Global market domestic capitalisation 1993-2009 ($ million)

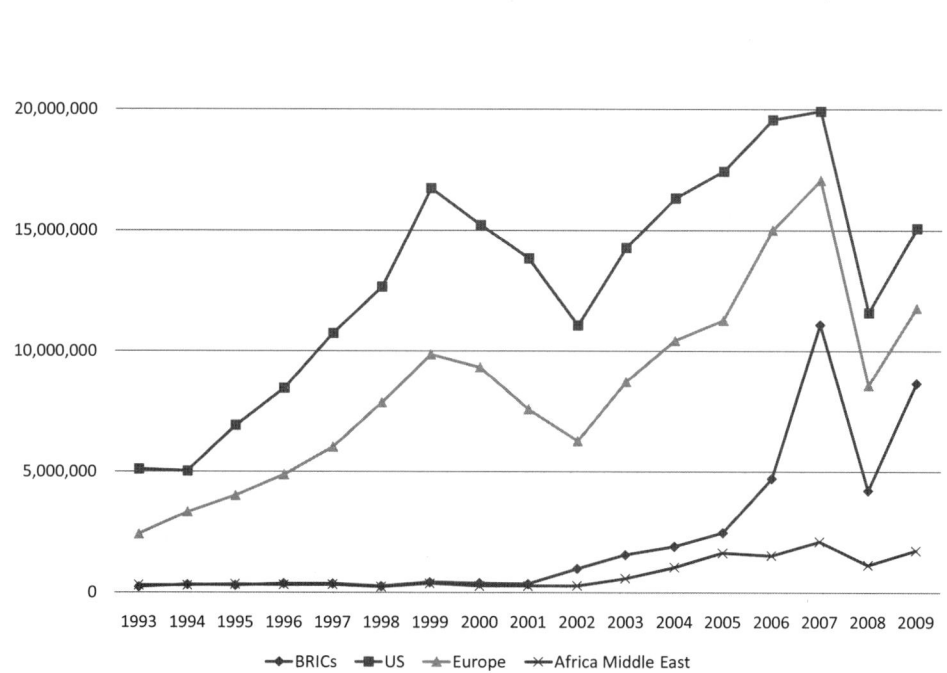

Source: WFE.

Table AIV.1 Market capitalisation ($ million)

NYSE Euronext (US)	11,837,793.3
LSE Group	3,452,292.6
Tokyo SE	3,306,082.0
NASDAQ OMX	3,239,492.4
NYSE Euronext (Europe)	2,869,393.1
Shanghai SE	2,704,778.5
Hong Kong Exchanges	2,305,142.8
TSX Group	1,676,814.2
BME Spanish Exchanges	1,434,540.5
BM&FBOVESPA	1,337,247.7
Deutsche Börse	1,292,355.3

Source: WFE.

Figure AIV.2 European (10 biggest trading venue) aggregate annual turnover ($ million)

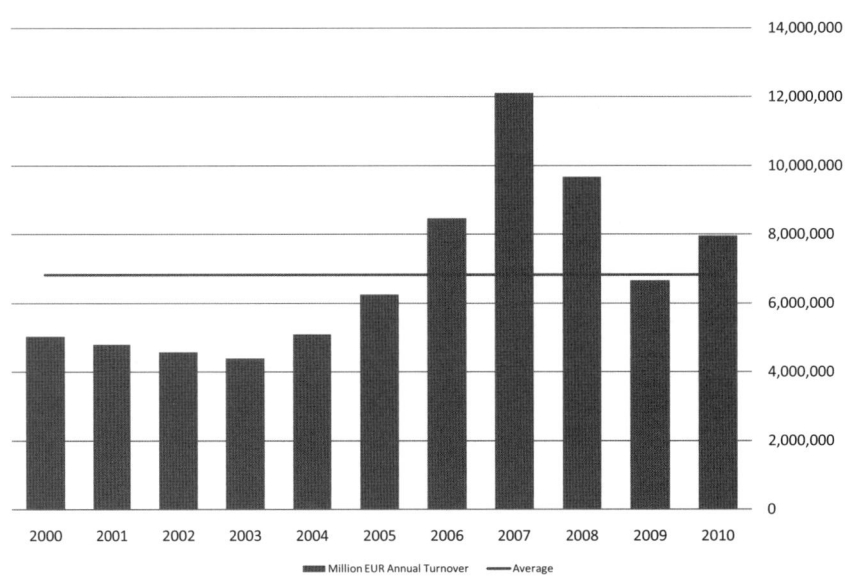

Sources: BATS Europe, FESE and Thomson Reuters.

Table IV.2 EEA market share by national market

London	22.385%
Frankfurt	16.474%
Paris	15.646%
Milan	9.652%
Zurich	8.443%
Madrid	6.752%
Amsterdam	6.318%
Stockholm	5.409%
Oslo	2.377%
Helsinki	2.065%
Copenhagen	1.128%
Brussels	1.119%
Lisbon	0.467%
Vienna	0.366%
Others	1.399%

Sources: BATS Europe, Thomson Reuters (Jan-Dec 2010, % turnover; lit and auction books).

Figure AIV.3 Trading volumes by trading venue, 2010

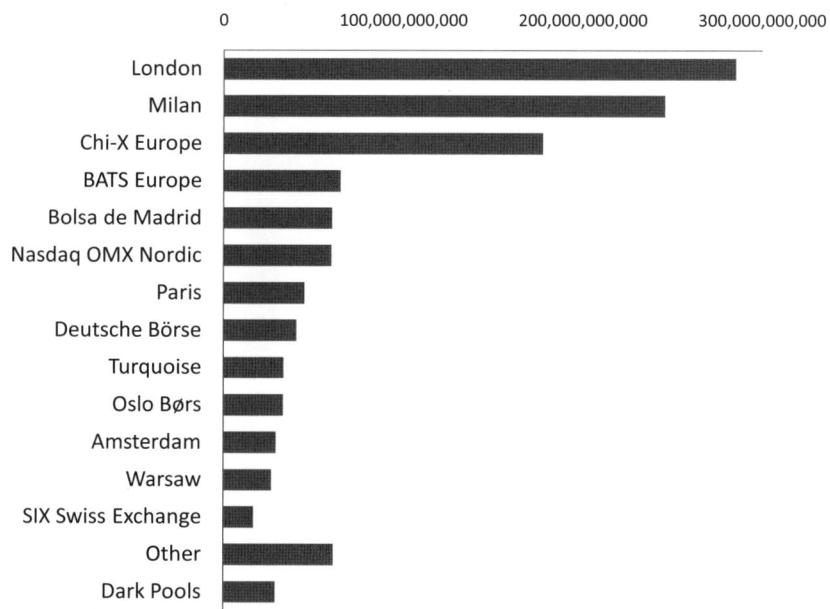

Sources: BATS Europe, Thomson Reuters (Volumes Lit, Auction, Dark Books).

252 | ANNEXES

Figure AIV.4 Turnover by order book, 2010

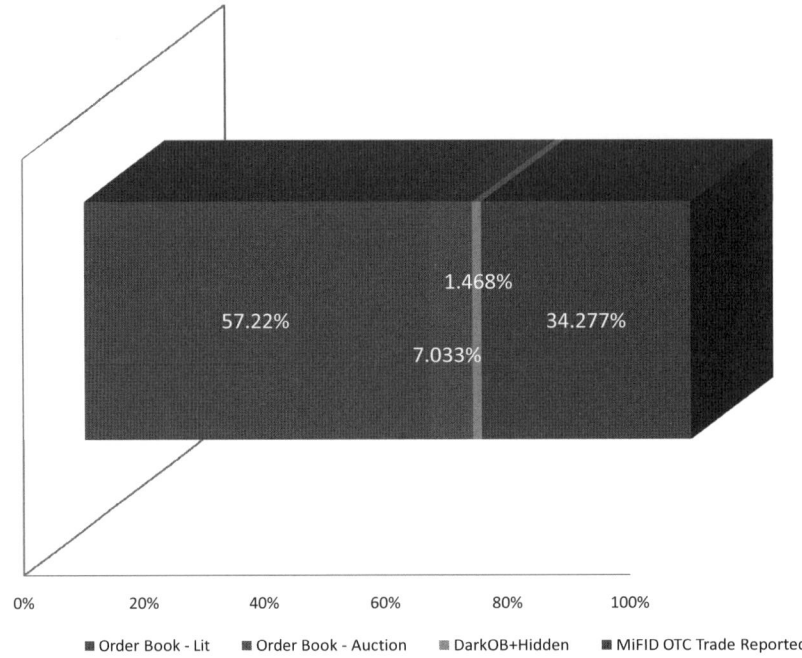

Source: Thomson Reuters (2010 turnover).

Figure AIV.5 EU27 debt and securitised financial instruments (outstanding; € billion)

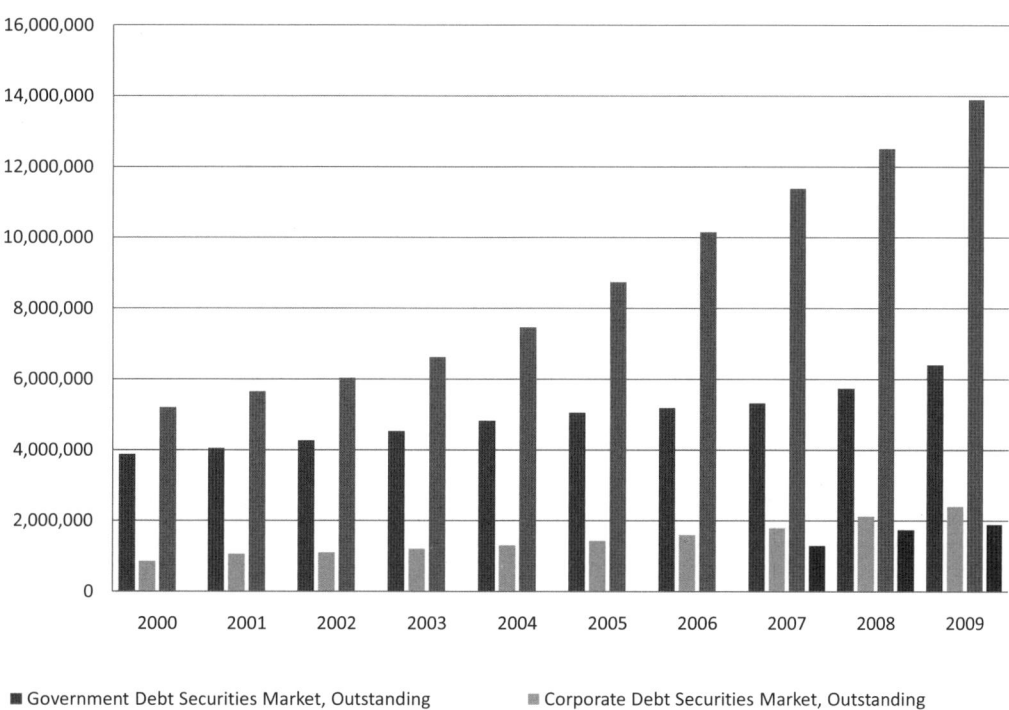

- Government Debt Securities Market, Outstanding
- Corporate Debt Securities Market, Outstanding
- Financial Institutions Debt Securities Maket, Outstanding
- Securitised products, Outstanding

Source: ECMI (2010), BIS, AFME.

Figure AIV.6 EU27 issuance of debt and securitised financial instruments (€ billion)

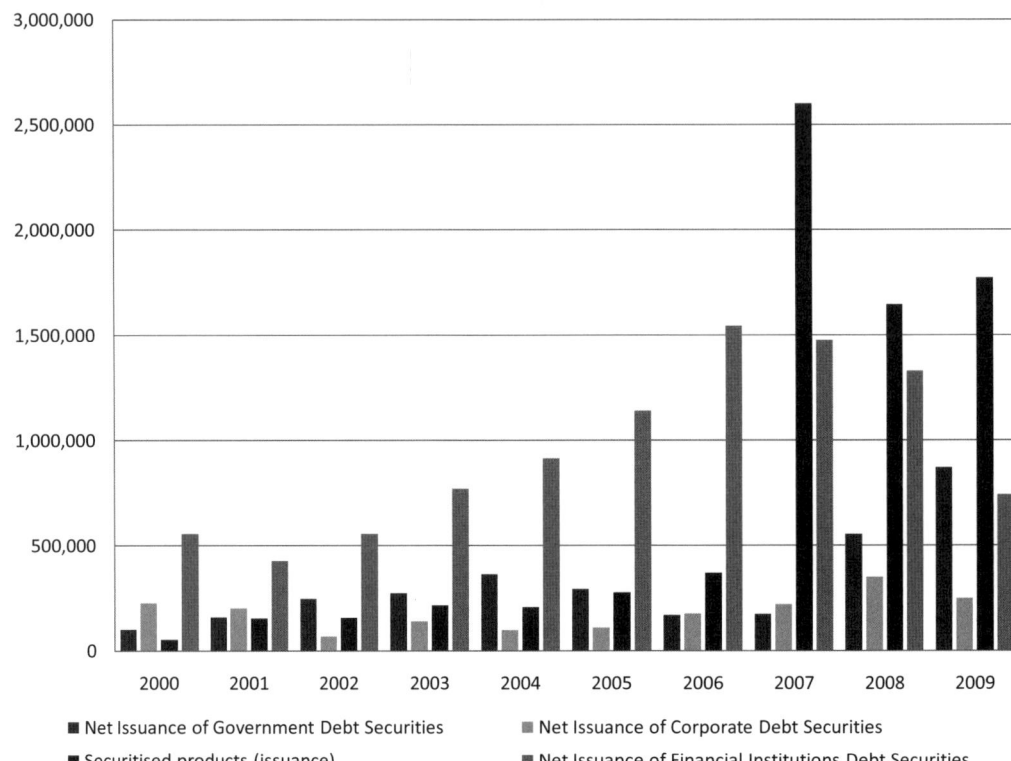

Source: ECMI (2010); data from BIS, AFME.

Figure AIV.7 EU27 financial highlights (1) (€ million)

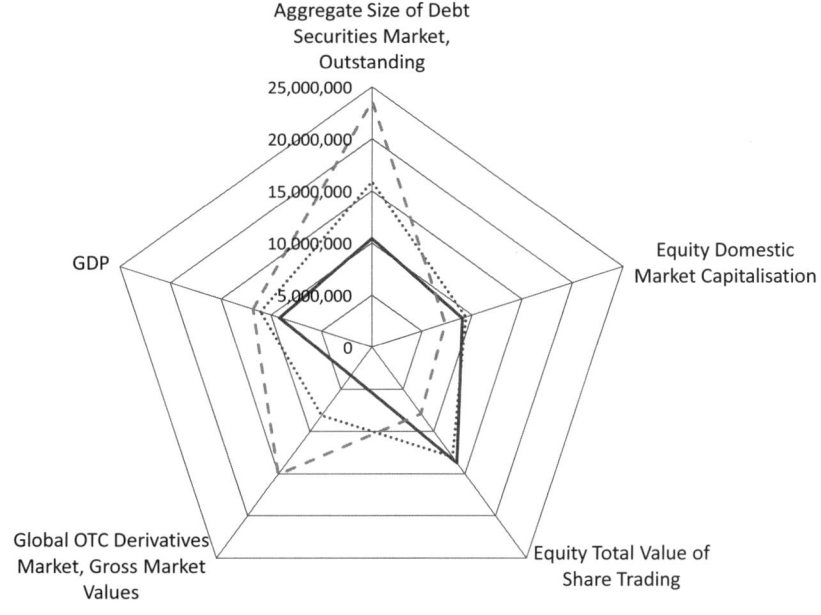

Sources: ECMI (2010) data from BIS, Eurostat, WFE.

256 | ANNEXES

Figure AIV.8 EU27 financial highlights (2) (€ million)

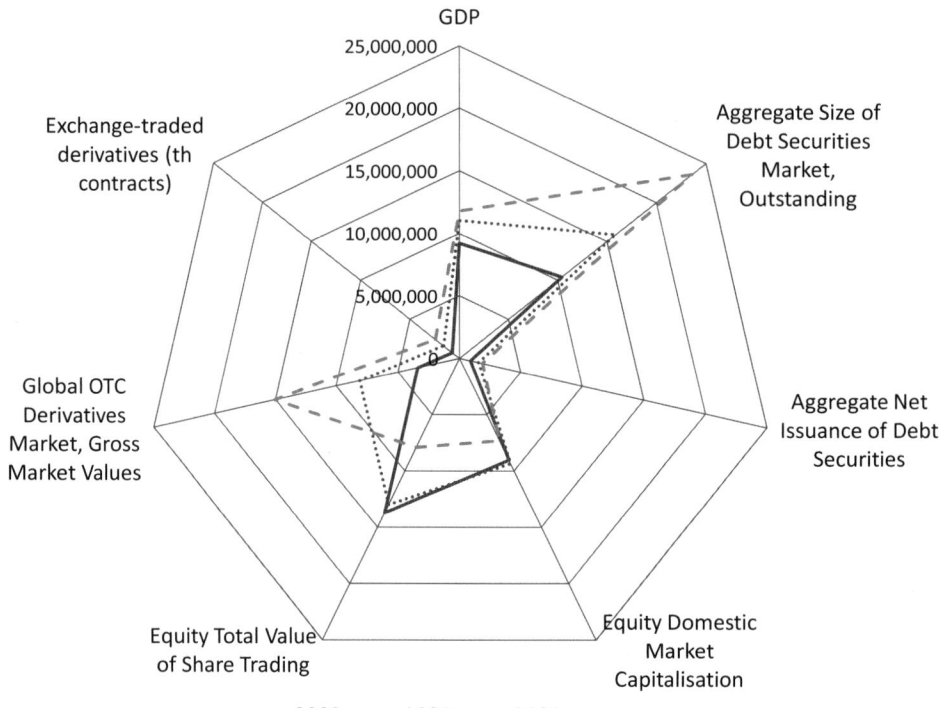

Sources: ECMI (2010) data from Eurostat, BIS, WFE,

Figure AIV.9 OTC (notional) vs exchange-traded derivatives (ETDs) (€ billion)

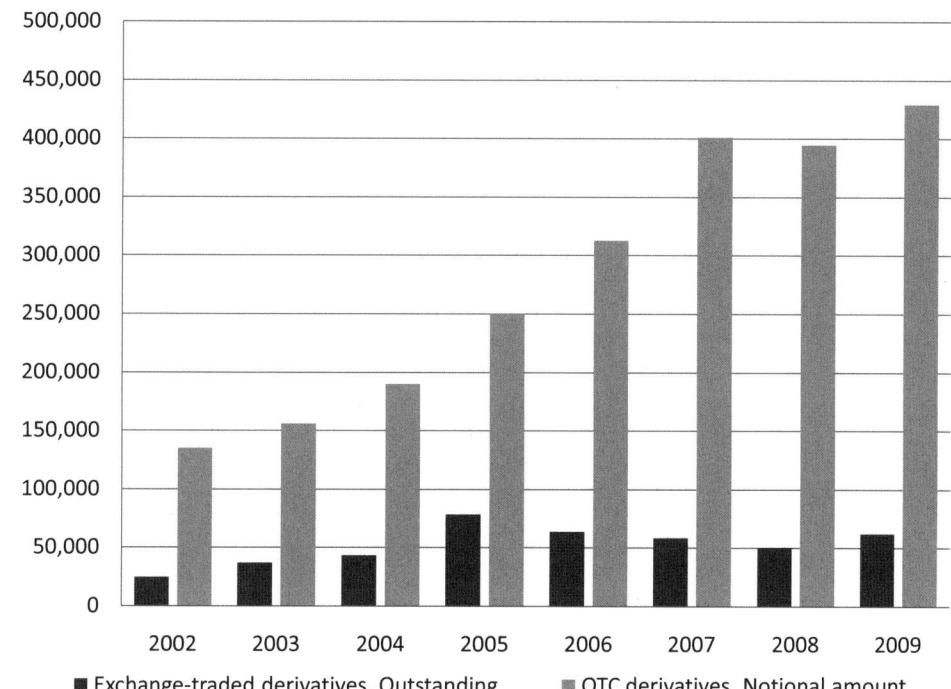

■ Exchange-traded derivatives, Outstanding   ■ OTC derivatives, Notional amount

Sources: ECMI (2010), data from BIS, WFE (ETD are estimations by default).

Figure AIV.10 OTC (gross market value) vs exchange-traded derivatives (€ billion)

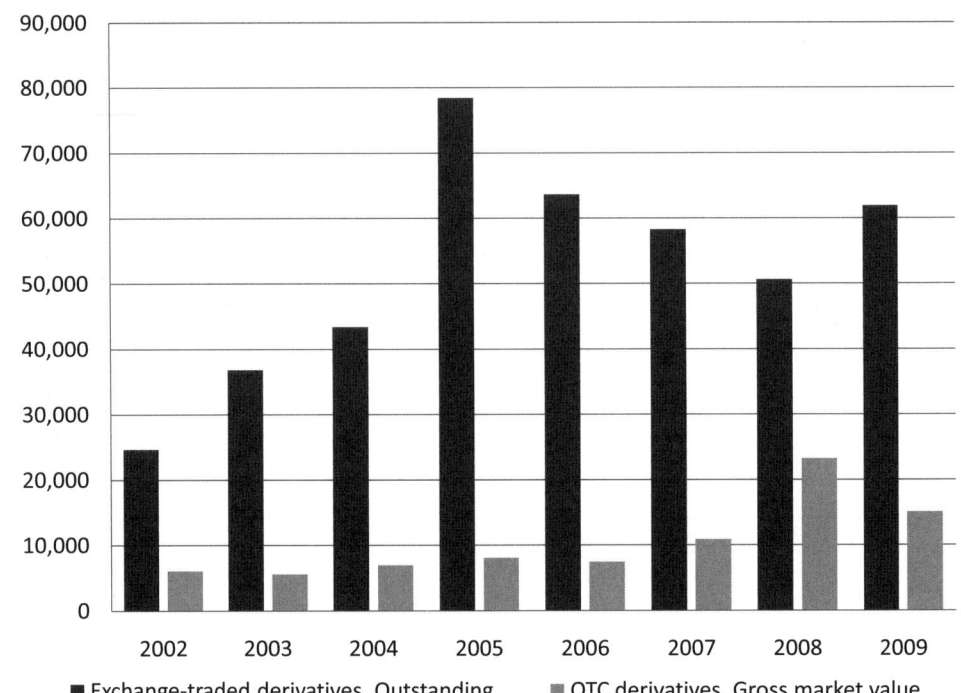

Sources: ECMI (2010), data from BIS, WFE (ETD are estimations by default).

Figure AIV.11 Global debt and derivatives markets vs world GDP (€ billion)

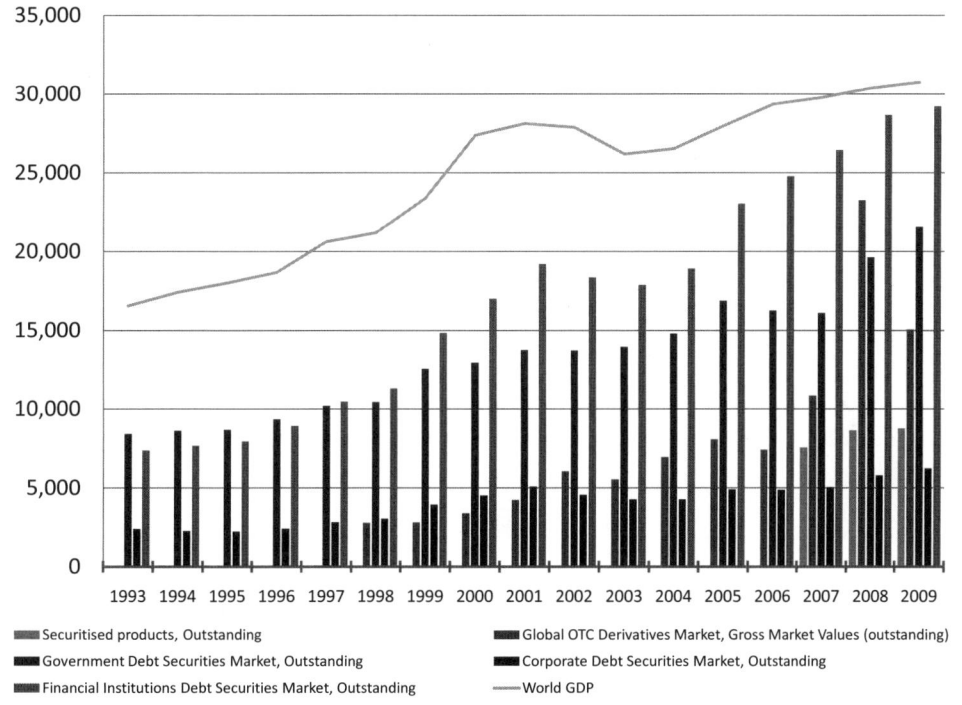

Sourcse: ECMI (2010); data from BIS, Eurostat, World Economic Outlook, AFME.

ANNEX V. TASK FORCE PARTICIPANTS

Disclaimer
The views expressed in this report do not necessarily reflect the views and positions of all members involved in the Task Force. Members do not necessarily agree with all relevant undertaken positions and do not necessarily endorse any reference to academic and independent studies. A sound and clear set of principles has guided the drafting process, in order to preserve a neutral approach to divergent views. All members' views have been heard and – if well-grounded – incorporated in the final text. When fundamental disagreement materialised, the Rapporteurs attempted to explain all views in a proper and fair manner. Finally, members have received enough time to comment and to contribute to each version of the Final Report, which can be only attributed to the Rapporteurs and no one else within the Group. Data included in the text have been generally considered as 'material and relevant'.

Chair
Pierre Francotte
Former CEO, Euroclear
General Manager, PLF International

Rapporteurs

Diego Valiante, Ph.D.
Research Fellow
ECMI-CEPS

Karel Lannoo
CEO and Senior Research Fellow
CEPS-ECMI

Members

Ludovic Aigrot
Head of EU Affairs
NASDAQ OMX

George Andreadis
Head of AES Liquidity Strategy
Europe
Credit Suisse Securities

Rosa Armesto
Head of Fixed income and
Economics & Statistics
FESE - Federation of European
Securities Exchanges

Georg Baur
Chair Securities Working Party
European Banking Federation

Catherine Blake
Legal Counsel
CME Group

Andrew Bowley
Head of Electronic Trading Product
Management
Nomura International

Bertrand Bréhier
Deputy Head Banking and Financial Regulation
Société Générale

Vanessa Bruynooghe
Compliance Officer Market
BNP Paribas Fortis

Michele Calderoni
Treasury and Capital Markets
ENEL

Simon Crown
Partner
Clifford Chance

Jérôme Desombre
Director - Strategy
Euroclear

Godfried De Vidts
Director of European Affairs
ICAP

Graham Dick
Head of Business Development
Chi-X Europe

Andrew W. Douglas
Head of Public Affairs
DTCC - Depositary Trust and Clearing Corporation

Florence Fontan
European Affairs
BNP Paribas Securities Services

Benoît Gourisse
Deputy Director
French Banking Federation

Huong Hauduc
Associate Director and Assistant General Counsel
CME Group

Samuel Hinton-Smith
Director Public Affairs
Nomura International Plc

Karl-Peter Horstmann
Head of Markets Regulation
RWE Supply and Trading GmbH

Bertrand Huet
Senior Policy Advisor
Fleishman Hillard

Henrik Husman
Vice President Nordic Cash Equity Products
NASDAQ OMX

Burçak Inel
Deputy Secretary General
FESE -Federation of European Securities Exchanges

Denzil Jenkins
Director of Regulation
Chi-X Europe

Sophia Kandylaki
Director
Markit Group Limited

Rene Karsenti
Executive President
ICMA - International Capital Market Association

Sacha Kumaria
Deputy Director of European Affairs
ICAP

Sonja Lohse
Head of Group Compliance
Nordea Bank

Graziella Marras
Senior Policy Advisor
EFAMA - European Fund and AM Association

Barbara Matthews
Founder and CEO
BCM International Regulatory Analytics LLC

Nick Miller
Associate
Morgan Stanley

Michele Morena
Associate Director
Kreab Gavin Anderson

Celia Neves
Representative
Nordea Bank

Francesca Passamonti
Representative before the European Union
Intesa Sanpaolo

Jeremie Pellet
Strategic Analyst
BNP Paribas

Frank Pottie
Director - Public Affairs
Euroclear

Cian Rice
Partner
Kreab Gavin Anderson

Donald Ricketts
Head of Financial Services
Fleishmann-Hillard

Tillie Rijk
Regulatory Affairs Analyst
Deutsche Bank

Julia Rodkiewicz
Policy Manager
International Swaps and Derivatives Ass. (ISDA)

Susanne Rompel
EU Liaison Office
RWE

José Manuel Santamaría
International Affairs
BME - Bolsas y Mercados Españoles

Marcus Schueler
Managing Director
Markit Group Limited

Guy Sears
Director of Wholesale
Investment Management Association (IMA)

David Self
Product Manager
Xtrakter

Martin Sjöberg
Manager European Affairs
CFA Institute

Enzo Stingone
Vice President Connectivity
Chi-X Europe

Steven Travers
Head of Regulatory Law and
Strategy
London Stock Exchange Group

Dermot Turing
Partner
Clifford Chance

Geert Vanderbeke
Head of Sales Europe
ABN AMRO Clearing

Jack Vensel
Managing Director
Citi

Hendrik van Vliet
Senior Adviser Markets Industry
ABN AMRO Clearing

Juan-Pablo Urrutia
Associate and Counsel
Goldman Sachs International

Helena Walsh
Manager
Cicero Consulting

Santiago Ximenez
Director Market Data
BME - Bolsas y Mercados Españoles

Elina Yrgard
Legal Counsel EU Affairs
NASDAQ OMX

Observers

Hans Degryse
Professor of Financial Intermediation
and Markets CentER - Tilburg
University

Salvatore Gnoni
Seconded National Expert
European Commission

Stephen Hanks
Policy Manager, Conduct Policy
Financial Services Authority

Hannes Huhtaniemi
Policy Officer Securities Markets Unit
European Commission

Valerie Ledure
Policy Officer, European Commission

Rhiannon Price
Assistant to MEP Kay Swinburne
European Parliament

Patrick Van Cayseele
Professor of Economy and Vice-Dean
Catholic University of Leuven

Hans Wolters
Head of Policy
Dutch Financial Authority

George Zavvos
Legal Adviser, European Commission